1848, BRIDGNORTH.
A FLOOD. A FIRE. A DEATH.

Mercy

EMMA
WOODHOUSE

CRANTHORPE
MILLNER
PUBLISHERS

First published by Cranthorpe Millner Publishers (2025)

ISBN 978-1-80378-309-3 (Paperback)

www.cranthorpemillner.com

Cranthorpe Millner Publishers

Printed and bound by CPI Group (UK) Ltd
Croydon, CR0 4YY

MIX
Paper | Supporting responsible forestry
FSC® C013604

This is a book about generations of women.

For the generations of women in my life:

Kayleigh Woodhouse and Ellie Hatton,
Marion Woodhouse,
Maisie Hatfield
and Hilda Woodhouse.

"Truth uncompromisingly told will always have its ragged edges." – Herman Melville, *Billy Budd, Sailor.*

"Stories have to be told or they die, and when they die, we can't remember who we are or why we're here." – Sue Monk Kidd, *The Secret Life of Bees*

"For murder, though it have no tongue, will speak
With most miraculous organ." – William Shakespeare, *Hamlet.*

""Take nothing on its looks; take everything on evidence. There's no better rule."– Charles Dickens, *Great Expectations.*

NEWTON FAMILY TREE

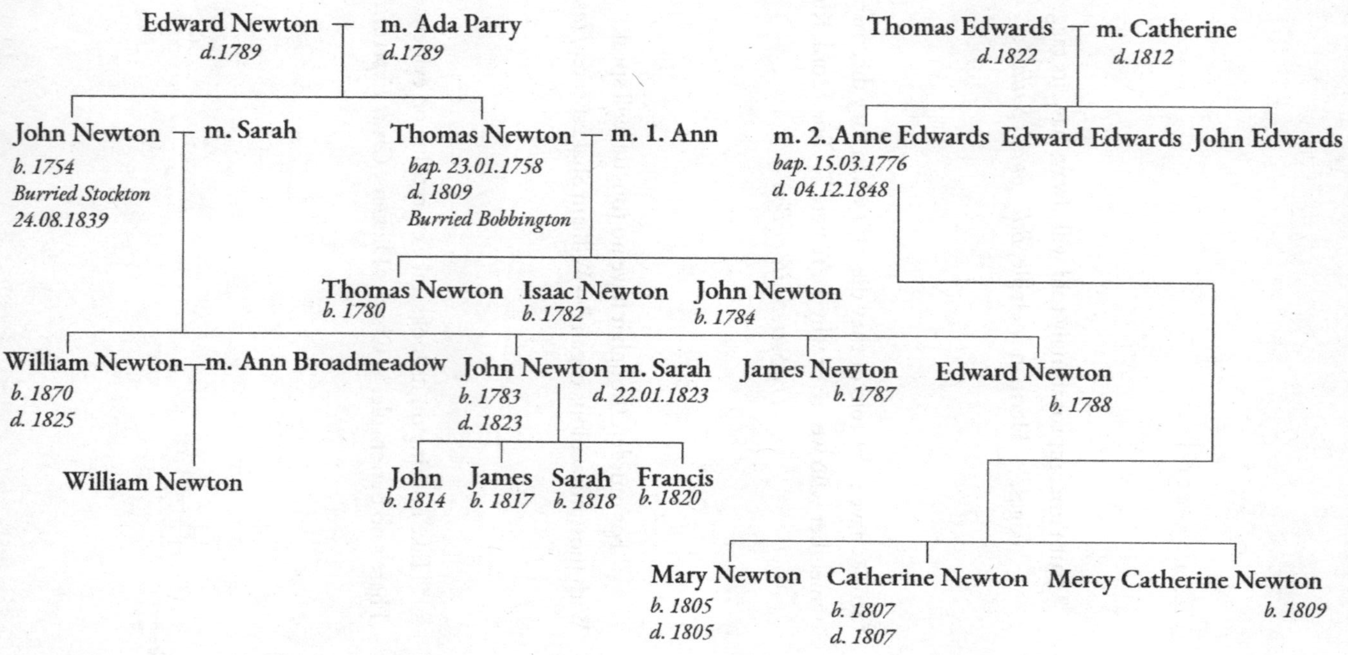

This is a story of three generations of women:
Anne Edwards, Mercy Newton and Maria Newton.

But this story has no heroine. It is a story of emotion and infamy; of the will to survive.

This is a true story.

Prologue

The Curse of the Newtons

Severn Hall

22nd of January 1823

Mary Jones's feet pound the earth. Her boots hit the hard, frozen ground, faster, faster, but not fast enough. The very moment the first scream pierced the darkness Mary knew she was too late. From her first lolloping steps onwards before she built momentum, skirts clasped in her fists and breath white in the frigid night air, she knew.

Just four fields, she tells herself, gulping down the freezing air until it stings her tubes and bites against her throat and nostrils. Four fields away. Her heart is racing too fast, not just from the exertion; here, in these uneven fields, feet pounding, she can guess what she is racing towards and her heart cannot pace itself. Already the screams have stopped, but now there is crying, sobbing; the noises of a child distressed somewhere out in the night air. Four fields have never felt so vast an expanse. She runs but seems to get nowhere. Time is working against her.

Behind her, the freezing, black, rushing water of the River Severn gushes, a vein that runs through this place, swallows the land when it rages and claims lives when it pleases. Thank God the moon is full, for these fields are illuminated in an eerie silver glow, enough that she can see her way, for the lantern she carried is dropped and gone, back when the first scream pierced the night calm. This moonlight is enough for her to ensure her pounding feet do not twist in a hollow, and there before her now lies Severn Hall, its white lime glowing against the black timber frame. Somewhere an owl hoots and she slows a little, the hairs on her arms and the back of her neck rising. She is afraid.

"Oh, Dad! Oh, Dad, dunna do it!" The cry floats across the last field towards her.

She hares across the last field, sobs growing louder in her ears, and there in the dirt is little John Newton, sobbing and shivering, and he turns to her, mouth agape and points, points to the open kitchen door. She pulls off her shawl and wraps him in it, then steps forth towards the kitchen of Severn Hall, unto what horrors she can only imagine.

Therein lies Sarah Newton before the glowing hearth, a widening dark puddle about her, pooling darkness on the brick floor. Already congealing at the edge closest to the fire, its tendrils ooze onwards in the crevices between the bricks, a darkening network of lines flowing, reaching forth to taint everything else about them. The reflection of the fire dancing, hellish, cavorts across the rest of the dark mass, fiendish, flames flickering in that dark mirror of blood.

"Good God!" Mary Jones is at her mistress's side in an instant, but the poor woman is barely conscious. "Mrs Newton, what can I do?"

She looks about her for something, anything, that might help, but only little John Newton remains, who has followed her inside, standing there quaking, dithering and sobbing, covered in snot and drool.

"Where is your father?" she whispers, glancing over her shoulder. "Where?"

John cannot reply. His eyes are like saucers, his mouth agape like a simpleton.

"I must raise her," Mary decides and tries to sit her mistress up, wrapping her arms about her and heaving, but the woman is a dead weight and the blood still flows from who knows where, and now Mary is covered in it too.

There is a clattering on the stairs and Billy Bache, the waggoner, staggers forth, catching sight of Sarah, whom Mary has laid back down for she cannot hold her weight. At the sound of him, Sarah's eyes flutter, and Mary sees a hand reach to him, and Sarah's lips move,

"God bless you, Billy," her split lips whisper. "I take my leave of you."

Billy is at her side now on his knees and he takes her hand.

"Where is *he*?" Mary asks of him, but he shrugs.

"He told me to come down to my mistress," he whispers, and his face is black. "Dear God, I did not think he had done her over this bad." He leans down to listen, for Sarah's eyes are closed again. "She breathes," he says. His eyes turn to little John, who is standing staring. "We ought to move her."

"What's to do?" Julia Oliver is in the doorway in her long nightshirt. "What's he done to her this time?" She rushes forth then at the sight before her, swearing beneath her breath.

"He's gone into town to fetch Sarah Lloyd," Julia tells them.

"Thank God he's done one thing good," Billy says. "Fucker."

They gaze down upon their mistress, her belly round beneath her skirts.

"It'll die," says Mary. "It'll never live."

They stand back. "He's done it this time," Julia concedes. "Never mind the babby, if Mrs Newton lives, that'll be a miracle."

They stand back. Little Francis is crying in his cot upstairs, but not one of them can leave their mistress. Her breathing is ragged.

"Did he kick her?" Billy asks, rubbing his chin. "Hit?"

Her eye is blackened, closed to a slit, and her lips are bloodied.

"I didn't see," Mary tells them. "I'd gone across the river, an errand. I was coming back across the fields when I heard her screaming."

"It was that George Edwards's fault," Julia opines. "Riled him up about that bill. The master said he'd given the mistress the money to pay it, but George Edwards swore he hadn't taken payment from her. They was drinkin' since one."

Mary takes a cloth from the table, folds it and places it carefully beneath Sarah's head. "Is there any drink?" she asks. "Brandy? Whisky?"

"There was rum, but George Edwards and the master drank it all," says Julia.

"Fucker," says Billy.

"He'd've hit me too but I ran." They all turn. Little John has managed his say.

"Went for you, did he?" Billy asks, beckoning for the lad to come near. John nods tearfully and scuttles over but hides his face in Billy's shirt so that he does not have to see his mother's blood.

"Dear God, I hope Sarah Lloyd ain't long in the coming," says Julia.

Mary has found some brandy. "Ought I give it to her?" she asks, pouring a little but dithering. "I inner sure if it's the right thing for her."

"It wunna hurt," Billy says, and so Mary steps forth, kneels and holds a small glass to Sarah's lips, but they do not part to admit the liquor.

"She won't have it," she reports and sits back on her heels. "Maybe we ought to wash her face."

This appears to be the best course of action. Mary sets about finding a fresh cloth and pouring water from the kettle. Julia takes the boy upstairs now for Francis is wailing like a cat, little

Sarah's voice can be heard complaining and James's voice too rises from his bed.

Billy stands guard, although if his master returns both he and Mary know that he will not be able to stop whatever fresh hell is meted, for John Newton, the master of this place, is a huge man, a strong, muscular man, and Billy Bache is but a lad. Mary brings her water across from the table and slowly, carefully, wipes Sarah's brow, and the cloth comes off red. Sarah groans at her touch, then turns on her side, her back to the grate, and draws her knees up to her rounded belly.

The light of the fire glows against the walls of the kitchen, like the inside of a kiln, and they stand there over her until they might be baked like clay in an oven, petrified and glowing, and through the window nothing but cold darkness all about them. And Severn Hall sits in its dip beside the river, beneath the silent, frosty moon, and along the dark track, at last, comes Sarah Lloyd, striding beside the huge, silent, frosty figure of John Newton, farmer of Severn Hall, husband of Sarah Newton, whose stick is the only thing that can be heard pounding on the ground, louder and louder, until inside the house Mary looks up from the bloodied form of her mistress and says, with a sickness rising in her, "He's coming!"

In through the kitchen door he strides, with a force so great that the door bangs off the wall and Sarah Lloyd has to catch it before it strikes her. He brings with him the cold, the dark and the deep, heavy scent of a man half-soaked with rum.

Mary falls back, and so does Billy, as their master approaches. He eyes his wife, then like a dog that cannot stop worrying sheep, he is over to her, looming, and growls,

"Which is the rogue now, you or I?"

And then he is gone, clumping up the stairs, and Julia sallies forth, and she and Sarah Lloyd somehow between them, like a miracle, lift Sarah Newton from the ground and heave her up the stairs. Mary follows shaking, but before she might follow them into the mistress's room, John Newton is bellowing to her to warm his bed, and she must away with a warming pan down to the kitchen before he loses his temper again. She's half-tempted to piss in the pan and hand it to him warmed and stinking, but knows she'd end up like Sarah Newton if she did. When she clambers up the stairs holding the warming pan before her and scuttles to the master's room thrusting the pan betwixt his sheets, she hears his tones, dark and belching fury in her mistress's room,

"A debtor you've made me, a fool, and who is the fool now? *Who is the fool*, you damned bitch?"

To Mary's horror, as she crosses the landing, John Newton stomps out of the mistress's room, but he does not see her in his haze. She shrinks backwards to let him pass, and he does and slams his door on the lot of them. Mary creeps over to Sarah's room. Billy has crept up the stairs, and they stand about Sarah's bed, silently listening once more to her wheezing breaths, which Mary is sure come shallower now. Sarah Newton's blood is upon them all, and even as she lies still in her cold white bed, it spreads itself about, red, and the mound of her belly, five months with child, lies high beneath the crimson sheet. Sarah Lloyd turns.

"He would not send for a doctor," she whispers. "But, William, you must go for one. This is the worst he's done to her yet."

Billy nods and is away. He will take a horse from the stables; he will be quick, Mary is sure. No stomping about the town for Billy Bache. He will be there and back in an instant. She says as much to Sarah Lloyd, and Julia looks around from her kneeling position beside the bed and nods in agreement.

"He'll ride like the wind," she asserts.

Still, these long, slow moments tick away, the children sleep in their beds and John Newton sleeps and snores across the landing as Sarah Lloyd does what she can to stop the bleeding.

At last, Mr James Barber, the doctor's assistant, arrives, but John Newton does not stir from his bed. He examines Mrs Newton's face, spectacles on his nose, spectacles off his nose, then back on again. Mary, Julia and Billy wait in the kitchen until Sarah Lloyd comes downstairs with him, and they all sit around the table. The hearth is dying now, barely emitting any heat, but Mary must stoke it, for she must heat more water to mop the mess from the floor.

"Apply vinegar to the wound," Mr Barber tells Sarah Lloyd. "Here is a draught which she must take." He pulls out a bottle: laudanum. Sarah Lloyd pockets it quickly. "Give her brandy," he adds, then turns to Billy. "I'll trouble you to take me back in the trap; it is too late for walking now."

Sarah Lloyd watches them leave. Her lips narrow. Her eyes do too. Mary can see that she is aggrieved. Suddenly, she turns on her heel and is up the stairs, her boots banging on the boards, and Mary and Julia stand at the foot of the stairs. Julia's eyes are wide. Mary cannot hide her shaking hands.

"What did you use, to do it to her?" Sarah Lloyd is yelling, yelling at John Newton. "What did you do it with?"

Mary strains but hears no reply, and then Sarah Lloyd is stomping again, back across the landing, and Mary creeps up the stairs to find her applying the draught to Mrs Newton's lips.

"What did he say?" she whispers. Sarah Lloyd gestures with her hand.

"He said nothing, merely showed me his hand," she mutters. "But a wound such as hers, a puncture like that, could not have been made by a hand alone." She points to Sarah Newton's chest, where a darkened, congealed mess lies. "I believe he's killed her," she breathes. "And the child too. It's murder."

There are hours yet, hours and hours until sunrise, but Mary wishes this night were over. She hopes that the sun might rise so that she might open her eyes to find her mistress well, and this whole night would prove to have been a dream. Each time she blinks, she wishes that when her eyes open, it will be the waking of her and none of this – the blood, the fear and the destruction of their lives, none of it – will be real. But each time she blinks, she is still standing there in that room, surrounded by the smell of blood, with the darkness and cold seeping in through the windowpanes and down the chimney.

Mary, Julia and Sarah Lloyd watch over Mrs Newton until the clock strikes two, and her last jagged breaths cease.

Everyone strains to hear or see if there might be one more, but there is not. Sarah Lloyd checks her pulse at her throat and wrist, listens at her mouth, and examines the chest for signs, but there are none.

"She's gone," she says. "He's killed her this time."

Mary turns her eyes away. She cannot bear to see her now, nor to imagine the child within her belly, suffocating and dying there inside its dead mother, that is if its father hasn't already killed it with his boots. She would give anything, in this moment, to not be enclosed in this room with death.

"Who's going to tell him?" she breathes. Julia shakes her head.

Sarah Lloyd clenches her fists. "I will," she says.

She strides across the landing. With all her might, she pushes the door and slams it open against the wall so that the huge man snoring in his bed is jolted and arises from sleep, gasping like a drowning man. Mary can see through the dark doorway the outlines, the silhouettes of the two.

"She's dead," Mary hears her tell him, then louder, "You've killed her. She's dead!"

John Newton is on his feet in his long johns, the blankets

flung to the floor, mouth open and eyes wide. For a moment, Mary thinks he will strike down angry, bold little Sarah Lloyd too, and she shrinks away herself as though from some ethereal fist, but instead he cries out in a whining, pitiful voice,

"Lord, have mercy on me! She is not dead. She is not dead; she has either fainted away or is in a fit."

Mary watches, listens and hangs from his passion. She hates his fear, for he is afeared only for himself and his neck at the gallows, not for his poor dead wife and child. He is afeared that he will hang.

Long before daybreak, Billy has fetched Elizabeth Ward, Sarah's friend, and the women have tearfully laid out Mrs Sarah Newton, sponged the cloying blood from her skin, taken from her the blood-soaked clothes, set some of them to soak and hung the rest in the closet. The words seem to stick in Mary's throat as she whispers a goodbye to the child within her, the one that was never born, and they all say prayers and shed tears, and cover her in a white sheet.

"What will become of the children?" Mary asks, as men begin to descend upon the place in the early hours, even before the sun rises. A gaoler's carriage arrives in the yard. They have set about their work already, demanding nothing be touched, berating the women for taking the clothes off Mrs Newton and sticking them in a water butt, for it has frozen now and the evidence they carry is lost. None of this matters now to Mary. All she cares about now are the four little Newtons and how John will remember this night his whole life as the night his dad beat his mam to death, and the three others will remember it as the night their mam left this earth.

"*He's* their father," Elizabeth says, wiping a tear on the back of her hand. Her eyes are red raw. "It is *his* choice what will become of them."

"He'll hang for this," Sarah Lloyd says. "Those kiddies have been through enough. They ought to be housed well away from anyone who'd bring them up the Newton way."

"Then where, Sally, where ought we send them?" Elizabeth is distraught. Her friend is gone, and her children will be thrown in the workhouse at this rate. "What relatives are there hereabouts that might have them?"

They go down to the parlour and sit, and Mary lights candles. There will be no sleep for any of them this night.

"What about Anne Newton?" Sarah Lloyd suggests. "She lives close by and is a mother herself."

Mary shakes her head. "Not her," she says.

"What relation is she to the children?" Sarah questions.

"She's aunt to them," Mary tells her. "Or great-aunt. Not that you'd tell they're family."

"Married to John's father's brother, Thomas," Elizabeth muses. "He's dead now. She's great-aunt by marriage. Not blood. She has a daughter, doesn't she?"

Mary nods. "Mercy. Though if you ask most Newtons, they'll deny she's one of them. Born well after the death of Anne's husband, that girl was. Anne isn't a one for taking on four children out of the goodness of her heart. She's a drunk and a pauper and the family hates her."

"There ought to have been five children," Elizabeth says dully.

They sit in silence until Sarah says, "Is Anne the only one? The only family? Surely not!"

Mary shakes her head. "They won't go to her, not if I have anything to do with it." She's seen Anne about, seen little Mercy Newton dragged up in squalor. Her husband is dead and Anne has nothing, eking out an existence in a tiny hovel of a cottage in the middle of nowhere. They've all heard of Anne Newton and how the family despises her. She traipses into Bridgnorth each market day, dragging her scrawny daughter after her, hollow-eyed, clad in clothes that are thinning, and Mary knows there is no money to support these poor sad children there.

The Newtons are men of means, but Anne's husband is dead and had three sons from his first marriage to leave money to, and Anne, his second wife, hadn't taken to them. John Newton had boasted time and again of how his Uncle Thomas had taken that young Anne Newton to hand with his fists. She'd birthed two daughters that had died soon after. Then, how Thomas had gone off to market in Huntingdon and died there; she'd birthed another daughter a good five months later, who survived, but has been ignored and denied by the rest of the Newtons ever since. 'A slut and a beggar,' John Newton had called Anne. 'A disgrace to the name of Newton.' No, Anne Newton cannot be responsible for the child she has, let alone four more.

"John has three brothers; the Newtons are a big family; we'll find someone to have them. For now, we'll take them in," Mary says finally. "Just for now. Me and my mam. Will you suggest it to Mr John, Mrs Ward, before they take him away?"

A sigh akin to relief passes over them all.

On the morrow, the four Newton children are packed up in the trap. George Littleford, one of the farm boys, takes them and Mary up the lane to Colmore Green, to Mary's mother's house, away from Severn Hall, where their mother lies naked beneath a sheet, her blood-stained clothes frozen in the water they have been left in, her fifth child dead in her waxy belly.

Thus is the name of Newton made infamous thereabouts, and thus is the curse of that name borne out across the Severn and over the valley beyond. It will weave its accursed threads into the land for a while yet.

The Arrest of Mercy Newton

Recollections of Thomas Whitmore, MP

Apley Estate, Bridgnorth
9th of December 1848

I have set myself the task of committing to paper the case of Miss Mercy Newton, for it is without question the most important case of my lifetime, and one which will infuriate me no doubt to my grave.

The name of Newton is almost as familiar to me as my own family name. There have been Newtons working for the Apley Estate certainly since I was a boy. Indeed, Newton Farm on our estate may well have been named for their clan, and I recall them, strong men, gamekeepers, farmers, always part of the landscape along with the other tenants and workers about the place.

Having lost my father the year before Miss Mercy Newton's arrest, I had, as the eldest son, inherited Apley Estate and all its tenants and land. I was heavily occupied in taking on the patronage of various local societies both in and around Bridgnorth as my father had, as well as overseeing decisions made regarding the land and its produce. Two days before the arrest took place there had been a large auction of oak, ash and elm timbers at the park, larch and fir poles too, and some of my time had been taken up with William Morris, the wood ranger, detailing the showing of the lots. People roundabouts fondly called my father 'The Old Squire'. I harboured a secret notion that they might perhaps dub me 'The New Squire', or mayhap 'The Young Squire'.

In order to understand this case, if it might ever be truly understood, I am convinced that a firm comprehension of the social situation in Bridgnorth must be had, along with a knowledge of the people who knew Miss Mercy Newton, upon whose whims she appeared to be buffeted about. Even with all of this information at one's fingertips, perhaps external factors – the way the wind was blowing at the time or the concentration of alcohol in their rum – might have influenced the outcome of the case. Certainly in my mind, common sense and the righteousness of the great British legal system had nothing to do with what unfolded here before the eager, ale-filled, gossip-laden folk of Bridgnorth.

The market town of Bridgnorth straddles the River Severn in South Shropshire, an industrious place with a foundry and its own river port. Since my father died, I have tried to make myself a presence about the town. Down by the river port, warehouses and the harbour master's house sit, damp and often flooded in the colder months, when the river bursts its banks, so that time and again the only way to traverse Underhill Street, which runs parallel to the river, is in a coracle. Public houses flank the hill up The Cartway, cheap ale by the barrel-load and brothels too, catering for the less choosy sailors. Donkeys, sad and wasting, pull carts filled with goods up the steep Cartway, past the tiny cottages and up onto Bridgnorth High Street, where the more expensive public houses sit, along with the butchers, the ironmongers, grocers, other shops of various sorts and the hotel. The fine old guildhall sits in the centre of the high street, wherein the business of the town is set out and where police trials may be held. And although one might imagine that the town is governed by those who sit within the Guildhall, when one sets foot within the walls of one or other of the alehouses, one realises that it is beneath the roof of these places, where the beer flows and the rum is sloshed about, that the real business takes place. The people of Bridgnorth work hard and talk hard. Many a deal is made over a pint and elections are swayed, as I have seen in my lifetime by the passing of words above and coin beneath a table.

On arriving in Bridgnorth on Saturday the 9th of December 1848, my carriage pulled up beneath the Guildhall. I was prepared to meet with Mr Deighton, the mayor, to talk over some business regarding rent payments. I alighted to find a rather worried-looking messenger boy wringing his cap between his hands.

"Please sir, Mr Whitmore," he piped, ever wringing, "The warden says, if it be not too much trouble, might you come to the gaol, for there is a mob!"

I stared at him a moment. "A mob sounds unlikely, boy, why might such a thing have occurred?"

His answer was instant. "Why, it be on account of the murderer that's banged up since last night," he reported.

At this, I was inside the carriage instantly and ordered him up front with the coachmen. The gaol, such that it was, was built to house criminals of a petty nature, for Bridgnorth was but a smallish town and crime here was nothing if it was not petty. Through the Northgate we went and already I could hear voices raised, irate, angry voices, and as the carriage turned left, I could see them. A gaggle of enraged townsfolk were gathered outside the prison warden's house, and someone had hurled an egg, no matter the cost or the need these people might have for food, at his window. The prison warden's house, a simple cottage within which he lived with his wife and their children, backed into the gaol yard and the warden was standing, his back against his door and his arms folded, barring their advancement. When he saw my carriage, I noted that his shoulders sagged with relief.

"Sir Thomas Whitmore will tell you all," he called out. "And like me, he will say you must bide on the side of the law!" Despite the December chill, I could see he was sweating. "Now step back and behave, and we shall see what he has to say on all this!"

I stepped down from my carriage and one man yelled, "Housing a murderer!"

"Stand by, gentlemen," I spoke loudly and politely but with gravity. "This matter is not of your concern!"

"They're all for lynching her," the warden breathed, mopping his brow as I took place beside him. "I'm afraid for my family, Mr Whitmore; something must be done."

I still had not heard the exact particulars of Miss Newton's crime, yet here I stood defending her stronghold.

"I'm afeared they'll break in," breathed the warden. "They'll scale the walls, I'm sure of it. I've never seen them like this, not in all the years I've been here."

At this, a pale, small face appeared in the window of the cottage for a moment, behind the slime of the egg that now coated the pane; it was one of the warden's children. It stared out for a second, wide eyed at this motley bunch of townsfolk, before it was pulled back into the darkness inside, and I found I could barely stifle a shudder. To bring up children so closely to those prison cells was not, in normal times, an unnerving prospect. Indeed, the usual crimes in Bridgnorth involved mostly drunk and disorderly folk or small theft of, say, a blanket or a turnip from a farmer's field. Murder was not, in these parts, something that occurred on a regular basis.

"I have two constables on their way who will assist in the removal of these people," the warden told me, and his voice was shaking. Never had I seen him so flustered. "When they arrive, they will flank you as you deliver a speech to these people about what is right and what is just. And please, sir, that they must leave my house alone."

We had only moments to wait before the two constables arrived. One, a Constable Evans, had been the man to arrest Miss Newton in the early hours of the morning, and sleep, it seemed, had evaded him. However, the four of us once prepared, stepped forth to face the angry multitude whose number had grown since my arrival, and the warden called for silence.

"Mr Thomas Whitmore is here to address you," he called out and his voice rang out in the winter air, and I knew that from inside her cell Miss Newton would be able to hear every word now uttered as clearly as the people gathered there beyond her walls.

I took upon me a severe look of gravity and cleared my throat.

"There is not a man or woman amongst you," I told the crowd, "who is innocent, utterly innocent, of any sin before God. This man," I indicated here, the warden, "undertakes that most sacred duty, to harbour those accused until such time as a trial, taken before God, may come to pass. His work is of the utmost importance, and his peace and the peace of his family must not be tampered with for the urges you feel upon yourselves this day."

A shuffling of feet on one side of me and a cough and a muttering from somewhere demonstrated that these people, whose eyes blazed black with murder, were hearing my words. The two constables flanked me, their hands on their coshes. I had heard of a thrashing or two given out in the name of the law by each of these men in the past, and those in the crowd would know too, perhaps may even have sampled, their concussive eagerness to dispense of the law to those who warranted it.

"If any among you seek to deter us from our work here," I told them in no uncertain terms. "If any tries to reach the prisoner, to tamper with what will be a rigorous and scientific trial before

God, then with the power I hold as your MP, I will see to it that you stand trial yourself. And there are witnesses here aplenty to testify to your guilt."

A few cries rose, but I had dampened their spirits now, and their fun for this day was at an end.

"Go back to your work," I told them. "Let the lawmen decide upon the fate of the prisoner."

"Hang her!" came a cry.

Someone threw an apple and it exploded beside Constable Evans, who drew out his cosh and made for whichever arm had hurled it, glowering, but between the shuffling and shunting of those amassed, from which hand it came he could not fathom and returned soon to my side, dissatisfied.

"Go home," I said again. "Or to your workplaces. And I promise, as your MP, as your landlord and as your friend, that Miss Newton will feel the full strength of the law. And if so she be found guilty, you will see her hang."

At this, they were sated for now and began to peel away, and the two constables held out their arms and drove them off like a flock of geese.

"Will they stay away?" the warden's wife called from the doorway, and I nodded to her.

"I hope so," I told her. "But the inquiry here will be over quickly, I would have thought. She won't bide here long and then you will be rid of her."

"Let me show you the cells, sir," the warden said once the last of the stragglers had been seen off. This tour of the prison, small that it was, was of great interest to me, for I had not been party to it in my father's day. I was sadly underwhelmed when, stepping through the gate at the side of the house, I was met with the small yard and the thick, wooden cell doors that led off it.

"Of course," remarked the warden, as much to himself, I

thought, as to me. "These bloody Newtons have been nothing but trouble ever since the murder at Severn Hall."

"Murder at Severn Hall," I found myself repeating his words. "Yes, I do recall that. In fact, I attended the hanging. How long ago must that have been?"

"Oh, a good twenty-five years or so," he replied, and I realised we had stopped and our attention, though subconsciously, was all focused on one door.

"John Newton," I said, and I recalled it well in that moment, remembered the sound of the rope and the roar of the crowd. There was something else though, something else that had bored a minute hole into my consciousness, a recollection of another Newton back in '33, perhaps ten years after the murderer John Newton swung, but I could not recall then, the event, whatever it was. There had been a hushed whispering all about the Apley estate, an urgent whitewashing of something – as often happens when a scandalous event might sully the reputation of a grand house. Suffice it to say, whatever vile circumstance had occurred, my parents, and those who worked for the estate, sought to hush it up and brush it away, so that the upcoming shoots and events the park so often hosted might not become tainted with an air of the obscene. I stood in the cold prison yard, and the residual knowledge that the name of Newton held no good tidings in these parts weighed heavily, suddenly, upon my mind.

"This is all there is," the warden told me, pointing to the second door along. "Miss Newton's in the cell yonder. Would you like to see her?"

I stood there in the yard and stared at the door. I could imagine a shadowy form inside, cold, hidden in darkness. She would be able to hear every word we said, standing there outside her door. I considered his offer for no amount of time and quickly shook my head. To stare at a woman awaiting trial for murder felt all too grotesque a sport.

"I will attend the inquiry at the Guildhall," I told him distastefully, turning back towards the gate. "It is not necessary for me to see the prisoner."

I knew not then, of course, that her case would make legal history. For a woman to be tried multiple times for the same murder was a case so extraordinary that the town of Bridgnorth, indeed, the county of Shropshire, indeed, the whole of our great country, had not seen the like of it before. And nothing could have prepared me for how intricately her future, and I soon ascertained her past, would become bound inextricably with my own.

The Hanging of John Newton

Mercy Newton

Batch Pool Lane, Bridgnorth

March 1823

Mercy Newton is annoyed with the world. She drags her feet down the lane and through the woodland path, towards the Severn. Everyone is talking about it. Everyone knows of the murder of her cousin's wife, Sarah Newton. The name Newton is synonymous with evil now, for all of Bridgnorth, Worfield, Oldbury and Chelmarsh, everyone in a twenty-mile radius knows what has happened at Severn Hall Farm. Mercy's own name is stained with it all.

For years, Mercy's mother, Anne, has regaled her with tales of her own thrashings from her husband, Thomas Newton, Mercy's father, who died before Mercy was born. Anne has recounted countless days and weeks spent nursing herself back from these beatings. She has also spoken of the two little girls born before Mercy, who died almost as soon as they took a breath. All because their blood was tainted and they took a battering in the womb because their father was a Newton. And Newtons are rotten, Anne has told Mercy, and Sarah's murder only goes to prove it. The only reason Mercy lived, Anne has told her time upon time, is because her father died five months before she was born, or else he'd have battered her out of there too. Those Newton men have ever been the villains, and yet their fortunes were good enough. Sometimes, Anne has also advised her, halfway down a gin bottle, that a woman has to choose between either a life of starvation or a life with a home, food, warmth and a purse of guineas held in an iron fist. To die from one or the other is a woman's choice.

Mercy runs a cold hand across her cheek and purses her lips. A man who raised a fist to her would be one who would shortly meet with the pointed end of a poker. Mercy suffers no fools gladly. Even at fourteen, she is sharp and hard, the way a person grows when there is little food and even less love. The way a person grows when life is for surviving, not living.

There are shop fronts leading towards the bridge on this side of the river, and she pauses to glance at her reflection in one of the windows and to adjust her bonnet. She is quick-witted, precocious, and she has been told on numerous occasions by her mother, an ugly, scrawny little piglet. This glance affirms all of these things, and she winds a stray lock back up into her bonnet and turns from the glass towards the bridge. Demolition work is beginning; soon the gatehouse, prison and chapel on the bridge will be no more. This place is expanding, and the bridge must move with the times too. Men are here swarming about the bridge like ants with tools and carts and plans, and Mercy is sure she can hear a hush wash over them all as she passes, for this is a small town and most people know each other by name, even though they won't admit to it. In weeks gone past, she has flashed an eye or an ankle at a few of their number, but now she cannot look at them. She is sure they all know that she is related to the wife-killer, John Newton. She is sure she hears the words whispered, 'Newton, Severn Hall'. She tarries not, makes no flirtation now that she is such a spectacle of the macabre, and instead bustles across the bridge, beneath which the brown, streaking water of the River Severn gushes. Horses trundle by pulling carts of skins, wood and coal. Down by the riverside, men call to each other as they unload cargo. A boy is standing on the other side of the bridge, on Underhill Street, flogging newspapers.

"Read all about it!" he yells, and Mercy hurries by, passing him as he pointedly relates the headlines at the top of his lungs, "Bridgnorth man sentenced for murdering his wife! John Newton of Severn Hall to hang!" She knows he's saved this for the very moment she passes and has to stop herself from going over and kicking his ankles out from under him. Her cheeks burn as she trudges past the sandstone cliff and up Church Steps, up, up and up, until she passes the fine house at the top where the magistrate lives, and out onto the Castle Walk where she stops a moment to catch her breath and look out across the valley.

The day is cold and grey, and the river high. The sandstone outcrop known as Queen's Parlour is away across the river, and down below the bustle at the river port emits a clanging and a shout every so often, and the formidable warehouses on either side of the river sit squat and bleak. Smoke rises from chimneys all about, and everywhere the people get on with their days; only Mercy Newton cannot. She watches the town beneath her, watches the workers, closes one eye and makes a motion with her thumb as though to squash one of them. She hates this place, these people, their earnest toil and their empty pockets. She cannot accept that this is all life has for her – to grow old quickly, to work her fingers to the bone, to be hungry and poor, perhaps to marry and eke out her days squeezing out brats and fending off the fists of a slurring, stinking husband. This town is awash with ale houses: down by the river for the sailors, up on the High Street, and every other man, her mother has assured her, is a drunk. She cannot accept that this is all there is.

She takes a deep breath and the air is sharp in her chest, sharp and cold like a knife. Then she sets her face to the wind and continues past the old, leaning Norman castle keep and out onto the High Street. She is set for the bank, where she knows her mother is to be found, for here she comes on this day at this time every month to pick up the interest from all her money in the world, and that which is Mercy Newton's obsession. Anne Newton has £500 which she cannot touch, left to her by her father that she might live off the interest. Upon her death, Mercy is to have two hundred pounds of it straight into her hand, and the rest is to stay untouched for her to gain the interest. Mercy cannot wait.

Up in the High Street is a cart outside the butchers unloading carcasses, and a couple of well-heeled gentlemen have stopped to talk outside the guildhall. Another damned newspaper boy is yelling at the top of his lungs,

"Murderer John Newton to hang! Leaves four orphans behind! Read all about it!" Then he stops, grins and winks. "'Mornin', Mercy," he says, and she scowls at him. "One of yours, ain't he?"

This time she really does lose her temper. She rounds on him spitting rage, takes him by the collar, and with a strength she appears incapable of with her stick-thin arms, she dashes him into the gutter, newspapers flying, to his cries.

"Watch your tongue, Edward Maiden, or you'll end up in the river," she hisses.

She steps back, and he scrabbles about, grabbing the papers up from the mire of the street, but many are already sodden.

"I'll 'ave to pay fer those, you evil bitch!" he mutters, but not too loudly, for he does not doubt she won't hasten to do worse to him. After all, her cousin is a murderer – might she not have it in her too?

Mercy Newton wipes her hands on her skirts. She glares about her, but those who have seen what has happened have lowered their eyes and are about their business once more; what is a scuffle between two nippers? All except one. Anne Newton is standing just outside the milliners facing the window but her head is turned and she has seen all. She shakes her head slowly, turns from her daughter and is gone, up the High Street towards the bank.

Mercy runs after her.

"Wait for me!" she calls. "Wait!"

She dodges a couple of older gentlemen conversing outside the public house and dashes between a woman with a little dog on a dainty leash and a shop boy carrying a box. Reaching out, she takes a firm hold of her mother's arm, so firm it makes her cry out.

"Kitty! You're hurting me!"

"Don't walk from me then," she retorts. "I want that money from you."

Anne turns a weathered face to her. "We can't afford it, Kitty. Not this week."

Mercy laughs but her eyes are cold. "Can't afford it? You always say that. But there's five hundred pounds in the bank!"

"Don't start this again," Anne returns, then yanks her skinny arm from her daughter's iron grip, wraps her shawl closer about her and makes to go past. "Selfish, that's what you are."

"I'm startin' nothin'," says Mercy, her thin lips pursed all the thinner. "But that money's mine, festerin' away in that bank 'til you die. And all I want's a ribbon."

"No," comes the reply, and Anne is moving, faster than she ought to be able to on those pin-legs, her clothes swamping her, her hair bedraggled and already grey and coming loose like a wanton woman's all down her back.

"All this town is talkin' of the Newtons!" Mercy yells after her. "I'll have no peace now! An' you won't even fetch me a ribbon for my troubles!"

She clenches her fists and looks about her, spies a stone

underfoot, grabs it, takes aim and lets it fly, but her aim is lousy and it clatters off the cobbles.

"A shocking business," she hears whispered somewhere behind her. She turns and there are two gentlemen, one with a newspaper beneath his armpit, and neither is paying her mind.

"Brutal," comes the other opinion.

"Those poor, poor children," comes the reply.

"And the one that died in her," says the second.

Another gentleman joins them with a lady on his arm. The voices do not even attempt to feign a whisper; they are all at it, talking about it, and the glances that come from them show they know who she is. She turns from them, eyes stinging, and stumbles, cheeks burning, across the road and up in the opposite direction to her mother.

Up to St Leonard's Church she goes, away from the High Street, and the black figure of the vicar is just disappearing inside. It is quieter here outside the grammar school where the little scholars are hard put to learn their letters, and Mercy sits upon the wall, cold and shuddering. She has no ribbon, only the tarnish of her family that gives colour to her cheeks and shame to her heart. She sits and stares at the ground, and only now that she's heard them mentioned does she start to think of those four little Newton children, the ones that had lost their mother and whose father would surely hang. She's spared them no thought until now, and it is only the words of those she has overheard on the street and the thought of the little scholars inside the grammar school that have swung her thoughts towards them.

These little Newtons will become orphans. She wonders what that's like. At the thought of them, she finds that her eyes are stinging and wipes her sleeve across them.

"As if it weren't enough that your own father went off and died like that," Anne's voice breathes, and Mercy turns to find that her mother has followed her and is seating herself on the wall beside her. "Now his kin are all at it, cursing this name we've had stuck to us, like shit on yer shoe. Cursed, the Newtons, all of 'em," she says in harsh tones, a cracked voice from a cracked soul. "You best watch yourself, Kitty, watch yourself and pray." She reaches out, uncharacteristically, to take Mercy's shoulder, but Mercy shrinks back from her touch; it usually comes with a sting at the end. Anne cackles. "Now hold your head high, my girl, and get off your arse and help me with business."

It takes little time to spend most of Anne's money on candles, bread and gin, yet as they pass the newspaper lad before the bridge, Anne gives in to a queer fancy and purchases a newspaper much to the lad's amusement. His eyes flash and Mercy knows that if he says a single word, one single word, she will hurl him into the river. The newspaper is tucked quickly away; Mercy knows it is all for John Newton and the gossip it contains. Later, Anne will no doubt expect her to read it to her by the light of a candle, for her eyes are weak, like the rest of her, Mercy thinks.

They reach home sullenly, trudging up the other side of the valley, Mercy far ahead of her mother, who wheezes, coughs and cusses to herself as the road steepens. She has already taken a few large lingering swigs of the neat gin and is slurring her words. Mercy strides ahead of her, for her mother is cruel once she's half-cut.

"A burden," she is muttering now, her words carried towards Mercy on the breeze. "Demanding. Ungrateful bitch."

Mercy's heart drops. It will be another evening of curses and rails from her mother, now that she has already taken down so much gin before the sun has set. Yet as they reach Batch Pool Lane, Anne's mutterings cease, for there is Edward Edwards, her brother, smoking outside their door, having tramped himself down that out-of-the-way, lonely lane, past the few scattered homes that house farmworkers, and he greets them with a cheery wave.

"What the devil do you want, Ed?" Anne asks, squinting into the daylight. He looks altogether an Edwards, almost as broad-shouldered as the Newtons, mean about the mouth.

"He's to hang, Anne," he tells her. "John is to hang. For certain now. I went to the trial."

She stares at him, her eyes aflame. Mercy sees her expression soften.

"You'd best come in," she says, for how dearly she wants to know it all, does Anne, wants to hear every last detail of that bastard John Newton's trial.

Edward Edwards, her brother, strides inside and looks about the place with disdain.

"I thought Thomas left you provided for?" he says, picking up a stool on its side and seating himself upon it but not without first wiping it with his handkerchief.

"Pfft, him? He left me nothing but the interest of £200, as long as the money remained in the hands of his bloody son," she tells him. "And that nasty piece of work has seen to it that I haven't had so much as a penny in many a year." She sucks her teeth.

Edward nods slowly. "I doubt it not," he admits sadly, though Anne had hoped for his outrage. His eyes stray to the bottle she has left on the table. "Pour," he says. "Pour and I'll take a drink with you, you little witch, and tell you all about the spring assizes and what is to become of your dead husband's kin."

Mercy sits in the corner unseen as Anne is pouring, Edward is removing his hat and coat and declaring loudly upon the weather. He seats himself on top of a chest that contains some moth-eaten bedding and listens.

"Well," says Uncle Ed, taking a swig, and Mercy glares at him, for she rarely sees a member of her family and she's been fairly convinced by her mother's ramblings that none of them are any good on either side. "It's a sorry tale, and our good brother John has been setting things to rights at Severn Hall, for he was close to John Newton, our John." He sighs. "It's a twisted old thing, and it seems one of ours aided in it all. George Edwards swears he told John to leave her be, swears on the Bible, on his mother's life, that he told John Newton he would rather forget the bill that was owed than John lay a hand on his wife for pocketing the money herself. They say John tried everything to get off, pleaded insanity, and a case of him sleep-walking was brought before the jury to try to prove his madness which stated that upon that instance, he shot off a gun from his bedroom window." At this, he puts his drink down. "Your Thomas was he, I mean, other than at the end, was he ever unstable?"

Mercy sees her mother suck in her lips. Thomas, her dead father, was a man she never met. She often when told of his great temper feels glad to have missed him. However, he has seen to it from beyond the grave that they are tormented – having passed his name of Newton like a disease to her mother and to her. There is evil in that name now and a curse in the bloodline. Everyone knows it.

"Unstable? No more than any Newton," Anne spits, glancing at her daughter whose face has caught her attention. It is so pale that it almost shines in the shadows of the corner. "John isn't mad. He's just a bastard."

Uncle Ed snorts and drinks some more. "He'd tried to get the witness, Mary Jones I think her name is, to lie to the court," he tells her. "But she didn't."

"Good girl," says Anne and slurps at her drink. Mercy nods.

Good girl to tell the truth, to tell the truth against a bastard Newton.

"Two people rushed into the court and were restrained," he goes on. "So desperate they were to see the trial. The place was a carnival, by all accounts." His eyes suddenly follow Anne's gaze into the shadows. "Don't hide yourself away, girl," he says and his eyes narrow. "Grown, ain't she?"

"Tall as you now," Anne says.

Mercy says nothing. She observes her uncle, who lives close by but rarely makes an appearance at their door; too mystified and disgusted, no doubt, at the meagre paucity of it all.

"Move forwards, come into the light and talk with us, Mercy," Uncle Ed requests.

"Call her Kitty," comes her mum's voice. "Short for Catherine. After Mum. And after..." She trails away dramatically. Mercy feels no pity. She knows she is named after her own dead sister, and she knows it has been sixteen years since the child Catherine Newton passed on to a better life. Enough people lose babies for her to have become hardened to a past that existed before her own birth. She feels no pity for the dead Catherine, for if she had lived perhaps Mercy would have been the one to perish.

"Mercy Catherine Newton, better known as Kitty," says this man's face and his hand reaches for her and gestures her to come closer. "Come out of the shadows and greet your uncle properly."

Mercy wrinkles her nose, but Anne's voice comes clear enough and she knows she can't evade it.

"Out you come, Kitty, and greet your Uncle Ed."

With a sigh and a roll of the eye, Mercy rises and shuffles the few steps toward him, standing there, smoothing her skirt for a moment. Every vein in her body throbs with distaste at this display her mother is forcing her to put on, this exposure of herself before this man she barely knows.

“’Mornin’,” she says gruffly.

“Uncle Ed,” her Mam pushes.

“’Mornin’, Uncle Ed,” she says in no less a gruff voice, and despite the filthiness of her hands, he takes one anyway and shakes it. Then he grips it hard and pulls her towards him until his face is but an inch from her own and continues his dramatics.

“The judge, he said, ‘You have deprived one of life who t’was your duty to cherish and protect, for what cause?’” His voice is deep and his breath is hot on Mercy’s face. She tries to pull back but is trapped, and this makes his words ever the more fearful. Not only that, but he reels off the words verbatim as though he were the fatal judge himself. “‘Why, because Sarah Newton, your wife before God, had misapplied the trifling sum of three shillings’.”

“Three shillings!” Mercy echoes lustfully; to her, three shillings is a portion of a fortune. She wriggles and pulls until she is free, and her uncle sits back with satisfaction at a tale well told.

“On Monday next, he hangs,” Uncle Ed says gravely, smoothing his hair and turns to Mercy. “Let that be a lesson to you, young Kitty Newton, to always hold your temper.”

“She’s got a temper like a cat, that one,” Anne sniffs, but her words are slurred. “She drives me to drink, she does.”

Uncle Ed purses his lips and strokes one of his whiskers. “This thin little thing? A temper? I believe it not, sister.” He throws back his drink and laughs more. It is a warm laugh, Mercy notes. A kind laugh.

Anne does not break a smile. Indeed, her face is stone. Mercy looks from one to the other, from laughter to loathing, and knows her mother takes no joy from her existence; she knows that if she had not been born, the money would stretch further and Anne might live closer to town or somewhere else entirely. She might even have found a new husband by now, but nobody wants a poor widow with a ragged, skeletal daughter hanging off her skirts. She knows her mum still cries in the night for the babies she lost, Mary and Catherine, those little girls, the ones before Mercy was born. She knows she wishes one of those had lived instead, and cold, hard Mercy had been the one to perish.

Uncle Ed is all for dramatics. He hunches himself and spreads his hands. "He tried to run in the end," he says in a hushed whisper. "Tried to bolt from the bar before his sentence was read. And once it was read, he wouldn't leave it, held on for dear life; they had to send in men to prise him away, and as he went he cried out..."

At this, Anne cannot help but clasp her heart, but Mercy does not know if it is from joy or pity.

"'Dona kill me!'" cries Uncle Ed, his deep voice so great he might be on a stage. "'Dona kill me!'"

Anne is silent as his words fade, but Mercy cannot bear to think of this man begging for his life, no matter what he did to his wife. She rises and flits out through the door, into the lane and through the leaves until she is quite hidden from view, and here she stands, remembering those words, 'Dona kill me!' in Uncle Ed's deep, pitiful voice until she falls to her knees in the moss and holds her hands over her ears. Her head is swimming, swimming as it has been all month, with the tale of John Newton of Severn Hall.

When Uncle Ed leaves at last, Mercy comes out of her hiding place near the gate post by the big house and slinks back into the cottage.

Anne picks her head up from the table and stares blearily at her. "You'll be staying here and if you need anything, you're to look to Mrs Littleford," she says. "I'm going to Shrewsbury with Uncle Edward and Uncle John." She cocks her head at Mercy's pout and winks. "I'm off to see a man hang."

Mercy flares and rants when her mother repeatedly refuses to take her to Shrewsbury, to the execution of John Newton.

"You don't want to see a spectacle like that at your age," is her repost, but none of this hangs true with Mercy. She's no child. Fourteen she might be, but she is sure that she can see a man hang and jeer with the best of them. Just as long as he doesn't beg for his life.

Anne never was close to Sarah Newton, but Mercy remembers visiting Severn Hall Farm when each of the four babies were born – though they were met each time with a frosty inhospitableness – and they'd have gone again if the fifth hadn't died in its mother's belly. One thing Anne said she had in common with Sarah was that they had both felt a Newton's fist. Since the murder, Anne has voiced the opinion no few amount of times that if Thomas hadn't gone when he did, her fate might have been the same as Sarah's.

"It's my duty to see that John Newton leaves this life," she tells Mercy.

"Mine too," Mercy tries, but Anne will have none of it and Mercy is left behind. On Sunday then, she stands in the lane and watches as Anne rides away in the trap with Ed Edwards and her other uncle, John Edwards, who had been good friends with cousin John. His face is pale at the prospect of watching him hang on the morrow. This family of Edwardses is together for the first time in as long as Mercy can remember. She hears her mother's uncharitable laughter carried on the breeze, while she is left behind in this hovel, alone and soiled with the name of Newton.

The Hanging of John Newton

Recollections of Thomas Whitmore, MP

Apley Estate, Bridgnorth

March 1823

My father having been the elected Member of Parliament for Bridgnorth swayed my interests somewhat as a younger man, drawing me towards following in his footsteps. Not only did I feel a draw to political and legal affairs, I was also deeply aware that, as his oldest son, I would inherit the Apley Estate, and all of the monetary benefits it carried., I harboured an interest in the affairs of the local area, for they were everything I had known in life up until being shipped off to Eton as my father was before me. At the age of sixteen, I returned to the homestead for Easter, which fell early that year on the 30th of March. I partook then not only in the celebration of the earthly demise of Jesus but also of a tenant of my father's, Mr John Newton. He was a farmer who oversaw the workings of Severn Hall Farm, across the river from the estate.

Allowed, at last, to dine amongst these men of authority thrice my age, I heard of the crimes my father had toiled over to find this man guilty and that man innocent. My father, ever diligent as an MP and ever caring about the welfare of his tenants, had been sorely vexed by this man's indiscretion, for it seemed he had killed his wife in a fit of rage over an unpaid bill. This man had attempted freedom in all manner of ways since his arrest – he had paid the coroner, Mr Whitcombe, a man my father knew well, to put together a jury that might be favourable to him, and he had feigned madness – yet neither of his schemes had succeeded in his efforts to dodge the noose. It transpired that he was to hang, and my father, his landlord and MP, was determined to go to the hanging. He had also decided that I, his first-born son and heir, was old enough to go too.

I was, by all accounts, fascinated and appalled by the idea, but my father would brook no excuses.

I remember it well, despite the years that have passed. I recall even the littlest details: the journey, the smells, the shades of colour and the heart pounding in my chest, as though to observe the death of another was to put my own at risk.

We set off directly after the Easter service. It took us over five hours to reach Shrewsbury in our carriage. My father and I wore matching greatcoats, with our collars up and warmers at our feet, for the late March chill was perishing. We paused at Much Wenlock to rest the horses and again at Cressage. It was growing dark when at last we came into Shrewsbury. We stopped at The Lion Hotel, the only place, my father told me, that gentlemen such as ourselves ought to stay in the town. We stepped down from the carriage, and a porter came to unstrap our bags. My father led the way; he was as confident here in Shrewsbury as he was at home. Every step was a stride, every word was firm, fair and absolute.

Monday morning, the day after the commemoration of the death of our Lord Jesus on the cross, would be the last morning John Newton would ever see, and it dawned bright. Monday the 31st of March 1823. My first public execution and it was a tenant of my father.

We rose early for my father was anxious to ensure that he might observe the proceedings well. It was a good course for by the time we arrived at the gaol, the crowd was already larger than any crowd I had ever seen before.

The hanging was to start at 8 a.m., and before us the multitude stood in the street, blowing on their hands and wrapped in their layers, all in position by seven, raring to roar and cheer as a man's life was taken from him. To my disbelief, a pie man elbowed his way between the people, and a baker's boy, and here and there people bought warm cobs and pastries stuffed with beef and potatoes. The tell-tale scents rose to my nostrils, and despite the overall aroma being more of potatoes than beef and I guessed more of hot air than either, I felt compelled to pat my pockets for coin, for it seemed the right thing to buy since those around us were already sinking their teeth into these steaming wares. My father reached to my wrist and shook his head.

"We do not eat what these people cook," he told me quietly. "Your gullet is more refined than theirs."

Many hangings were, he had told me in the carriage, done inside the gaol, but that day there was a scaffold set up, and the crowd were certainly not disappointed by it. I strained to hear the conversations of those about us. There was talk of nothing but the prisoner: that John Newton murdered not just his wife but his unborn child. People said he sought a coroner who was not to be trusted and that the jury had been selected to be favourable to him. Yet still, he would hang here today, for no jury on earth could find this man innocent.

Talk rippled throughout the crowd of Newton's plea of insanity and of his last night spent praying with the chaplain. Then suddenly everyone fell quiet. I hardly dared look up.

John Newton, a huge great bulk of a man, was being conveyed up the scaffold.

"Bloody hell," breathed a man close by; his companion shushed him.

"Burn in hell," a woman called out.

The death penalty – the hanging part of it anyway – was only the start of the torment the soul of this man who stepped out upon the scaffold would endure. The body of a convicted murderer would be cut up for medical research and then denied a Christian burial. This man climbed the steps up to the boards in full knowledge that this would be his fate. He trod slowly, as though to delay his end, a frightened shell of a man, hands tied and shoulders about his ears as though to protect his neck. All eyes were upon him as he reached the top step, and I recall the goosebumps that broke out across my arms. It suddenly seemed barbaric to me that this crowd would amass to witness the suffering moments of his last breath. Depraved. I glanced up at my father, and he read it in my eyes.

"It must serve as a deterrent," he told me. "Without such threats to a man's liberty, there are many more assembled here today who might, in a fit of passion, take the life of another. For them to witness this here, is for them to be chastened and tamed."

I glanced about us; indeed, there were rogues aplenty in this melee of expectancy. Up on the scaffold, the sad figure of John Newton turned to the crowd, searching for a friendly face no doubt.

"John Bolton of The Hem!" he cried hopefully, but someone else shouted back:

"He is not here!"

Newton shuffled his feet, then tried again,

"John Edwards, are *you* at least come over from Severn Hall?"

The crowd was deathly still now; no matter that this man had murdered his heavily pregnant wife, the spectacle of his piteous last moments weighed heavily now. This was not the rip-roaring quick-drop of an unrepentant murderer. It was the ghoulish observation of a man who was petrified to die.

"'Tis a sad death, my lads, for a young man like me!" Newton called out to the crowd now, pitiful at the last. "God bless you all!"

Inconceivably, a few cries of "God bless you!" were returned, fuelling Newton to nod, as though he believed God actually might bless him after all he had done.

"I would give all the world that it had not happened so!" he called out.

The crowd remained silent, but the hangman was waiting. I felt nothing but pity. Perhaps, I had started to suspect, I might not be cut out for my father's shoes. The distaste I now felt for the current situation was almost more than I could bear.

"Lord God, have mercy upon me!" Newton tried. "Don't hang me! I pray you, gentlemen, do not hang me yet!"

At a push from one of the prison guards, he kicked off his shoes and a bag was applied to his head. I found that I was gulping in the air, air which was ripe with pipe smoke and sweat even in this early morning cold, as John Newton was taken firmly to the noose.

All eyes were on the prisoner. All eyes but mine.

I did not watch as the trap door opened, and the crowd then, once the prisoner swung, roared. I could not. I wanted justice, but this was no more civilised than the burning of a mediaeval heretic or the public decapitation of a French aristocrat. This was a mob. They were like the hounds braying at the kill.

I wanted to chase them all away then, to see them off like a pack of curs, but my father's hand upon my shoulder kept me still and gave me my wits once more.

"Sometimes," he spoke wisely into my ear. "You will feel that the law is harsh. Sometimes you might feel it is more barbaric than the crime itself. Yet still we must uphold it, to save all that is civilised."

I turned away from the scaffold and knew he had seen my disgust.

"There is a clear choice," he said, and his words I have carried with me throughout my life; "The law or the collapse of society. These people need you to have a firm hand, Tom, when you become squire."

My eyes, ever certain in their path that they might not veer towards the man hanging from the scaffold, met his.

"I will," I promised, although every part of me was reviled now by it all. It would be my path and I must follow it. It was in my blood. I must live up to my father's legacy when the time came. "I will."

Mr Deighton, the Mayor of Bridgnorth, leaned over to me at the commencement of the coroner's inquiry into Mercy Newton's arrest and whispered,

"You will recall back in '24, the hanging of her cousin...?"

I glanced at Miss Newton, her dark figure beneath the stained glass and it all came flooding back. My disgust. The braying onlookers. The mob.

Now she had a mob of her own.

She was following in his footsteps.

And her past was my past.

I remembered the words of my father, 'There is a clear choice: the law or the collapse of society'.

I had seen it already in the people of Bridgnorth, in the rabble outside the prison and the guildhall. Indeed, they were crammed within these walls and they milled about without waiting for justice.

I know that I shuddered. For we were, myself and Mercy Newton. We shared a past and, I was beginning to perceive, a shared future.

Whatever the outcome might be.

The Hanging of John Newton

Mercy Newton

Batch Pool Lane, Bridgnorth
31st of March 1823

All day, on the day of her cousin's hanging, Mercy Catherine Newton is alone in the little cottage down Batch Pool Lane. She is taken by an urge to be useful now that her mother isn't around, and boils up some water and mops at the brick floor as best she can. She beats out the rag rug, then dunks it in the water butt for good measure and slings it over the gate at the end of the lane to dry. She spends a while reading the Bible, the only book they own which Anne took from her parent's farm when she married Mercy's father. The longer the day stretches, the more intent Mercy becomes to clean this place until it hardly resembles their home at all.

It isn't the first time she has spent a night without her mother, but there is no fodder for the fire and little left to eat. She must chew a hard crust and make it last whilst she watches the embers die taking with them the last twinkling of light.

Her head is pounding with the desperate words of John Newton given life by her Uncle Ed's deep imitating tones, 'Dunna kill me! Dunna kill me!'

As the day grows old, she stands in the darkness near the glass of the small windowpanes and thinks she can see in the darkness an outline of herself, a ghost, there in the glass. She shifts her feet, and the rough surface of the glass distorts the ghost – it might be

Mercy, but then it might be Anne. She lifts a hand to her neck, and the ghost in the windowpane does the same. She places her fingers about her throat and feels the bones and its soft skin. How easily a rope might squeeze the life from this neck, she thinks. Her lips part.

"Dunna kill me," she whispers to the ghost. "Dunna kill me!"

Somewhere outside a fox shrieks.

When Anne returns the following day it is late; Mercy is already sleeping. The cottage is tidy as though she has spent her time scrubbing and mending, filling her hours. Anne hopes the work has quelled her spirit, for she is growing afraid of the girl and her temper.

As she pulls off her skirt and clambers into her bed, Mercy stirs.

"Is there food?"

Anne has brought back a bun wrapped in her pocket and she retrieves it and passes it to her daughter. A thin hand comes out from beneath the blankets, takes the offering and pulls it back inside.

"How was Shrewsbury?"

Anne pauses, one foot in the bed, one foot out. "It was magnificent," she says finally, and snuggles down into the blankets, pulls a flask from somewhere and swigs her gin, as Mercy crams the bun into her mouth beneath her own blanket. One eats, one drinks, to celebrate the purging of John Newton from Severn Hall and this earthly paradise

They lie there in the darkness, the room growing colder by degrees, the fox out there somewhere, screaming into the night.

As she at last closes her eyes and drifts into a cold, cold

slumber, Mercy cannot help but hear those words again.

'Dunna kill me,' she hears, as her breathing slows. 'Dunna kill me.'

Chapter One

Mercy Newton

The Shrewsbury Road

December 1848

Mercy is rigid, stiff and chilled to the core as the carriage that takes her through the streets of Bridgnorth jolts against ruts in the road. In these last weeks, she has been transferred to the 'House of Correction', where at least she is inside a proper building. Although she sleeps on the harshest of pallets, lacking the luxury she is used to, this has set her joints solid. She aches now all over with an intensity that burns, and the jolting of the carriage sends waves of pain through her as she traverses these streets, away through the town and out towards the countryside.

She cannot look out, cannot bear to lift her eyes, for surely these streets will be thronged with people all vying to catch a glimpse of her, angry and throwing things, just as they have been every day as she was transported by cab and escorted by police officers to push back the hollering mob around the guildhall for the inquiry. She has never felt as though she belonged here and now she knows the hatred the people of Bridgnorth have for her; she has felt their spittle on her cheek and been deafened by their vitriol. Now they will be out there waiting to see if this is the coach that carries her, and she sits back, her bonnet low, wishing she could sink into the shadows so they might not see her.

To no avail. Word travels fast in this town. A magistrate's warrant and a coroner's hearing that failed to reach a verdict at Bridgnorth Guildhall has led her to this, and now thanks to the gossip wagon and to those who can read the printed word, everyone within a ten-mile radius knows the name of Mercy Newton. Line the streets, they do. The town is at a standstill for once, so all might come out and abuse her as she passes.

Opposite her sits a police constable, stern and still, his eyes piercing her skin as though he is reading her, seeking out the truth, glaring into her soul. She does not lift her gaze from her lap wherein lie her trembling hands, thin, white hands, delicate and slender. These are hands that have touched the skin of a lover, nursed old men on their deathbeds, hands that have held a newborn baby, polished silver and counted gold; now these hands will be forever tarnished and all good that they have achieved will dissipate. The police constable is staring at her hands too she notes in a glance, and she knows he is seeing not hands that have nursed others but instruments of violence.

"I know your mother," she snaps at him. "I doubt she brought you up to stare."

He glances at her coldly for a moment, then turns his eyes to the view.

Mercy's breath rises in white clouds, even here inside the carriage. This December is cold and wet. The River Severn has flooded, and still the rain persists, battering the carriage. Out, out of Bridgnorth they go, and at last she lifts her eyes and lets her gaze fall upon the fields, the familiar hedgerows. She casts her mind across this land she knows so well, traverses it in her head, the land she has walked these past thirty-nine years. She knows that just over there across the fields and down behind the hill, beyond sight towards the river, sits Severn Hall, where her cousin John murdered his wife, Sarah, back in 1823. It has been over twenty-five years since the murder at Severn Hall, but it is as raw today as ever it was.

"Oh, dear God!" the words rise from her belly as they did the night of her arrest, although as soon as they are said, she wishes they'd stayed buried. "This will be like Severn Hall again!"

She looks down again, back to her hands, and finds she is wringing them. She wonders what it is like to choke on the end of a noose. She wonders if she could fling herself from the carriage somehow and run into the hills. John Newton tried to bribe his way out, she remembers, and promised the coroner, Mr Whitcombe, money to build a jury of men who would announce his innocence. Even that hadn't worked; he had still been hanged, and Mr Whitcombe's name had been in all the newspapers too that summer months after the hanging, found guilty of misconduct, his career ruined. Besides, Mercy has no money, not now they've taken it from her to pay for her defence. She has nothing to bribe anyone with.

What will they tell Maria, she wonders. What exact words will they use to tell her what has happened? And what will Maria think, what will she do? She was ever a girl prone to the doldrums, prone to shadows in her mind, and who wouldn't be, stuck with Anne in that dreary little cottage. What will this news do to her?

Will she come to see her mother hang? Will she make the journey like Anne did when John went to the gallows?

Will she feel the want that Mercy once felt, to witness the demise of a blood-tied criminal?

Hour upon hour they go, without words, until the rhythm of the horses' hooves beats within her aching bones, a throbbing she can hardly endure, until at last, finally, she is numb to it.

Over and over, she asks herself how she came to be here, but the question is a stupid one; she'd seen this, foreseen it, in dreams and in words. Down she goes into herself, past the coldness that has become part of her, to find tears, but for now there are none. She does not weep, not for her soul, not for anyone else's.

Her heart, she finds now, is ice.

Shrewsbury Gaol gatehouse sits high above the town. Only the red, sandstone castle sits at a similarly prominent pinnacle. It is a place of awe and dread, a place of death, and it looms over the town, a threat to all who might dare disobey the law.

Mercy has never seen it before. Its squat gatehouse and impenetrable walls are the most terrifying things she's ever seen.

Will Maria stand out here as Anne had done, she wonders, when it is her turn to swing? Will Maria watch as her mother's feet dangle?

"Do you know what happens to the bodies once they've cut them down?" the police officer asks suddenly. She looks up at him but does not lose her dignity. She gives no response. The corners of his mouth are upturned and the set of his jaw is square and cruel. He has waited for a while to say this, she can tell, and he's expecting to enjoy her response. She will not give him the satisfaction. When her cousin John was hanged, his body would have been taken for dissection and then thrown in a pit most likely.

"You won't have a good Christian burial," he tells her, and she can see a sadistic merriment in his eyes. "You'll be dissected on the table, cut apart, naked, all your bits on show, skin all open and whiskery old men furtling with your guts." He clears his throat and spits out into the lane. "Imagine that," he says, raising his eyebrows, then sits back to observe her response.

"They stopped dissecting murderers more than ten years ago," she retorts primly. "Don't think just because I'm accused of murder that I don't read the newspapers."

He eyes her a moment then curls his lip. "Stuck up bitch," he growls. "Won't be so stuck up when you swing."

Outside the carriage now she hears voices and the clanking of locks undone, of hinges moving. The gatehouse is opened and the carriage is admitted, jolting forwards. Mercy casts one last look at the sky from the outside of the prison, then closes her eyes as the clattering of the horses' hooves echoes within the gatehouse. The prison gate shuts behind them and the definite, deafening metallic clangs of the bolts announce her incarceration.

Would it be worse to hang with Maria watching or without her, Mercy wonders, as she is led towards the governor's house. If she were Maria what would she do? But she already knows the answer before she has asked it of herself. Just as Anne Newton had to see John swing, Mercy would want to see, would want to witness the hanging of the person accused of her crime.

Maria has Newton blood through and through, she tells herself, as she is taken into that prison. Maria will come. Maria will want to see it through to the end, just as she herself had begged to go to cousin John Newton's hanging.

Will she cry, she wonders, or be overcome with a sickening thrill?

Whichever reaction, she is sure.

Maria will come.

Chapter Two

Mercy Newton

Winscote Hills, Apley Estate

1831

Bridgnorth and its environs are crawling with the names Newton and Edwards. They reach out, out into the countryside, out to Claverley, Chelmarsh, Stockton and Worfield, the strands of a web, interlinked, feeding off one another. Mercy is 22 years old and works in and out of service, ferrying between houses, cleaning in the big house on the lane, then over to an Edwards' house, helping at this relative's and that. When a baby is born she cleans and cooks and swaddles, she provides extra hands in a farm kitchen until the neighbour, aunt, second cousin's wife, third cousin or whatever relation they might be is back on her feet again. She is glad to be out and away from the shadows and her ever-tart old mother in Batch Pool Lane. She is happy to be about in the world, spending months on a farm over in Claverley, baking and scrubbing, until her cheeks are red and rounded. Then, months more over in Allscott to help keep house in an Edwards-run farm.

She sees people.

She sees *women*.

She sees what they marry into and how they can be ground down or held aloft, depending on the husband. She observes how women may marry up in life and how they may marry down. Each new place reveals to her more and more of the secret manner of marriage and life; each community bears the same scars and the same rhythms of life. She observes the contented, plump wives of the sober, hard-working men who have married their way into some sort of satisfaction, and the insect-thin, pursed-lipped, sad-eyed women who have married a drunk or a wastrel or a wife-beater. She learns and she observes. After each assignment, she returns for as little time as possible to her own mother. Her mother is her own insect-thin reminder that her father was a violent Newton who died before she was born. He left her mother with nothing but one sour, condemnatory, living daughter, and the ghosts of two dead ones.

She will not end up like this, she vows. She will never stoop so low as to be like Anne Newton. Life is for the taking. She will rise.

Mercy returns one Saturday from the market in Bridgnorth town to discover a horse and cart in the lane outside the little cottage. It is not Uncle Ed's nor Uncle John Edwards's cart, but a neatly packed cart of provisions. She stops in the lane and stares. There are grocery items boxed and packaged: flour, dried fruit, sugar, jars and bottles crammed into crates. She runs her hands across them, cocks her head and listens. She can hear the reedy tones of her mother, the slurring of her words, the detested effects of the gin on her ability to converse in a dignified manner. She cannot recognise the voice of the man who speaks with her. Absent-mindedly, she pulls out a jar from a crate and slips it into her own shopping, wriggling it down beneath her candles and another.

Then she passes by the cart and enters.

They are sitting close by the fire, this man and her mother, and Anne is ten sheets to the wind, making little sense and does not even notice that she has entered. But *he* does. He stands whilst Anne still sits, eyes rolling, cheeks red, mumbling something about firewood.

"Mercy," the man says and he nods in greeting.

"I said, you'll never be short of firewood, not there!" Anne burbles, then, "Kitty, that you?"

"Of course it's me," Mercy snaps and sets down her sack-cloth bag on the table. She cannot unpack it yet, for this man will see his jars amidst her things. She eyes him and undoes her bonnet. "Who're you?"

He smiles and his eyes seem familiar. "I'm James," he says, holding out his hand. "I'm your cousin. I'm lookin' for a housekeeper, and word has it that you keep house well." He refrains from looking about the place, for Mercy does nothing to keep this hole nice. She won't keep house when her mother ought to rip herself away from the bottle and do it herself.

"Another Newton then," Mercy says shortly, and hangs up her bonnet.

"He'll pay a good wage, he says, Kitty," Anne announces. "You said, didn't you, you said, you spoke of the terms?"

James Newton nods. "I did," he says.

Mercy casts her eye to her mother. "Wages you'll be wanting *your* cut of," she snaps, but Anne is reaching for her drink once more. "Where's the house?" she asks, sitting herself on the corner of the table. "Is it far?"

"Winscote Hills," he says. "Or thereabouts." He smiles again.

"He's a gamekeeper," her mother pipes. "At the Apley Estate."

"I live in the lodge house," James says. "I don't have a wife to take care of me. I'm alone, traipsing about all day in the mud. I need someone to cook, clean and keep house, a housekeeper, and people say that you are amenable. And efficient."

Mercy sucks her thin lips. She looks down at her mother,

lolling in her chair. The fire is burning low, and there is no wood stacked inside to dry.

"How are we related again?"

He meets her assessing gaze. "I'm your cousin."

She calculates. A cousin. So was the killer, John Newton, the son of her father's brother. She does not tarry with her inquisition.

"And what are you to John Newton, late these last few years, of Severn Hall?" She knows this question might be the end of the job offer, but she finds that she wants to know more than anything.

James Newton clears his throat. He stands and he is tall, so tall that he almost hits his head on their low ceiling. He has the Newton stature. His shoulders are broad and he looks down on her now from his great height and breadth and breathes, "I'm his brother."

There is a stalemate. Mercy's heart jolts then beats faster. The fire spits pathetically and Anne Newton burps a little as she readjusts herself in her seat.

"You needn't fear," he adds slowly, deliberately, pre-empting her thoughts. "I'm not like him. I won't strike you, not ever."

Anne Newton snorts. "You're a Newton," she burbles. "You all do it. She's no fool, my girl. She won't end up 'neath the fist of a Newton. She'll take the poker to you!" She starts to cackle, and Mercy's cheeks glow at the noise, like a crow, harsh and nasal.

"I'd deserve it too," he remarks charitably.

Mercy stares at him. He is perhaps forty or a little over, well-looking in the Newton way, strong, charming. It will just be a job. She can always walk away. He would not batter her like a Newton batters his wife. The terms are good. And she hates living here with her mother.

"When would you like me to start?" she breathes and her eyes sparkle a little in the gloom, for she can sense that there is danger to be met and dealt with, and she likes the idea of it.

Once he's gone Anne's cackling ceases and she takes on an altogether more sinister tone.

"They're all pigs, these Newton men," she tells Mercy. "Pigs. Don't you let him ruin you."

Mercy is chopping carrots and potatoes at the table. "Don't you talk of pigs," she tells her mother. "You live enough like one."

Suddenly Anne is beside her. "Don't go, Kitty," she breathes in her ear, contrary as the drink makes her. "He'll kill you, like his brother killed poor Sarah."

Mercy stabs her knife into a potato. "He can try," she says. "And I'll stick him like this spud."

Anne cackles again.

Mercy sits next to her cousin, the gamekeeper of the Apley Estate, the nephew of her dead father and the brother of the hanged John Newton, as he bears the cart off the road and up the lane, where a cottage sits on the hillside, looking out towards the looming trees, great, tall, ancient things, dark, abiding.

"Keeper's cottage," says James, nodding at it. "Not mine. Another keeper."

She is determined not to speak of John Newton again, not to ask, not to mention him, but his existence has been more real to her, more jibed at by anyone hearing her name, more spoken about by any of her Edwards relatives, than this man. In fact, she had not even registered that he existed before his appearance at their little cottage, for John Newton's legend has overshadowed them all for these last seven years and no Newton will ever claim such notoriety again, she thinks. None of them will be remembered in a hundred years, none but John unless another cracks and murders. But now, she bumps against the bulk of his brother as the cart hits a rut, and listens as he talks, and he does not seem to be a monster, a legend or a bastard.

"I spend most of each day out on the estate," he tells her. "Some nights too at different times of the year. On the lookout for poachers too, so we'll not cross paths for much of the day. But I bring in the leaves and the mud no matter how I remove my boots, and I've always a hankering for a hot tea and some stew or the like after a long cold day. It's tedious to make shift for myself."

"I'll keep house well enough," she tells him. "If there's things I do that you don't want, tell me so. And if there's things you want doing that I've overlooked, likewise tell me."

She has taken care of other humans and other houses now for years. Her quick efficiency has made a name for her, to Anne's amazement – never has she extended her skills to care for her undeserving mother, who wallows in her own inebriety back in Batch Pool Lane, never lifting a finger to help herself, living off her interest from her damned five hundred pounds. How she struggles to live with five hundred pounds in the bank is beyond Mercy's comprehension. She grits her teeth.

"We won't be always on our own," he continues, beside her. His voice is confident, kind. "Edward is here too, and there's John and William Barnfield over at Ewdness Manor, we'll see some of them. And there are other gamekeepers and families that live on the estate."

"Edward?" she thinks for a moment that he means her uncle, Edward Edwards, but he is quick to tell her, "My brother, Edward Newton, he's got a farm close by."

She nods; another brother of John Newton then. "My uncle, John Edwards, was a friend to your brother John," she says, belying her thoughts. "So many Johns, Edwards, Newtons and all." She lets the words drift away, over the hills. The air here seems different, not tainted by foundries or chimney after chimney; even in Batch Pool Lane, they seem to bear the brunt of Bridgnorth's industry in their lungs. Here though it all seems fresher, cooler, better. Upriver, up into the Winscote Hills. She turns to him. "Do you not have any sisters? Is it all men that you know then?"

He snorts. They hit another rut and she bounces off him. He smells of carbolic and woodsmoke. Mercy is used to living out of the way, to being far from town. However, even in a damp, solitary little place like Batch Pool, there were other cottages in shouting distance, and she only had to cross a field to look down across the valley at the town. She cannot spy a single house here now they have passed the first keeper's cottage.

She is silent, for her thoughts are heavy in her head, but he is determined to break the silence; she can sense his unease at her quietude. He clears his throat.

"Are you happy to come then? I mean, it's a way from town."

She shrugs. "It's a way from my mother too. And that's never a bad thing. She's harsh when she drinks."

He nods.

They round the top of the hill. The wind hits them as they crest the top. The view spans down, over the valley, across trees, green and luscious, the red stone of the land piercing the emerald spread at intervals and the river snaking along at the bottom. He stops the cart and they look out, and there away across the river, tiny, so small yet so conspicuous, sits Severn Hall, white and piercing.

He knows she's staring. She can sense him tense beside her.

"You don't have to fear me," he tells her again softly. "I'm not like John was."

During the week she took to prepare herself for her departure, Mercy has heard tales from anyone and everyone she could gather them from about these Newtons, these cousins of hers. She knows of the reputation these men carried in their youth: strong, powerful, unstoppable, charming and determined. Unstable. He turns to her now and catches her by the chin.

"Not afraid, are you?"

She stares at him and wonders which parts of his face resemble his hanged brother, and which resemble her dead father. He does not look unstable.

"Why is it *I* who ought to be afraid?" she asks darkly, and the corners of her mouth turn upwards. "I'm a Newton too. Perhaps *you* ought to fear *me*."

He snorts at this, takes up the reins and on they go away, two Newtons together.

Mercy wakes in the night to a storm. A crack of lightning overhead and a flash so violent that it lights the room, pulls her to her senses quickly and she throws a shawl about her shoulders and treads over to the window to see outside. All is darkness, shadow, shifting blackness against blackness. The might of nature is crashing about, cracking branches in the wind, and rain lashes down hard against the pane.

This cottage is not what she expected. It is nothing like the hovel her mother lives in. Mercy had wondered how she would fare with this unknown cousin, living on top of each other, but the gamekeeper's lodge is spacious, and James has installed a bolt upon her bedroom door that she might seal it and have some security of mind. She wonders if the storm has stirred him but can hear no sounds from across the landing. She goes back to bed, back to the warm spot she has made, and curls up in this bed all her own, in this room all her own, in this house which is four or more times the size of the little cottage in Batch Pool Lane. There is no incumbent wife and no brood of children, just two dogs, whose pawprints now adorn her skirt. She hugs herself gleefully and prays that this position might last.

She next opens her eyes at a knock upon her door and the sound of clumping boots taking themselves down the stairs. Opening her door, there is a glass of milk standing outside it. She smiles, takes it in and goes to the window, to see him, her cousin, striding out into the early morning, whistling to his dogs, who come flitting past, a shotgun on his shoulder.

She takes her time to ready herself. There is a little scuffed looking glass on the old chest of drawers in her room, and she squints into it to tidy her hair, pin it up, smooth her dress down, and she tries to rub off the dried paw prints and uses cold water from the jug to wash her face and hands.

He will be back by ten, she knows this. He has told her his routines and informed her of his needs. He will require a breakfast of a substantial nature and a pot of tea. He will expect the kitchen to be warmed by the range. These then, are her first tasks. She finds that he has already filled two buckets with water, for he is, as he told her on their first meeting, used to making shift for himself. The range is clean and lights easily enough, and she sweeps, boils water and mops the tiled floor, which is thick with dried mud. She takes out the mat from the doorway and beats it in the fresh, sharp morning air, the air of a world that has been cleansed by a storm. She puts the rag rug that sits before the range to soak in a bucket, for its colours are quite hidden with dust and caked mud from his boots. Then she finds bacon in the larder, and eggs and bread, and goes by the clock that ticks on the mantel to time it all for his return.

When he arrives home, she is waiting at the door smiling, and the dogs come flying in before him, paw prints skidding across the clean floor and he grins ruefully.

"It'll always be like this," he tells her. "You'll find that the mopping must be done, but that the effects are fleeting."

He sits, boots flaking vegetation about the place, and she takes his tin plate which has been warmed over the oven and places it before him with cutlery, and watches him tuck in. He closes his eyes to savour the bacon.

"Ah, the taste of food when it has not been cremated by my own rough hands." He looks to her for a moment. "Are you not eating?"

She shakes her head and places a mug of tea before him. "I will eat when you are back out there. I did not think..."

"But you must eat with me," he says perplexed. "We are family."

And that is that. Each meal now is eaten together. Each day he leaves early, comes home for breakfast, then leaves again, often carrying some sort of net or fishing tackle, and always with dogs and a gun. Her days are filled with scrubbing, dusting, washing, mending, cooking and plucking, and then he is home. She ensures, however, on that first day, that once he is gone, she explores the house.

Up to the very top she goes first, to the attics, of which there are three, so huge is this house in comparison to anything she has ever known. They are filled with boxes, gun boxes, nets hung from the walls, fishing rods, strange, long spear-like things, dog leashes and muzzles, powder and shot flasks. She stands amidst it all and knows better than to touch any of it. Each item will have its place. James will know exactly where each thing belongs, and she ought not to alter a thing. Besides, the paraphernalia of the gamekeeper holds little interest to her. She descends the stairs, checks at a window to make sure she will not be discovered and lets herself into his room. It is orderly, bare. A bed, with a smear of mud on the sheets near the footboard, which indicates he has fallen asleep on top of the covers with his boots on. A chest, a set of drawers. A pitcher and ewer. A block of carbolic. A small fireplace with a log basket. Little else.

Another room lies up there, made up as though for a guest, but simple again. No comforts. Swathed in dust.

Downstairs there is the kitchen where they eat, and a best room covered in a layer of dust – she doubts he comes in here. There is another room made out for dining, but more dust. Hard chairs, a hard bench, a stone floor and the sort of chill that belies the abandonment of a room. She takes a stick of black lead and makes the little range neat, then makes up the fire in here, sets it burning, dusts and lays the table. They will eat in here tonight. She will help him to enjoy, to inhabit, this place, she decides, and with his enjoyment she will have her own. She will be mistress of all these rooms not just the kitchen.

When he returns, he is filled with the news of his day – how he will be busy with a partridge shoot in a few weeks, that Thomas Whitmore, the squire of Apley, is having guests over and that he has met with him today to go through some of the details. He tells her of the beehives he keeps and indicates the jars of honey that came from them in the larder. He is all talk: of the ferreting that's happened at Long Hill, the children from the village he's tasked with collecting acorns to save for the deer for winter and of the beer delivery that will be coming tomorrow from the

Hundred House – he's ordered a barrel.

Mercy smiles to hear him, opens the oven at the side of the range and takes out the potatoes she has roasted, along with chicken and parsnips. She dishes it up, with carrots from a pan, and as he sets to seat himself at the kitchen table she says, "Dining room," and sweeps her way through and into the open door, where the fire is crackling and there is beer poured and waiting. She sets down the plates and pulls back the chair she has chosen for him.

"Well," comes his voice from the doorway, and he sits wordlessly as she sits opposite, he casts his eyes about the place and sees that the dust is gone, the floor is mopped and the grate is newly black-leaded. He smiles at her, his eyes creasing and his lips parting to say, "What a surprise," before taking up his knife and fork and tucking in.

There are outbuildings here hidden at the back of the house, occupied by other workers in the daytime. Stable workers arrive each morning at six to take care of the five pairs of horses who require feeding, exercising, mucking out, rubbing down, hoof picking and shoeing, and the cleaning of the tack often takes them beyond their twelve-hour shift. Mercy sometimes takes them a jug of beer, for which they are always thankful.

She has time one afternoon that first week to explore the grounds of this place. James takes some terriers and goes rat-catching leaving her to wander. Out into Spring Coppice she goes, exploring her new territory, through the trees, the sounds of skylarks and stock-doves in her ears. Down the valley, towards the River Severn, across which she can see the startling white of Severn Hall staring back at her. She sits, thoroughly alone, long enough for the rabbits not to notice her. Tentatively they come out from the bracken one by one, eyes darting at first until they settle in the long grass. She sits listening, breathing, watching. Their movements are quick; they exist merely to prolong their existence. She has lived like one of them for too long already. It tires her just to watch their twitches and their starts every time the breeze catches a blade of grass too closely for comfort. Like her mother, she thinks.

The grey sky is reflected in the water, grey above and grey below, and yet though it is grey it is teaming with life. At the edge she can see small shoals of roach flitting this way and that. The river is deep and strong enough here that it could carry her away if she slipped. There are tales that all along this riverbank on both sides, all the way down to Bridgnorth and beyond there are underground caves, spaces where the river can hide a person so that they are never found again. So easy for a life to disappear, she thinks. She looks over to the rabbits again, over where the bracken grows thicker. They are playing, she realises, one bounding at another, one diving in between the bracken stalks, before popping out a few feet away. Suddenly a laughing cacophony of duck calls echoes about her.

There is joy to be had from life, she decides. *Existing is not enough for me. I want to live.* For the first time in her twenty-two years, she thinks perhaps this is possible, here with James.

On Saturday, he returns with the dogs at ten for his breakfast, and with him he brings a horse and cart. Mercy sits with her eggs and asks, "Are you to town?"

"*We* are," he tells her and smiles. "How is your sewing?"

"You need something mending?" she asks, but he laughs.

"I want my house to be a home," he says. "I will buy fabric, and you will make curtains and the like. Comforts. Now there's a woman in the house, we need a bit of colour and some niceties."

She smiles. "That will be easy enough."

"Then you must come with me," he tells her. "To choose the fabric. I have no eye for that sort of thing."

They ride into town together, jolting along the lane and out into the road, the river on one side and the red sandstone cliffs rising on the other. Over the bridge and up into the town, where they leave the horse and cart at the back of one of the public houses; James tipping the landlord and promising they will drink there once their shopping is complete. Mercy strides beside him out into the High Street, until he gives her his arm and with pride she takes it. Then they go as one; her lips curl up in the corners and she delights in meeting the eye of those who have ever snubbed her or made comments about her family, those who have turned up their nose at Anne's harsh curses, bad-mouthing her on market day as she tags along, hoping for sixpence or a penny even of that five hundred pounds but never seeing it. Her heart is soaring. James tips his hat to one man and calls a greeting to another, and about there are cries of "'Mornin', Jim," and "Newton, how's the pheasant population looking?" Working men and men of property alike seem to know him.

She indulges him and persuades him to buy the necktie he sees in the window of Bowen's outfitters, tells him the colour will suit him well, and he in turn declares she must have the ribbon that sits next to it that they might match.

Boot polish and beeswax, dusting cloths, herrings, flour, raisins, treacle and wine he buys before they even reach the end of the High Street. As they walk bags now filled and heavy and Mercy's heart sky-high with pride that this is her cousin and that this is what he can afford, they pause outside the hotel at the corner of Whitburn Street, where men turn to greet him and include him in their gossip, and with him, her.

"Up the Stoneway Steps, he reckons," one is saying. "And round Castle Walk, all on horseback. He'll do it, too."

"No wonder they call him Mad Jack," another says.

"I'll wager good money that he'll fall," another adds, but James shakes his head.

"He'll do it," he says. "He'll do it, and I'd bet five pounds on that."

"There'll be time for betting on the day," another says.

James turns to Mercy. "Then come we must," he says. "I'll not miss this for the world."

"Who is Mad Jack?" she asks as they reach the place James is intent on buying his comfort material from.

"Mad Jack Mytton," he tells her in hushed tones. "From over Oswestry way, Halston Hall. He's a drinker, and a gambler, and a mad, mad bastard." He stops and turns to her. "Oh, I'm sorry," he says, casting his eyes to his boots. "I don't curse in front of a lady. I've been too long alone."

She laughs. "It's nothing I've not heard my mother say." She squeezes his arm. She does not add that it's nothing she hasn't said to her mother in return.

He pushes open the door and gallantly guides her inside. "Then we will see this man carry out his feat? I want to see it," she breathes.

As they drive the cart back, packed with their things – Mercy's ribbon that matches cousin James's neckerchief and a bundle of fabric she has chosen from Bowen's – along with the promise of betting, drinking and the spectacle of a mad man riding a horse up Stoneway Steps and around the precipitous Castle Walk, they return. Mercy can feel a fire in her belly like never before.

Sunday, Mercy rises and prepares for church. They are to go to Stockton church where she will set eyes on more Newtons and perhaps the Whitmores of Apley Estate, James's employers. She must look her best, and she ties the ribbon he bought her about her throat and hopes that it sets off her eyes as well as she thinks, although in the tiny, scratched looking glass, it is hard to tell in the dim light of the morning. She feels, for the first time in her life, pretty and as though life here has made her bloom.

After a breakfast of porridge and honey, they walk through the estate together. It is the first time she's seen him walk about without the dogs or a shotgun, and she smiles to herself as he points out a building here: Ewdness Farm; a line of buildings there: Newton Farm, though no Newton lives there now; Winscote Cottages, where some of the land-workers live; and all the while, others are walking or riding in the same direction. They spot a person in the distance that James says is his brother, Edward. When at last they come to the church, a fine carriage and two horses are halted outside, a smartly-dressed coachman sits waiting patiently, and James calls a greeting to him as they pass; they are some of the last to enter – Mercy realises that James's natural gait is much faster than her own and he had not set off with this in mind. There is a pew waiting for them, and James takes his place in it and nods to those about him. However, to Mercy's disappointment, there is no time for him to point out who is who. She is content, though, that James is wearing the kerchief. It suits him as well as she hopes her ribbon suits her.

The choir is made up of boys who sing well enough, but who,

partway through the sermon, begin to ripple. Then out flies from somewhere a sparrow, and the boys cry out in delight and a woman at the front of the church shrieks. Laughter rises from the choirboys and the rector shoots them a frown, but Mercy is laughing behind her gloved hand, and she can feel that beside her James is chuckling too.

Afterwards, she is introduced to the Whitmores themselves as James's new housekeeper, and she makes herself humble and friendly as Sir Thomas Whitmore, the Old Squire himself, smiles and his wife tells her how pleased they are that James will have someone to take care of him. In return, she tells them that she is honoured to work on their estate and receives approval, but of Edward Newton, James's brother, there is no sign; he has escaped without their notice. James looks about for him amidst the departing churchgoers, but he is gone.

"That's a pity; you might have met another cousin," he says. "Still, there is always next Sunday."

A pity indeed, however, Mercy finds she is not disappointed for it means that she can stroll back with James undisturbed.

She makes the curtains in moments between trips to fill her buckets, boiling, stewing, mopping and black-leading. She savours those moments, the evenings once they've eaten, and she sits with an oil lamp to light her stitches, talking with James of whatever sermon they've heard the Sunday before, the upcoming deer cull or the whelping spaniel bitch that is kept out with the horses and from whom James is hoping to make money from.

The day of the partridge shoot, James strides out with his dogs and takes two of the terriers from the stable block. He is gone all day and does not return for breakfast, taking with him a bundle of cheese, bread and boiled eggs. Mercy walks up to the Long Pool, where there are otters, and stands watching the reeds blowing in the wind.

Somewhere out on the estate, she hears gunshots, the echoing explosions as the partridge shoot begins. She imagines James walking out with Sir Thomas Whitmore and his guests, beaters from the village before them and the dogs nipping forth to take up the fallen birds. She imagines them sniffing, taking up the bleeding bird, a head lolling from one side of the mouth and the tail feathers from the other. Is there real cause for so many of them to die, she wonders; are the rich so in need of a bit of meat? It seems excessive killing when there are just a few rich men at their sport. The land echoes with gunshots.

"Shot so many we'll never get through them all," James tells her as he follows her through to the dining table where she has prepared them a meal of cold meat, pickle, homemade bread and butter and a jam roly-poly. He sinks half a pint of beer, declares his thirst must yet be quashed and sinks another.

"What will happen with the rest of the birds?" she asks.

"Whitmore'll use up what he will and his guests will take what they will and then they'll be fair game for his tenants," he says. "He'll pass them on, will the Old Squire, they won't be wasted."

She nods at this – they will feed the villagers at least and have not died for nought, they will go in the pot, along with whatever rabbits or salmon or eels they can boil – and takes up her knife.

When at last the new curtains are hung, James announces that it is time she meets her cousin, Edward Newton, the other brother of the murderer John Newton properly.

"To show off these fine items," he says and pats one of the

cushions. The fire is crackling and there is a rabbit stew bubbling in the kitchen, the dogs are inching closer to the pot. Mercy is sitting with a little glass wherein lies red wine, viscous like blood, and she can feel it going to her head.

"I'll make something, something good to eat," she tells him. "A sponge pudding. A fruitcake too."

"There's brandy," he tells her. "It'll go well with a fruit cake." He jumps to his feet. "Let us try some," he says and goes to a cupboard on the wall in the corner and pulls out a bottle and two small glasses. "To a house of comforts," he says, pouring and handing her a glass. "We will show it all off. Perhaps I ought to invite my father too." He knocks his drink back, but Mercy is calculating again. She does not touch her little glass and lets it sit on the table before her. Just the smell of it reminds her of Anne.

"Your father," she says. "My uncle?"

He puts down his empty glass and sits quickly. "Perhaps," he says, and then he pours himself another drink and takes that too. The dogs shift at his feet.

"What is his name?" Mercy pushes, but James is uncomfortable now.

"I shan't invite him," he says and runs his tongue across his lips. "It would be a wrong idea."

"But what is his name?" she wants to know; her mother has said little of her genealogy on this side of the family other than that old adage, of course, that all Newtons are evil bastards. This, Mercy now believes, cannot be true for them all, for her cousin James is kind and giving, and strong and grateful.

"His name is John," James says slowly. "He is undecided with regards to you." He stands once more, goes to the pot and stirs it with the ladle. "You must know that he loved his brother Thomas, your father, dearly."

Mercy feels her face change, feels her lips tighten. Like her mother's. "And he loves the half-brothers of mine, those three that were born to my father's first wife," she says, those pursed-up lips dredging up the complaints of her mother. "He loves them enough. But pays no heed to me." She sets her hand on the little glass before her. She has not partaken of liquor for months; the last time she did, she and Anne came to blows, for it fires her up, does the hard stuff, and then she finds she cannot stomach her mother's slanderous tongue or quick slaps to damage her any longer. Now she thinks of her uncle, her father's brother, and his antipathy for her, and she finds heat rising within her. Slowly she sips the brandy, though it may be more fuel than to quench it. It is strong. She feels it in her belly directly.

"You must understand," James says and he is beside her now on the trestle bench upon which she sits. "There were circumstances about your father's death and your birth. He died without knowing that you would be born. And then there was your mother and the question of her fidelity, and your brothers, those motherless lads who she refused to love because they were not hers."

"They're no brothers to me," she bursts out, cheeks hot from the wine, hotter still from the brandy, and burning from the fire. It is rare that she feels compelled to stick up for Anne, but she finds she cannot hold her tongue. She sips again quickly and then lets fly. "They were almost as old as she was! And they saw my mother out of the farm before the bed was cold."

He sighs, puts his arm about her shoulders and pats her awkwardly. "Anne was treated unfairly," he says. "I'll grant you. But nobody knew she was carrying you. You were born five months after your father died and she was keeping it close, having lost the other babies so soon after they were born. She'd grown superstitious, I expect; I've heard many women do that after they lose their babies. Did she tell you much about her marriage with your father?"

Mercy sips again. Her words are thicker now. It takes little time for spirits to take hold of her. "That he beat her. That she had two girls before me that died, and no wonder, with his heavy fists. That those boys, John, Isaac and Thomas, were unruly and unlikeable, but my father expected her to mother them anyway, and she was only a few years older than them. They hated her. And then my father went off to Huntingdon, to market, and died anyway."

James nods. "I remember it well," he says. "It was the talk of the family, of course it was. Those three boys got the lot, all but the settlement Anne's father made for her on her wedding day. She could've stayed at the farm though, she didn't have to leave."

Mercy knows well her mother's complaints, repeated religiously throughout the years, and recites, "She had two hundred pounds settlement money, a dowry, which she'd come with, that's true enough, to be kept in my brother John's hands, so that she might have ten pounds per annum interest, a choice of which bed she wanted and some goods she'd brought over from a family death in Trysull a few years earlier. Bits of sticks that are falling apart now or sold off." She rubs her eyes. "And John saw to it that the £200 wasn't long in his hands, so she's lived off what her father left her in his will ever since. I've heard of it often enough."

"Did they do nothing for her, those stepsons of hers?" he asks. Mercy shakes her head, sets down her empty glass and indicates for him to pour.

"I don't even know what they look like," she tells him. "She couldn't stay, of course she couldn't, not with them. They hated her. She went back to her parents' house in Chelmarsh to birth me. Sutton House, do you know it? A big place, a good house, for she came from a little money, but my father saw to it that she lost her value all right. Lucky that when her own father died, he left her money too, five hundred pounds in the bank, or we'd have starved."

The fire crackles. James stirs the stew whilst Mercy sips some more and descends into doldrums, dwelling on her mother's poverty, the selling of the furniture and the days of little to eat, but she does not voice her memories. She watches the fire in silence for a while and she knows her mother had it harsh, but still she knows only too well that her mother might have done more with her money if only she could lay off the spirits. She might have fixed relationships, might have been kinder to those stepsons and might have saved them both from the degradation of Batch Pool Lane. She stares into the flames and drinks the rest of her brandy.

"Nobody knew she was carrying you," James says again at length. "I remember seeing Anne in Bridgnorth at the end of the year with a baby strapped to her. I must have been sixteen or seventeen at the time. I did not greet her, and for that I am sorry. There is a good deal of guilt in this family." He places a hand on her wrist and squeezes. "The stew must be done," he says. "Let us eat."

She stays once he has risen, stares at the spot on her wrist that he has touched and feels his fingers upon her skin, a lingering pressure that she does not wish to fade, but the wave of his pity is already becoming too much to bear and she must rise above it. She comes to the table, where he places tin plates of stew, there is bread and butter waiting and he takes more wine.

"You'll not go back there now," he tells her firmly. "To Anne and hardship. There'll be no more guilt either as far as you are concerned. You're with family now." And he reaches over the table and squeezes her wrist again.

The day of the wager draws in and Mercy rides with James in the cart back to Bridgnorth, to see the feat of this famous gentleman, Mad Jack Mytton. James regales her with tales he has heard of the man, and she listens to his voice and feels the warmth of him beside her as they go.

"Rode a horse into a hotel in Leamington Spa, they say," he tells her chuckling. "Right up the grand stairway, out onto a balcony and then jumped it, on the horse, straight over the heads of the people dining below, and out the window. Won that bet."

She cries in delight, "But what of the horse? Would it not be damaged from such a height?"

He shrugs. "They say he has two thousand dogs and feeds them steak and champagne," he says. "Damaging a single horse is the least of his worries. Imagine."

"He sounds like a fool," she tells him. He snorts.

The streets are thronging when they reach the bridge. People are gathered making bets, and at first she scans the crowd to seek out her mother, for she is bound to be here somewhere, but there are so many people, so many faces, that she cannot see her. Word has spread far and wide, and there is nothing the people of Bridgnorth like better than an opportunity to drink and gamble upon a spectacle. Mercy is dressed in her best and she holds her head high, when she spots Anne among the people, her mouth pinched. She must have been here a while, Mercy thinks, for her eyes are narrow and her mouth tight with the outrage that falls upon her after a few hours of drinking. She is berating someone, a stranger most likely, expletives rising from her. Mercy rapidly guides James away by the elbow and loses sight of her before Anne can notice them.

They laugh as a lad juggles little sackcloth balls standing on his father's shoulders just before the bridge, and James throws them a coin. Men go about the crowd selling things: pies, sausages, bread, tobacco, anything a crowd might hanker for. Outside the grim little public houses at the foot of the Stoneway Steps, there are men and boys taking orders for beer, rum or whatever might whet a man's whistle. There is someone singing at the bottom of Cartway, and the crowd joins in. Someone else is playing a fiddle and another the spoons. Mercy cannot be at ease now, for she knows Anne is out there somewhere in the crowd, that she's been drinking, and that should they happen upon her, she has, no doubt, a wealth of stored-up vitriol ready to pour over Mercy's head. Her eyes dart this way and that. Each time James casts a glance at her, she smiles, but her heart is pounding. Her mother has spoiled this day without even trying.

All about, ribbons from bonnets and silk flowers bob and flutter in the breeze, heads upturned to seek out the madman on his horse, and when at last he appears and rides by, there is a cheer. Mercy grips James's arm in excitement and feels him place his fingers upon hers. He has not, she realises, made a bet himself, although she knows he believes this man will complete his wager deftly. They see Mad Jack high up on his horse, a valuable, muscular Arab, and he salutes the crowd for another cheer, then turns to the Stoneway Steps, which have been cleared for the proceedings. With a "Yah!" he spurs his horse towards them and off they go, clattering up the steps. The crowd gasps as they disappear between the buildings, up, up into the town, until, so soon, they appear, high up on the Castle Walk, which drops down perilously towards them. Now he is spurring it on, round the walk, and the crowd is rushing forwards, hurrying up the Stoneway, others up Church Steps, and others towards Lavington's Hole to mount the steps there to see the madman at the finish.

“Ought we to follow them?” she asks, but he laughs.

“We’ll see nothing up there,” he says. “He’s won his bet already and will be at the other end of town by the time they get to the top, quaffing beer with some of the toffs. Let us, instead, buy you a new bonnet.”

She turns to him and he to her, and for a moment she thinks he might kiss her. She wants him to kiss her. And she wants a new bonnet. She wants it all. Their bodies are close, so close she can feel his breath upon her cheek. It would take hardly any movement to tiptoe, to press her lips to his, or for him to lean down to hers. For a moment, she wills it with all her heart. James gazes down upon her, brushes a curl from her cheek and smiles.

“After you,” he says politely and ushers her onwards towards her new bonnet.

Winter is fast upon them. Mercy has transformed the lodge with the comforts she had always wished her mother had bothered to provide. Colourful draught excluders keep out the worst of the chill, and she has lined the curtains so that they might keep more of the heat within. There are rag rugs now upon which the dogs make their beds, for James refuses to allow them to sleep outside, and wherever he might set his feet she has placed a small rug that the cold stone floors do not chill his toes. He sits and polishes his shotguns in the evenings, whilst she polishes his boots or mends his socks as the fire dies in the kitchen. Then they take a little port in the best room, and by candlelight with the fire crackling, he reads to her, and she, although she reads a little, tries in return and grows in confidence each day with the shaping of words upon her tongue. There is a fire in every room at different times of the day. It is the richest she has ever been, and she cannot imagine ever returning to Batch Pool Lane.

Although James always tells her to take a half day after church to visit her mother, she does not. She cannot bear to break from this existence and go back to see Anne in that dismal little ditch. She does not miss her – the sharpness of her tongue and the after-sting that rings in the ears and the mind long after the words have ricocheted. No, she will not visit her. She cares nothing for her mother, for the depths to which she has sunk, when she might have been part of this man's life and family instead. She has come to see Anne the same way that the Newtons do.

The winter is long, but they are prepared. There is coal delivered and a log pile that never seems to dwindle. Mercy has set eggs in waterglass in preparation, they have sacks of potatoes in the cellar, apples stored and salted and smoked fish from the river. There is corn and flour, and Mercy has a store of pickles, jams and honey. Cheeses sit in the larder, their rinds thick and hard to slice into.

James goes out in the dark and comes back in the dark. He talks of the deer, the sacks of acorns gathered in the autumn coming in handy and the maize and beans they have stocked for them. He whistles to them and they come in a herd expecting to be fed.

"You can train any animal," he says. "If they're hungry and you have food."

In January, the Long Pool freezes, and James sets forth to test it. Mercy goes with him, wrapped tightly against the sharp air, but even so, she is dithering. Everything glitters; it is a world of diamonds coating the grass and covering the trees. She watches him poke and prod at the ice with a stick, and then, satisfied that it will hold, step out onto the ice.

She observes him and knows what he is doing is dangerous, but he is so sure of himself that her fears seem diminished. He is as bold out there on the ice as he is anywhere. When he slips a little and she gasps, he merely grins back at her and waits to see if anything cracks, but the ice holds.

"It's ready," he calls, turning to her with a wink, and she finds her own lips, though almost numb, reciprocating the curve of his. "Come out!" he encourages, but she shakes her head.

"No fear!" she calls back. "You'll not get me on there!" But she is laughing now, and as he slides flat-footed towards her holding out his hands, she shakes her head but takes the tips of his fingers in hers and he coaxes her forwards until she feels her feet sliding.

She gasps and his face is close to hers. He breathes, "Relax and you'll enjoy it!"

She is so close to him that their bodies glance off each other, as slowly and smoothly he guides her forth. Her legs are locked and she curls her toes as though they might grip the ice beneath her, but still her left foot seems to be drifting away from her right.

"I shall fall," she says. "I shall fall soon!"

"I think it's too late to worry about all that," is his reply, and he takes her by the waist, turns her round, making her shriek with laughter and terror, and then guides her back to the bank, where her left foot really does drift too far out and she feels her legs suddenly give way and she lands in a heap.

When his hand reaches down to help her up, she takes it unabashed and allows him to pull her upright and brush down her skirts.

The Whitmores spend the afternoon skating, strapping metal blades to their boots, muffled and giggling; the men showing off, the women on sledges, one daughter of Sir Thomas Whitmore quite the little acrobat. Mercy watches from a distance, but James is there with them, overseeing the ice, checking for cracks and helping the fallen back to their feet. Indispensable.

Cousin Edward brings a couple of pigeons for a pie one Saturday in early spring, and is greeted by the barking of the dogs and James's booming laugh, and sits near their fire to warm his hands with the greeting,

"There's cholera about." He takes the tin mug of tea from Mercy and nods. "Uncle Thomas's girl, then?"

As if he didn't know. As if he hadn't touched his hat to her at church every Sunday, hadn't taken beer at Norton with James and they hadn't spoken of her many Saturday nights in these last few months.

"Can you see a resemblance?" she asks, smiling thinly, but he shakes his head.

"You're more like your mother," he sniffs, and she purses her lips the way her mother does, but then pulls them straight again. "Cholera," he continues. "About the country. Only a matter of time before it hits round here."

"It won't come here," James says. "Not here, not to Winscote Hills at any rate. Bridgnorth maybe. Wolverhampton assuredly."

"It'll go where it likes," replies Edward, his eyes darting too blatantly towards her. "It'll come down the river. Like the plague."

Mercy listens to the brothers as they tuck into the brandied fruitcake she has set before them. If cholera does hit, she thinks as she watches the cake disappear between the two of them, she might see that five hundred pounds she has been waiting for sooner rather than later.

When the spring finally thaws the land, the cholera does indeed come with it. The first few cases in Bridgnorth are spattered over the newspapers, bringing terror and dread to the streets. James stops suggesting they ride into town each Saturday, and for provisions he gathers as much as he can from the farms about: eggs, seasonal goods, chicken and pork. When he must venture to town he goes alone, and Mercy is left to herself. She is used to spending time alone, but now she begins to wander the estate more, calling the dogs to her, for James has given her permission to take them now that they know her and will come for her. She traipses about the Spring Coppice, down to the river, from whence she can spy the barges mounded with coal or barrels, cargo heading to Bridgnorth Quay and beyond. She watches the men on board, hears them shouting and swearing, watches the slightest details from them, their shapes, their accents, imagines their scent, and plays a little game with herself – which man, she wonders, on each boat, will die of cholera first? She observes their stature, strength and attitudes, but none of them compares to James. Sometimes they spy her, call to her and wave, and sometimes, just sometimes, when she is in a flirtatious mood, she lifts her skirts and flashes an ankle, a portion of leg, and laughs to hear them cheer but knows that they are worthless to her. She wants James. These men are nothing.

Deaths come now to Bridgnorth, choleric cases rising quickly, everyone afraid for their lives. James tells her when he hears of a death, and they toast the life of another victim together solemnly with brandy or port.

"Another one gone," James says. "Thank the Lord that we are safe here." One evening they toast six new deaths, all north of the river in Bridgnorth, and James says, "Thank God I brought you here."

The port is thick on her tongue. "Thank God you did," she replies. He reaches to her and presses her wrist, and she reaches to him and presses his. And with that he has her in his arms, scoops her up, this strong, broad-shouldered Newton and carries her up the staircase, kicks open the door to his chamber and lays her on his bed. The two of them clutch at each other, fumble and pull at each other's clothing. Mercy is all for undoing his buttons and peeling off his shirt, but he is all for what is beneath her petticoats, and soon, still clothed, he is in her, and she gasps to feel him there, but pulls him closer until he buries his face in her neck and falls onto her in relief.

Then she kisses him, kisses his neck, his cheek, the part of his skin she can find betwixt shirt and neck until he rolls off her and lies very still.

"It is all right," she tells him, but he is frowning.

"I oughtn't to have done that," he says, fumbling with his breeches.

"You ought," she says. "I have such feelings for you." She strokes his back through his shirt and feels his muscles taut across his shoulders.

"We're family," he says. "Edward said it would go this way and I told him he was disgusting."

Like a stab to the heart, Mercy sits up. She is shivering now, for the fire is not yet lit in here and James's words chill her to the bone.

"It's not disgusting," she says. "I've been a wife in all ways but one to you, this past year. Now in all ways." Suddenly she is pulling at her clothing, tearing at her stays, and piece by piece she throws it all in a heap on the floorboards. "Look at me," she says, pale in the growing gloom. "Look at me. I'm yours."

Slowly, he turns his head to her and then he is upon her once more, and this time she takes off his shirt for him, and he removes his boots and breeches. Their bodies entwine and rock until he lets out a cry and a shudder, and Mercy cries out too.

Edward Newton comes calling within a fortnight, but sits outside because of the cholera, smoking, and Mercy brings him tea but he refuses it.

"Can't be too careful," he says, eyeing her disapprovingly, so she tips it all out onto the ground at his feet.

James has asked her to say nothing of their relations, although they sleep in the same bed now and he refers to her as his wife when they are together. He stands beside his brother, and they talk of the cholera, the estate and the winter that has passed, and Edward admires the shotgun James has propped beside him. Mercy takes a last glance at the two of them and then strides away down to the river to skim stones.

Later in bed, after he has had the taking of her, Mercy talks to James of marriage, but he shakes his head.

"I do not think it would be approved of," he says. "My father..."

"Your father does not believe me to be a Newton," she snaps. "Your father then ought to have nothing to say about it."

He is silent for a while. "It's not just that we are kin," he says. "My father disapproves of your mother. Of her behaviour when she married Thomas and what she was like to his sons. And Edward; he said this was wrong."

"There's no law against cousins being together," Mercy says into the darkness. "But still, I'm not welcome."

They lie in silence for a long while. Outside, the noises of the hills, a fox, an owl, the wind.

"I love you," he says at last. "You mustn't leave."

She turns to him then, up on her elbow. "I'll never leave," she tells him. "Just so long as you want me here."

She lies beside him now, heart pounding as though it will explode. How will she keep this place, this life, this home if she cannot marry him? She must persuade him then, she thinks, and places an arm across his chest, pulls herself closer and presses her whole self against him. He sighs, a contented sound, and lays a heavy arm over her.

He loves her, she tries to tell herself, and so there is hope. But as she lies there in the darkness and thinks on his words, 'I do not think it would be approved of', and she could shake him. The deeper his breathing and the further into sleep he falls, so too does she fall, into introspection, and now she feels that this happiness, this hope, must be a lie. For out there in the blackness, there lurks the cholera. She knows that the curse of the Newtons is with it, and these dark apocalyptic forces will work together, she thinks, surely. She has never felt such love as this, and it must only be a matter of time before it is cruelly ripped from her.

The Coroner's Inquiry

Recollections of Thomas Whitmore, MP

Apley Estate, Bridgnorth

December 1848

The coroner's inquiry of Miss Newton's crime was, undoubtedly, the largest spectacle the town of Bridgnorth has ever seen, and there were incidents of unrest outside the gaol from the moment the Newton woman was incarcerated to await her hearing. Indeed, I myself sat in upon the hearing at the guildhall and the place was uproarious, packed to the hilt with spectators. Out on the High Street, the masses loomed, jeering and hooting upon the prisoner's arrival and departure. No doubt she must have felt their presence sorely, for they booed and spat such hatred that it was unpleasant to behold. An uprising amongst the common man against one of their own.

I knew well the coroner, a Mr W.D. Batte, a fair man, who oversaw the debacle. Mr Newall too, the esteemed surgeon and ex-mayor of Bridgnorth, as well as Mr Thursfield, surgeon, whose report it must be noted did go some way to complicate matters. Without his conclusion I do believe the whole matter might have been over and done with rapidly, and Miss Newton might well have been hanged in the spring.

Nevertheless, as a Justice of the Peace, I consented to work for the prosecution alongside Mr Phillimore, whose intelligence and prudence in all matters concerning the case was a boon. Many days and nights we worked to bring our case together in preparation for the assizes, considering all aspects of the coroner's report, as well as the tactics used by Mr Hazlewood at the coroner's inquiry for the defence – tactics that proved substantial enough for a jury of thirteen men to come out with no clear verdict, when in my opinion and an instance as condemnatory as this, the jury ought to have been unanimously in favour of the prosecution's case. The astounding nature of the thing, and the historical import of the case, meant that our joined intellects were greatly burdened by responsibility, for the outcome of such a trial would surely, we postulated, create a precedent for decades to come. The peculiarities of the case, I will relay in time, but for now and forever I will be struck by that first sight of the prisoner upon entering the coroner's inquiry at the guildhall as a spectator, and this I must relate now in order to put my thoughts in order and demonstrate my position from the outset.

Mercy Catherine Newton.

She stood in the guildhall, dressed all in black, with a black bonnet and a dark veil before her face. Shrouded, one might describe her, and a more ghoulish figure I have never encountered in my life. A silent, still figure, face hidden from view. Were one to meet such a thing in a dark alleyway, one would fear for one's life. She slowly sat in a chair proffered to her by one of the constables and looked down into her lap, her veil hiding her features. All about us the hall hushed, and there was a creaking of pews as people strained to see better. Up on the dais sat Mr Batte, readying himself for the evidence which was to be put towards him.

When the proceedings at the guildhall began, Miss Newton finally reached up and pulled back her veil. Her face was stony, pale and utterly devoid of feeling. Upon reflection after that first, chilling observation of her features, I found I had some small recollection of the woman who stood in the dock. Her face was one that might be considered memorable for its sheer lack of femininity. Hard-faced, one might surmise. A younger vision of it swam within recall. I remembered her, of all places, in our little church in Stockton, perhaps fifteen or so years before, those black eyes and that unfeeling face staring out of the pews as my father led us out after the Sunday service. My uncle, Charles Blainey Cavendish Whitmore, was rector back then, and my family often stood by after the Sunday service to talk with him or went back to take a glass of something with him in his garden. I could recall, I found, this woman coming forth from the church in her younger days but still cursed with the look of one who lacks a soul. One has seen such a countenance in those who have returned from war, having observed horrors of the most unimaginable. This woman, however, was, I believed already the creator of her own horror and her looks were entirely of her own making.

Impartiality is most difficult, one finds, when faced with a case such as that of Mercy Catherine Newton.

And yet during the coroner's inquiry, I found myself feeling sorrier for her the longer it went on. The whole thing dragged on in such excruciating detail that it spread to four or five meetings, and between each, Miss Newton was again taken back to the gaol amidst the yelling and general uproar of the masses. So indignant were the indigenous folk of Bridgnorth regarding her accused crime that she had to be protected by additional constables. Throughout it all, she held herself with a commendable control, having the professional defence of the much-revered Mr E. W. Hazlewood Esquire, who it transpired afterwards extended his aid to Miss Newton gratuitously. Even so, the thing was a shambles.

Indeed by the time it was all over, Mr Thursfield had complicated matters and a Reverend W.K. Marshall had appeared for the defence and complicated things further, the jury could not come to agreeance. Mr Batte was forced, having received no verdict, to write to the Secretary of State for advice on whether Miss Newton ought to proceed to the gaol at all. We were all, despite being men of the law, utterly perplexed at how to proceed, no matter which of us he spoke to on the matter. Upon her final moments in the guildhall, her last occasion there, beneath those rather striking stained-glass windows that let in shards of coloured winter light, Miss Newton looked utterly bereft as she was informed that she would be taken from there to Shrewsbury Gaol, wherein she would await the spring assizes.

The money she had saved – £13 in ready money and a further £30 in the Bridgnorth Savings Bank – would be given up to a relative (not her uncle, Edward Edwards, I might add, for he was a witness for the prosecution. I would come to know him further, in time, for happily would he relate his niece's words and deeds for the purpose of her prosecution, and so had no cause to help her) – in order to pay for her defence.

The newspapers, of course, abounded with speculation and reported in detail the particulars of the case. I collected them, as many did, for this was a famous case, and therein I read that the prisoner had a daughter aged about sixteen years. As the coroner's trial went on, I found myself scanning the pews for a face that matched the prisoner's and I thought at times she was doing the same, for at points her eyes would rove those seated, but always her gaze fell back to her lap. That child of hers had not come to observe her mother here. Indeed, the more I considered the daughter and the more I heard of the accusations against Miss Mercy Newton, the more I wondered, how could this child ever look her mother in the eye again? Not only had she been betrayed by her mother's temper, but the newspapers had seen to it that the poor girl's history was spattered into every article.

The prisoner's daughter, Maria Newton, is aged 16 years. The father of this girl was the cousin of the prisoner.

Ah! These journalists did well to jog my memory. I recalled further the incident at Apley Estate now. The thing that had to be hushed up. The history of the woman did something to explain the harshness of her features, perhaps.

This then, I knew, when I took on the prosecution of Mercy Catherine Newton: there was just forty-five pounds to pay for the men who would stand against my prosecution, in a case so unheard of, so twisting, so rare, that it would create legal history.

Chapter Three

Mercy Newton

Winscote Hills, Apley Estate
1832

The cholera is rife. From Wolverhampton to Birmingham and Worcester to Kidderminster people are dying. Recommendations from The Board of Health include the stringent cleaning of bed linen, clothing, stockings, the sanitary disposal of refuse, the cleaning of sinks and the abstention of 'ardent spirits'.

Mercy scrubs and cleans, more so than she has ever done before. She burns herbs and lavender to drive out the illness. She beats the mats every day, scrubs the windows and burns every last bit of rubbish that cannot be sent for the pigs. James's stash of liquor is banished to the attic until the epidemic is over.

She will fight the Asiatic cholera. She will keep it from her sanctuary at all costs.

She spares little thought for Anne away in Batch Pool Lane soaking in her gin. There will be no cleaning going on there, she considers, but Batch Pool Lane is far enough away from Bridgnorth to be safe. Perhaps.

They keep away from the town, away from the villagers in Norton even, and church services are still avoided; everyone both in and around Bridgnorth is petrified.

"It is bad air, has caused this," she tells James, mixing a concoction of carbonate of soda and ginger at the kitchen table, and standing over him as he downs it to keep her happy. She will not allow this plague to take him from her. She will keep him safe. He grimaces, pulls her to him and buries his face in her neck.

"The scent of you, wench, that'll protect me," he tells her, for she smells of lavender water now that she has him. She never owned a scent when she lived in Batch Pool Lane. Everything there smelled of damp.

When the wind first blew over from Bridgnorth filled with the pestilence of the cholera, she slammed every window and door, blocked all the gaps with cloth and burned away at her stock of dried lavender. So far her ministrations have kept them safe. Mercy will fight this plague with all she has.

"Take care not to stand close to anyone," she instructs James each morning, as he leaves their bed. "Do not share a flask, nor a pipe, not anything with anyone."

"And you," James asks her, laughing, pulling on his shirt. "What shall I forbid for you? What small pleasures can I deny you in the name of cholera?"

"I shan't be dying any time soon," she tells him, curling her lip, flicking back the blankets and poking him with her toe. "I have much too much to do clearing up the mud you cake the place in each day and feeding you."

Visitors do not come to the house anymore. When Mercy ventures forth to the stables to take the lads beer, she leaves it on a log and steps away. She does not tarry to watch them shining the horse brasses or to enquire after the training of the gun dog puppies.

Nobody will come under a roof that is not their own unless they must now. Nobody has been to church for months, and as the year grows cold, Thomas Whitmore, the Old Squire himself, comes a-knocking, though he stands well back beside his horse and speaks to them from the gate.

"Newton," he nods, as James steps forth and Mercy comes to

rest on the step behind him. "Don't come closer, I'm doing the rounds of my tenants." He tips his hat at Mercy. "Miss Newton," he adds genteelly. "I am come to inspect your health and give word to my tenants about a new Act which has been passed in Parliament."

James grins as one of his dogs darts out from between Mercy's legs. He whistles it back, and it runs round in a circle and comes to rest at his feet.

"The rudest of health, that's how we are keeping, Squire!" he calls. "And ever onwards with the groundskeeping too. The land don't stop for cholera!"

"Indeed," replies Sir Thomas, nodding his approval. "And there is now The Act for the Prevention of the Cholera Morbus. Some houses must be cleaned, Newton; those known to be unsanitary."

"You needn't fear for cleanliness here, Squire," James pipes up, leaning against the doorpost. "This cousin of mine is scrubbing and washing all day long. She's shredding her fingers to ribbons in the process."

Mercy looks down at her hands; she's barely noticed, but they are indeed red and chapped. She hides them in her skirts.

"No, not here," concedes Whitmore. "Some of my tenants in Bridgnorth will be forced to allow cleansing to take place. Perhaps one in Norton too."

James nods. Mercy does too. She knows the house. Everyone does. A tiny place filled to the rafters with bare-footed children, chickens and mice. Stinking.

"I'd say that one'd best be done sooner than later," James calls back.

Sir Thomas taps the gate with his cane. "I'd need workers to clean it," he says at length. Mercy can feel that he is looking at her. "It would pay a good wage for a few days of work."

She will not do it. She will not step foot in a contaminated hovel and endanger both her own and James's life.

"I won't do it," she whispers. "I won't risk my life and yours."

James nods. "I can't spare Miss Newton," he calls out. "This time of year, I'm treading mud thick as my arm through the place. And we need to keep this house clean and the lads in the stables fed and watered whilst they're here."

Sir Thomas stands a while longer, then nods. "Noted, Newton," he says. Then he tips his hat. "Pounded myrrh and camphor," he says. "The newest advice. Carried in a silk pouch in the waistcoat and jacket pockets. Do you have silk, Newton?"

James glances at Mercy. "We have camphor," she says. "No silk, no myrrh."

"We will find some, Squire," he calls to Sir Thomas, who nods and turns back to his horse.

"You cannot go into Bridgnorth," Mercy tells James that evening, as she mixes him more ginger and carbonate of soda. "People are dying there. You will get ill. I won't lose you!"

James knocks the potion back as soon as she hands it to him. "You'll not lose me that easily," he tells her and wipes his mouth on his sleeve. "There's plenty of life in me yet!" And he grabs her about the waist and hauls her off to bed.

By the time she wakes in the morning, he has gone already.

She struggles out of bed and into her clothing as quickly as she can, for the room is chilly and she can see her breath in the air. She crosses to the window, opens the curtains and stares out into the early morning light. The mist is low between the trees, a layer of gossamer, of cloud, and she imagines it to be the cholera spreading across the land, reaching out from Bridgnorth, hemming them in on all sides, and if so it be, it has swallowed James already. She stumbles down the stairs and checks that the cloth she uses to keep the draughts out from under the kitchen door is rammed back into place.

Then she sets water to boil on the fire. She will scrub the place again, ensure that wherever the mist might have crept in when James went out is cleansed.

By midday, the mist has receded from the little clearing within which the lodge sits, but still James is not home. Mercy has run out of things to clean inside the house. She takes to the yard, heaves out the dolly tub and grates in some carbolic, ready to wash his clothes when he returns. She will strip them from him before he sets foot in the house if she has to. She will brook no plague within her walls.

But as she sets down the soap block and turns to the house to fetch the pan of water, she hears a noise.

Somewhere out in the woods, someone is crying. A faint, eerie sound, and no matter which way she turns she cannot fathom the direction from whence the noise comes. She turns this way then that, cocks her head to one side, but still it seems all about her, one plaintive, quiet moan after another. As though the mist receded and left sadness in its place. She looks towards the stables, but the boys are all out now with the horses. There is nobody here. Nobody but her.

"Who is it?" she calls out. "Who is there?"

The noise ceases.

"Are you hurt?" she calls out and steps towards the gate, but the same fear that kept her from helping Sir Thomas Whitmore with the cleansing of his tenants keeps her now from opening the gate. "Are you injured?" she calls instead to the trees.

Somewhere, a rustle of bracken, and then in the opposite direction, a twig snapping. A tree groans. The birds are silent.

Then the crying starts again.

It is, Mercy is sure now, a child. Too soft and high-pitched for an adult, it pulls at her heart now and she is fighting the urge to go to it, to find it. She lays one sore, red hand on the latch of the gate.

"Are you lost?" she tries again. "Come to the gate, but not too close, and I will see if I can help you. Only, for now, I cannot see you and I cannot come to you for fear of the cholera."

She realises her hand is shaking. She steps back from the gate, for if this child comes forth she must have space between her and it. She must not breathe contaminated air.

Between the trees, where the late autumn sun cannot penetrate, remnants of mist still linger, and try as she might, Mercy cannot contain those thoughts once more – that it is the cholera, lurking between the trees, so silent and still and deathly. Then, as she stares into the shadowy depths of the woodland, out of this layer of ethereal matter steps a child with long, lank hair, bone-thin limbs clad in filthy rags, and hollow cheeks.

Mercy steps back. "Stay where you are," she calls to the child, but the child's mouth is open, eyes streaming. "Stand still!" Mercy orders, but still this child walks towards her, and now, one of her hands reaches out to Mercy from the mist, and she might be, for all Mercy knows, the bringer of death. "If you come any closer, I'll knock you down!" Mercy cries, and this, at last, stays the child. She stands swaying in amongst the rotting bracken.

They stare at one another for a moment. Then the child says softly in a voice that rings between the trees, "Do you have any food, missus? We're all starving."

Mercy stares at her. The girl is perhaps eight but could be six for how small and skinny she is. Her hair is dark, her skin is caked in the dirt of late autumn and mud halfway up her dress. Her boots are too big for her, as though they belong to someone else, and one is open at the end. She is shaking or shivering, or both.

"Where is your mum?" Mercy calls. "Your dad? Your kin?"

The child does not speak, only points away through the forest towards Norton or, Mercy thinks, perhaps towards the graveyard at Stockton church.

"Do you have any food?" the child asks again. Then she stands, staring out from those deep dark sockets, through that long, dank hair, quivering like something newly born, her boots swathed in the choleric mist.

"Wait there," Mercy says, and turns to the house. She means to walk, but her feet will not obey her; she stumbles and breaks into a run, grabbing her block of carbolic soap as she flits past the dolly tub and into the house, slamming the door and bolting it. Panting, heart pounding, she does not know what to do. She moves to the window and peers out from behind the curtain. There the child stands between the trees waiting, waiting. Death can be patient, Mercy thinks. The curse of the Newtons might be working through this child for all she knows. She might be here to deal Mercy a hand she will not be able to bluff her way out of. She peers again. The child is as still as a gravestone out there in the silence.

If these were ordinary times, she would share her bounty with this child gladly and send her home with a loaf perhaps, or a jar of something or both. But these are not ordinary times, and the child is the living breathing cholera, risen from the mist to steal all of Mercy's happiness and all her contentment away from her. Offerings must be made to appease the curse, to appease death, Mercy decides. She must make good on her promise, not just hide away here and hope that the child goes away. She grabs a cloth and spreads it out. From the larder, she snatches the first bit of meat that comes to hand and a bit of cheese. There is bread left over from yesterday's loaf and she puts that in too. There are a few eggs and she wraps these carefully and places them inside the bundle. Then she glances at the bowl on the side and thinks of Sir Thomas Whitmore and his hope that his tenants would be cleansed. The child is certainly covered in filth. She prises the bit of carbolic that has stuck itself to the inside of the bowl and wraps it in a bit of an old flour bag, which goes into the bundle too. Then she ties up the corners, takes up a half-empty jar of blackberry jam and unbolts the door.

The child is gone.

Mercy calls out, but there is no sound.

She steps away from the door, and looks about, left, right, but there is no sign of the little girl, only a breeze now that brings with it the scent of the foundry all the way from Bridgnorth. Mercy treads warily towards the gate.

"Where are you?" she calls and places the bundle on the wall. "I have food for you!"

Out in the trees then she hears a whistle – James's whistle – notes that rise and fall as the hammering of her heart comes to a standstill. He is coming home.

"Thank you, missus," says a little voice, and a cold hand descends upon her own, and she yelps, falls backwards, stumbles over her own skirts and lands in the dirt, as the child, who is now somehow inside the gate and who has touched her skin, leans down and kisses her on the cheek.

"Get away!" Mercy cries and lashes out, but the child is quicker than lightning and is away through the gate with the bundle and the half-jar of jam. Mercy is left in the dirt, struggling to her feet as the child disappears between the trees.

James is coming and she has been kissed by the living dead. She staggers to the dolly tub, takes up the carbolic and starts to scrub her hands first where the child touched her and then, once they are stinging from the carbolic, she rubs up a lather and is about to slap it to her cheek where the child touched her with its cold, soft lips, but then James is upon her, laughing, catches her about the waist and plants a kiss himself in the self-same spot.

"No!" she cries, pushes him away and searches the trees. "There was a little girl from Norton I think, from that hovel, she was here..."

James slings his bag over his shoulder and shrugs. "I saw no one," he tells her, and she looks down at the lather between her fingers and then impotently rubs it against her cheek. What damage is done, is done. She has killed him, she thinks, without even trying. "Just you, scrubbing yourself ragged, was all I could see. Come inside and let's warm your bones before the fire," he tells her, catches her wet fingers in his and pulls her towards the cottage door.

Mercy serves James the old, salted meat for supper after giving the last of the fresh stuff away. They must replenish the larder tomorrow for that was the last of even the salted meat and now there is nothing left. After supper, Mercy sews little silk pouches and stuffs them with camphor and myrrh, which she has pounded into smithereens. She makes six of these little pockets, two for James's jacket, one for his waistcoat, one for the pocket in his breeches and two for herself. Then they sit before the fire with the dogs at James's feet, until, as Mercy finishes the sixth little pocket, James declares he feels unwell. Mercy goes cold.

"I will mix you more ginger and bicarbonate," she tells him and begins to boil up water, but James waves her away.

"Go to bed," he tells her. "If I am to be ill, it is not for you to see." She can hear his stomach now, hear it gurgling and churning.

She shakes her head. "I shan't leave you," she tells him, though she knows what is to come. The cholera deals out a nasty end, and she will not surrender him to it. She takes up the silken pockets and thrusts them all, all six of them into any indent she can find in his clothing, but as the sixth is applied he rushes past her and is out of the door.

Mercy closes her eyes. It is well known across all England since this plague began what the end is like for those who die of it: violent diarrhoea, and the hands and feet turn blue just before death. She will not allow it. She mixes the ginger and bicarbonate of soda and leaves it to cool. Then she takes up the carbolic and scrubs James's plate, knife, fork, the arms of his chair where his hands grip it and the mouthpiece of his pipe. Yet still, despite her scrubbing, James Newton is caught by the cholera.

It is the longest night of Mercy Newton's life. No doctor will come, and she has no way to send for one anyway. The cholera kills within hours. If she leaves him alone to try to find a doctor or someone to help, he might be dead by the time she comes back. She can do little but mop his brow, pass him the ginger and bicarbonate of soda and plead with him to drink it. He writhes and moans, twisting the sheets about his legs, and she falls back in horror; it has come on so quickly – she could lose him in an instant.

When at last he lies still and she can hear his breathing ragged and shallow, and after she wets his lips and bids him take in some of the moisture, she has time to blame, time to garner her guilt. If he dies, she has killed him. She has killed him with the filth from her own cheek left there by that child of the mist. She ought to have scrubbed her face first, not her hands. This is, she is sure, the decision that has infected him. That the curse came from the forest, came from the mist, and is taking him from her.

Yet still for now he lives.

She checks his hands. They are not blue. She pulls off his boots and thick woollen socks, and his feet are a healthy pink.

She strips him and puts everything he has worn into a sack. He groans but is still breathing. This is everything. Then she takes the bowl and the carbolic and washes him down, dries him and covers him with the blankets. She disposes of the water, refills the bowl and scrubs herself over and over again driving out the foulness of the girl from the mist.

If he dies she does not know what she will do.

If he dies she has nothing to live for.

The curse dictates that a Newton will either take their own life or that of another. She stands shivering in the doorway watching him. If he dies, she will die too, empty and alone; this she knows to be true. Her heart will stop, either of its own accord or by force.

The place is cold, the freezing tendrils of winter are fast taking grip, but she is too afraid to leave him to fetch wood to build the little fire in the tiny grate. If she leaves him, he might be dead by the time she gets back. She stands there through the dark hours until she realises that beneath his blanket James is shivering too. Then at last for his sake she breathes,

"I'm just going to fetch fodder for the fire, my love."

He does not respond. She swallows.

"Do not leave me," she says, and almost trips down the stairs, plunders the kitchen for fuel and carries it back up the stairs in her skirts. She stands for a moment outside the door and listens. He breathes yet. With a shaking tread, she enters the room; James has turned to his side. She kneels before the fireplace and fumbles with the wood, the twists of paper and the matches. At first it does not light, and she curses and pokes it and adds more paper twists to the bottom, and then at last, a flame takes. She suddenly realises how petrifyingly cold it is in here. She blows gently, and the flames begin to thrive before her, blindingly bright in the darkness. When at last she is satisfied, she turns from the blaze and realises that there is light outside – the night is over. And she turns to the bed and James is lying there quite still, but his eyes are open.

"Are you still with me?" she asks him, and slowly he nods.

By Easter, the cholera is abating, and their solitude which Mercy has adored is over. Holed up together, as James's strength returns and she has nursed him back to health, they have been lovers night after night. She knows him, she thinks, better than she has ever known any person. He *will* marry her one day, she thinks, for he tells her that he loves her every day. Every single day he tells her, until Stockton church welcomes back its parishioners and James spies his brother, Edward in the pews. On this day her heart sinks. Edward's expression as he sees them together, smiling, close and her hand upon James's sleeve, is a face of disgust.

Then the words of love are pruned back, and the brothers go to Bobbington to visit their father and see what members of their family are left over now that the cholera has departed. The newspapers report that at least one in three who are infected have died. He leaves her at the lodge, and he and Edward go in the trap, expecting a third of his family to be dead.

Mercy watches them go. Perhaps she ought to seek out her mother... yet she does not.

A young man turns up one day on their doorstep. James is off out with the dogs about the estate with Thomas Whitmore, detailing a shoot that is to happen next month. Mercy opens the door to find a young man standing there staring to see her.

"James Newton?" he asks nonchalantly, but she can tell he is examining her.

Her heart is suddenly thudding. Who is he? A long-lost son? Who? "He is out, but will be back presently," she tells him with curt politeness. "Who should I say called?"

"William Newton," he replies. "He's expecting me."

James has said nothing of this boy. Mercy is certainly not expecting him. She hesitates to shut the door.

"I'll wait," he adds and takes out a clay pipe and seats himself on the log pile. Mercy closes the door.

She takes up a cloth and scrubs at the table. She can smell the smoke from his pipe permeating their home. It reminds her of her mother and she hates it. She considers who he might be and what sort of relation. He appeared a similar age to herself, in which case, it is a possibility that he might be James's son. But James has never mentioned having children himself and as she scrubs the table, she decides that this cannot be the case. She knows that the murderer, John Newton, had four children, but there was not a William amongst them. The son of his other brother perhaps, the live one, Edward. She stops scrubbing and heaves a sigh of relief. She has narrowed it down. The boy has come to visit, that is all. There is nothing to fear – he will not disrupt them. He will take tea, share his news and leave.

At length, she hears the barking of the dogs and a cry of welcome from James. In he strides with the youth behind him.

"My housekeeper, Mercy," he introduces her as, not as wife, lover or even cousin. "This is William, my brother's son."

"Edward's?" she asks tartly. "Not John's?"

"William's," comes his reply, but she knows of no brother called William, and he is already too busy detailing his morning and showing off his double-barrel shotgun to this William for her to press further.

That evening they all eat together, and James asks about others, names she has not heard before: Jane, Sarah, Matthew and others. William replies with details that Mercy cannot focus on, for she is too irritated. She must make up a room, James says, for this William will be stopping with them for the foreseeable future. All in all, she still does not know who he is.

This night she waits for James in his bed, but when he has finished drinking with this William, she hears his boots clump up the stairs and pause, and then perceives him open the door to another bedroom and close it behind him. He is not coming to his own bed tonight because she is in it.

When she lays his breakfast before him at ten o'clock the next morning whilst this William is toileting, he is distracted and distant. She tries to find a way to speak to him, to open a conversation, but she can sense she must tread carefully, and so she asks, "I didn't know you had another brother?"

He chews and swallows his mouthful. "William? He's dead," he says shortly.

"Oh." She stands fumbling with a dishcloth. Another Newton cousin. Dead. How does she not know of him? "Recent?" she asks, awkwardly.

He shakes his head. "About seven years hence. This William's his son."

"I'm sorry," she says, and she is, for if this brother William wasn't dead perchance his son wouldn't have interrupted their bliss.

"He chose the end of it himself," comes the reply. "Hanged himself. Fit of the melancholies, they say." He wipes his mouth on the napkin she always lays by his plate and rises. "After John was hanged, he never was the same. We were all close, us Newton brothers. William left all his kiddies and a good wife behind." He takes another bite and stares off into the trees for a while. "We've all got a touch of the morbs, deep in our veins, us Newtons," he says, and turns to her. "Can you feel it too, sometimes?"

Mercy stares at him. "No," she tells him. "Not enough to take my own life, no."

He eyes her awhile, as though seeing her anew. "Then you must have benefitted from a most uncommon dilution of the blood," he says after a while. "Or else those rumours about your mother were true and you're not a Newton after all." She opens her mouth to retaliate, but he is already speaking again, "Whichever it is, you ought to be thankful."

And then he is off, whistling to the dogs again. She watches him stride away, this brother of two hanged men, a man whose blood runs with morbidity, and she can all but feel the coldness emanating from his retreating form.

When at last one night William retires early, Mercy seizes the opportunity and hands James an overly large glass of brandy and takes some herself for courage.

"Do you not love me now?" she asks and takes his hand and places it on her breast. "Do you not wish me to lie with you anymore?"

He lets his hand linger. "I oughtn't to have lain with you in the first place," he says, but he does not take away his hand from her. "It was wrong of me."

"I miss you," she tells him, but now he takes his hand away.

"I miss you," she says again, lifts her skirts and straddles him in his chair, but he turns his face away until she starts to move upon him, and then he pulls out his cock and is inside her so fast that she could cry out, but she rides the pain until she softens and coaxes him to finish.

"Oh, Mercy," he says and then puts her from him, reassembles his breeches, rises and takes himself to bed without a backward glance.

This usurper is in their midst now all the time. With him come visitors: Benjamin Newton, his brother, a pig farmer who stinks like one a mother called Ann who is nothing like her own mother, but is neat, sober, wholeheartedly Christian and prim; a sweetheart also called Ann, who is all smiles and coquettishness, and is come to see her beloved's new home; and a little sister called Jane, precocious and pretty, who asks Mercy why she looks so tired and ill. And if truth be told, Mercy feels tired, ill and old too. She has been suffering quietly for weeks now with some sickness that stops her from eating Her sleep is punctuated by her broken heart, for James passes her no looks now and no lingering touches. She is growing thinner and her lips are narrowing like her mother's. She can see the resemblance now in the scratched looking glass and she knows James must see it too. What is worse this month she has not bled.

With two men in the house and the guests they must entertain on William's behalf, Mercy has more scrubbing, mending, cooking and drudgery than before, and the house seems colder than it ever has been even as the late February sun begins to feebly attempt to warm the place.

Now when James eats it is with William, and she takes her own food on a tray in the corner by the fire. The cholera epidemic is waning, and although Bridgnorth has lost many lives to it, James ventures forth more readily now but he does not offer to take Mercy with him. She is stuck here, trapped far from town, and must live with this man who cannot bear to look at her, with his prodigious nephew, who is civil but treats her as a housekeeper, not a family member. And now, her stomach is starting to round and protrude. She has not told James and does not know how to.

At the beginning of March she knows she must tell him for the sickness has passed, but she has not bled now for four months and he is to be a father. She finds him at the wood pile one morning. He has sent William off with the dogs who now respond to him. He looks worn, she thinks, as she draws near. She has brought with her a parcel of cheese and bread, for he did not eat much of his breakfast. He looks up as the movement of her catches his eye, pauses and then brings the axe down to split the log beneath. Then he stands and wipes his brow.

"What is this?" he asks; she reaches out the bundle to him.

"Bread and cheese," she tells him. "You did not eat enough at the table."

He stares at her and wrinkles his brow. "You care enough, still then? After all I've done?" and takes it from her. She seats herself upon a log and he settles beside her.

"I care more than anything," she tells him. "I love you and I will never stop." She pauses. "Even if you have."

His hands, which have been unwrapping the food, freeze. "It's not that," he says. "I'd give anything for it to be right, Mercy, but it *isn't*. You know that, don't you? My father, he'd disown me, he'd..." his voice trails away.

She looks down at her feet. This father of his whom she has never seen, this man who is her grandfather, this man who despises her mother, her father's father and who considers her an illegitimate bastard carrying the name of Newton, this man is what stands in the way of her happiness. If she knew where he was it would be the worse for him. She clenches her fists. Then she thinks of her mother – if she had been a different woman, if she'd been able to show affection for those three boys, Mercy's half-brothers, and if she hadn't ended up a gin-swilling foul-mouthed old stick, then maybe things might have been different.

"And Edward," he carries on. "Disgusting, he said, it would be if we..." He sighs. "They'll all say it was wrong," he tells her. "My father will never see me more and my brother will disown me, and Mercy, I cannot fathom a life without them." He turns to her. "I can't lose more of my family. I've had two brothers who've swung from a rope one way or another," he tells her. "I cannot be the one to bring more shame upon this family. *Our* family." He turns to her and lifts her chin so that she is looking at him. "And by God, I've prayed that you will forgive me, but there must be an end to it." She feels a tear, a damned tear that escapes and belies her emotion, and he wipes it away with his thumb. "Don't cry," he says softly. "I couldn't bear it."

"I'm with child," she breathes. "I've not bled these four months, my love. We could marry. We *can* be family still, with you at the head. The father of my children."

But he is already stumbling back, and the look upon his face is not the look of love, but of a horror that makes Mercy fall away and all that is hopeful turns to dust inside her.

"It isn't true," he gasps. "It cannot be!"

She stands and smooths her skirts across her burgeoning belly. The tears are running freely now, and she curses them for her weakness. She must win him back now, any way she can, for she cannot go through this pregnancy without him. She feels strongly now that things will go wrong – that he will dispel her from the house, from this home she has created for them both, and that he will deny the child. He stands there next to his axe, staring at her.

"I love you!" she cries. "How can it be wrong?"

Stumbling he turns and grabbing his axe strides away. She watches for a moment, then staggers after him, the cheese and bread forgotten and left to the birds.

"Wait!" she cries, but he does not, veering instead towards his horse which stands at the stable door at the side of the lodge, and into the block he goes and begins tacking.

"Where are you going?" she asks him. "Why are you leaving?

I'm carrying your child, for God's sake! Why are you going?"

"I'm going to set things right," he growls, pulling the stirrups down, and fastening the girth another notch. "This is the decider now, once and for all."

And he leads his horse out, mounts and is away, leaving Mercy standing in the grass quaking.

She waits for James to come home, jumping up from the fire when she hears a whistle outside, but it is just William coming back, gun over his shoulder, with the dogs.

Bleakly she places a plate before him and fills it, and he thanks her, but there is no love lost and she goes to sit by the fire unable to eat herself. She can hear him clattering his fork against the tin plate – how she'd love to take it from him and stick him with it. Instead, she stabs at the burning logs with the poker, sending sparks showering onto the rag rug at her feet. Again and again she thrusts the poker into the burning heat, and her skin feels tight about her head, her skull pounding. There are brothels in Bridgnorth, all up the Cartway from the river, and this is all she can think of. Stab, stab, stab, she goes, and the flames rise before her until her skin is burning.

When at last James returns it is dark, and she waits to give him time to stable his horse and then sets out his meal, but he strides in, ignores the plate, takes up the bottle of brandy and mounts the stairs two at a time.

"Where did you go?" she calls after him wildly. Her tone heightens with each word, as the panic rises from her. "Where did you go? What did you do?" But there is no reply, just the slam of a door so forceful that the whole house shakes. Her world is falling apart and she stands helpless for a moment, tears and panic rising, but she cannot let it grip her, not yet. Perhaps there is something she can do to claw it back, surely there must be – she is carrying his child. The food he has left, she dashes into the fire.

There is a week of drinking then, of meals left untouched, of coldness and silence, until one day after he has stumbled out of the house mid-morning stinking of rum, she is hanging the washing and she hears out in the woods a gunshot.

William is shining tack and he falls out of the tack room, across the yard, mouth open. "There's no shooting today," he says.

They stare at one another, and both of them know what the other is thinking. It isn't unusual to hear a shot, of course it isn't, but this is an unexpected shot that ought not to be heard after a week of drinking and a morning where James threw his breakfast straight into the fire and insisted that the dogs be locked in one of the stables. The dogs are howling now and Mercy clutches her stomach with one hand and William's arm with the other.

"Find him!" she cries. William sets off at a run. Mercy cannot take a step. A huge wave of sickness engulfs her. Clutching the stable door she struggles to breathe. Time cannot play tricks like this, she tells herself. History does not repeat like this. This thought must steady her, she tells herself. Coincidence, fate, whatever she believes in, cannot happen twice, in so similar a design. Her own father died in the spring, buried, they say in the March of 1809, whilst she was born in the August. This child she carries, she has calculated, will be born in August. The father of her baby must not die in the March. History surely, *dear God surely*, cannot be so cruel as to smite her with the same fate as her mother.

Her breathing seems shallow, no matter how she heaves for it, as though this child who is still so small is taking up all the space within her. She is suffocating.

And then William returns and his eyes are red, and he holds out his hand before him, warning her not to come near, and there is blood, the reddest blood, upon him. Mercy clutches at her stomach. She knows by his face what he will say, but she cannot hear it, she will not hear it. She turns from him, but she can hear his feet on the ground, hear his ragged breathing, coming closer.

A Newton takes their own life or that of another.

When the cholera struck, Mercy knew that if James died she would gladly kill herself. But now there is a baby inside her. *His* baby. And she must live.

William reaches her and he smells of blood.

"He's dead," he stutters and his eyes are wild. "He's shot himself." And he retches there by her side, but she cannot comfort him, for he, the usurper, stole James from her, and now he is dead.

"We're all cursed," she tells him, for there must be blame and she will not carry any of it. "The Newtons. Cursed. Every last one of us." She chokes on these last words.

Somewhere in the woods the howls of the dogs rise to cover her sobs.

The night before the funeral, William eats the meal she has prepared alone at the table, for she cannot eat and refuses to eat with him. She returns to the fireside, to stare into the flames, watch them lick up about the coals and she feeds it, stokes it with the kindling and her food, listening to the fat on the meat sizzling in the heart of it. James lies in the parlour, waiting for his grave to swallow him, and she cannot bear the oppression here. The silence. It is suffocating.

When she stands to take away his plate, William pats at the

table for her to sit.

"I am to marry," he tells her abruptly. "Ann and I, we are to wed. Soon. And I will have no need for a housekeeper, Mercy." He takes out his pipe. "I'm sorry Mercy, I know James kept you here because he considered you family but..." his voice trails away.

"But what?" she mutters, gritting her teeth.

She can see him steeling himself. She knows the gist of what will come, but she must hear him say it.

"My family do not believe that you are a Newton," he tells her firmly. "You are not family, not to me. And I do not need a housekeeper."

She stands. "Let me give you a lesson that you will benefit from once you are wed," she snarls. "It takes nine months for a woman to bake a baby. I was born five months after my father died. I *am* a Newton. And you're bloody lucky I've got no heart left in me or I'd teach you something else, something you'd never forget." Even so, she takes hold of the table and tips it, sending his plate, the teapot and cutlery clattering to the stone floor, his clay pipe smashing into pieces. He opens his mouth to cry out, but she rounds on him with such a look that he does not continue. She glares down at him and casts her eyes about the room, so familiar, the most homely place she could ever imagine. This interloper will wed and will live here in this house with a wife, when it ought to have been hers and James's. She thinks of the child within her, of the life it might have had. Everything is gone. Everything is ruined.

James Newton is buried at Stockton church on the 4th of March 1833, twenty-four years and a day after Thomas Newton, Mercy's father, was buried. Mercy is numb. The church is filled to the rafters. The Whitmores greet Newtons from all over the county and beyond. There is Edward, who tips his hat to her, knowing nothing of the child within her. She sees William greet brothers, sisters and his mother, others too, and she wonders, perhaps, if some of them are those children who witnessed their mother's murder at Severn Hall, but she is too sickened, too weak, to discover if her theory is true. And then, when it is over, all the platitudes and meaningless hymns, and James is interred down into the cold earth, up steps an older man to the graveside. This man, she realises, can only be her Uncle John Newton senior, James's father, the brother of her own father. He throws the first handful of earth, and his wife, who must be her aunt, moans on his arm and is taken away to sob upon a bench. She has dreamed of tearing strips off these people and daydreamed of the ways she would denounce their ignorance towards her and her mother. But she finds that she has nothing left within her to ignite her temper; she is cold to her very heart. So she stands there and watches this father say goodbye to yet another of his sons, unnaturally taken from this life, and says nothing.

She will take something of his son away with her, she thinks. This man will never know his own grandson.

She strokes her belly surreptitiously.

Once the funeral is over she knows she must leave the lodge house.

Whilst the rest of the ghouls go from the funeral to the public house at Norton to toast his life, Mercy stands in the kitchen, *their* kitchen. She imagines the three of them, her and James and the baby, seated at the kitchen table, laughing, the baby plump and gurgling. What a magnificent life they might have had together.

But instead, the grate is empty and the place is cold and silent and dark. The curse of that Newton blood has taken him from her.

"We could have been happy," she says out loud. "We could have made a life together." She gives the place one last glance over to seal it in her heart. He feels so close here that she almost thinks if she turns quick enough she'll catch him striding up to the door with his dogs. But no dogs bark and no figure comes. The dogs are locked up again out in the stables, and James Newton lies rotting in Stockton churchyard. All is still, wan and grey.

One last thing there is for her to do. She upends one of her bags in the dirt. It is filled not with her things, but with the clothing of William Newton, gathered from his room, and his spare shirt, breeches, socks, two white cravats and best jacket land dumped in the dirt. She pours James's rum and the last of the lamp oil over it all, then pulls out a box of matches and strikes. The flames take quickly. She stands for a while watching the stuff burn, then returns to the house to retrieve her belongings. As she walks past the licking flames, a small, wan smile spreads across her thin lips.

Hooves sound outside the gate and a voice calls, "Having a bonfire, miss?"

"Just burning some rubbish," she replies and hauls herself up into the back of the cart with her bags. One of the lads from the stables has offered to take her and her things back to whichever lodging house or relative she intends to stay with now. Of course, there is only one place for her to go.

Back then goes Mercy Newton, pregnant, bereaved and dried up, back in the same cart that brought her here, except now she sits in the back and stares at the lane as it passes away. Every jolt, every hole that sends the cart sideways reverberates through her body, and the little grub inside her is turning somersaults, or perhaps it is the last of whatever food is wallowing deep in her gut rising.

The boy driving the cart is whistling, and sometimes he clicks his tongue to the horse and calls to them; his noise never ceases, and it is grinding Mercy's patience to threads. By the time they reach the sandstone cliffs that overlook the river, she could easily put her hands about his throat and throttle him.

"This will do," she snaps. "I'll get out here."

"Whoa!" he calls to the horses and pulls them up. "We're a good way off yet, Miss Newton, and there's the hill yet to come; are you sure you don't want me to take you to the top?"

She shakes her head. "No," she tells him. "I will walk the rest of the way."

"With all those bags?" he tries again.

"With all these bags," she tells him and clambers down and takes her things. She stands in the road for a moment and then reaches out to pat the noses of the horses, but when she feels that soft, nuzzling warmth in her hand her eyes sting.

"Goodbye then, Miss Newton," says the boy and she nods, but cannot make more words come, so he clicks and sends the horses on to turn where the road gets wider, and Mercy starts her walk. Back to Batch Pool Lane. Back to her mother, who is thinner and more like a mayfly than ever. She opens the door to her with resignation, and from whom the waves of alcohol are so thick they are almost tangible.

Mercy has lost everything. She sets eyes on her mother and wonders what it would be like, just for a moment for her to wrap her arms about her and tell her she is loved. Instead, Anne demonstrates her usual maternal dissonance.

"I wondered how long it'd be before *you* came back, now he's dead," she slurs. "Didn't care to send me any money, did you? Then come marching back in here when he shoots himself because he is sick of you." Her voice is harsh, shrieking, bird-like. She sways in the doorway, hair bedraggled, spots of spittle on her lips. The drink has her in its grip. "You'll always come back to me in the end, Kitty, because this is what you are worth. Bugger all!"

Mercy drops her bags. One hand shoots up and slaps her mother's cheek with so much force that her head knocks into the doorpost. Anne Newton stands, shocked and open-mouthed, but Mercy has already picked up her bags and is pushing past her.

"I shan't be putting up with your poisoned words any longer," she tells her mother as she passes by. "I won't end up like you. And I'll be using your bed from now on."

The First Trial: Spring Assizes

Recollections of Thomas Whitmore, MP

Apley Estate, Bridgnorth
17th of March 1849

The spring assizes were soon upon us, and Phillimore and I had prepared what we believed to be a distinct case for the prosecution. The witnesses were all in our favour – by God! – and even the woman's own uncle was prepared to testify against her, to see his niece swing.

As the prisoner stood, aloof and self-possessed in the dock, she appeared, from the straightness of her back and the set of her shoulders, to be calm. She wore black once more, as she had in the guildhall, and the veil on her bonnet again covered her physiognomy for all who were not directly before her. The gallery was an ignominious crush of gossip-hungry spectators; flat caps and top hats, bonnet after bonnet, a fan flickering here or there, and unfortunately, such a crush did nothing to dispel the odour of the masses. The sheer intensity of bodies brought forth waves of smoke, sweat and dirt.

Despite the entertainment prospects for the onlookers and the possibility that the whole thing might degenerate into little more than a freak show, Miss Newton was clearly determined not to give them cause to ridicule her. She was dressed fashionably enough for one of her status: a black silk dress, mourning wear, with fur Victorine cuffs, a black straw bonnet and that black veil giving her the air of something risen from or soon to repair to the grave.

At length the place twittered to a standstill and all eyes focused solely upon her. I found myself wondering if she could feel the weight of them all beneath that veil, whether she could feel the pressure of all those eyes bearing down upon her. Perhaps she wore it not merely so that they could not observe her, but also so that she could not see them.

Since watching her coroner's inquiry, I had done a little more research and of course read the newspapers and been apprised of the unfortunate events in her family preceding the suicide of her cousin, James Newton. I was aware that this was the very place her cousin, John Newton, of Severn Hall, was taken to trial for the murder of his wife. I could not prevent myself considering, when I thought I observed her emit a little shudder, that she must be thinking of him and perhaps wondering if her feet stood in the self-same spot as her own cousin when he was meted out his death sentence. I remembered only too well those words reported in all the newspapers that her cousin spoke as his sentence was meted out, strong in the local dialect, 'Dunna kill me! Dunna kill me!'

I couldn't help but wonder what her response might be when she realised her fate would go the same way. Would she need to be prised from the place as he was? Would she cling to the bars, hold on, literally, for dear life? Or would she accept the inevitable with quiet grace? For I was beyond doubt sure that this woman was for the noose.

Chapter Four

Mercy Newton

Batch Pool Lane to Morville

1833 – 1838

That first day she arrives back in dark, damp Batch Pool Lane and sweeps in past her mother who stays standing in the doorway nursing her cheek and rapidly darkening eye, Mercy has not told her mother that she is pregnant.

To give her mother fuel for her ravenous taunting would be too foolish. No, Mercy must hold this secret for as long as she can. Sometimes she loves this little grub inside her more than life itself, for it is half *him*. At other times she cannot stand it and wishes it gone, ripped from her and thrown in the depths of the river, boiled in oil or suffocated in her own birthing fluids, for it will ruin her life.

The first day, however, once she takes to her mother's bed, she finds she cannot rise from it, though her mother rails and rallies at her,

"You lazy little slut, I shan't be keeping you!"

"For God's sake, Kitty, get your fat arse out of bed and put some food on the table!"

"It's no wonder he killed himself, living with you!"

Mercy cannot even summon the energy to retaliate. She lies, staring at the whitewashed stone wall, each dimple and crack forging its impression into her eyeballs. She is exhausted. She lies there in a mist of sleepless loveless limbo. She is a rock, a stone, a shell, cold and hard and broken. Only the child bubbling inside her reminds her she is a warm, breathing creature.

Anne grows aberrantly worried as the drink wears off. She sits timidly on the edge of the bed and puts a hand on Mercy's arm.

"Kitty," she says. "What is it? This isn't natural and it's not you." She waits for a reply but none comes. "I've got some eggs," she tells her. "I'll make us some and some toast, Kitty, how about that? You'll like that, won't you?" She waits again for a reply, but Mercy merely sighs and closes her eyes.

Anne sets the eggs to boil, slices bread and stabs it with the toasting fork. "You loved a boiled egg when you was a little 'un," she calls to Mercy as she works, in the sing-song tones she normally saves for little children. "You wouldn't be as big and strong today if I hadn't kept you in eggs."

Once the eggs and toast are ready, Anne puts it all out on the little table proudly.

"Kitty, it's ready, come and eat with me," she says. She approaches the bed. "Come now, Kitty, sit with me, please," she pleads and takes her arm. Mercy allows her to sit her up and guide her to the table. She sits, and Anne cracks her egg for her.

"Eat up," she tells her, as the scent of boiled egg wafts heavily up to her.

Mercy takes a breath. Then she dives for the bucket by the fireplace and throws up anything she has left inside her.

"Please take the eggs outside," she manages to whisper. "Please."

Anne stares at her. Slowly she rises, takes the eggs from the table and opens the door. Mercy sits, sickened now by the stench rising from the bucket, and lets the cold air encompass her. She can see Anne outside peeling eggs, throwing the shells in the little vegetable patch and biting at the white, sucking the yolk out. She spits into her bucket. She cannot imagine ever eating eggs again.

She is normally so strong, so brittle, so enduring. Now though, she feels that she is shutting down. The little thing inside her is leeching away her strength.

Then at the doorway, there is a cry. Anne is standing there, a bit of egg yolk glistening on her chin, staring, pointing at Mercy sitting there, the bucket between her legs, her skirts stretched across her belly.

"You didn't!" Anne cries. "Oh Kitty, you haven't!"

Mercy raises her head slowly.

"You're in trouble, girl!" Anne growls. "Was it that nephew of his? William? I heard he was staying there. Him who found the body. Was it him?"

Mercy narrows her eyes. She looks down at her belly. It is bulging beneath the folds of her skirts. She looks back at her mother and slowly shakes her head.

Anne stares at her for a moment, then cries out again and steps backwards. Her hand flutters to her mouth. "No!" she says. "Not him! Not your own bloody cousin?"

Mercy tries to quell the next wave of sickness, but it overwhelms her for a moment. Once it has passed, Anne is still there in the doorway, and the place is cold.

"It's James's baby," she tells her mother defiantly. "There's nothing wrong with it! We could have been married!"

Anne stares at her for a moment. "You could have been, but he shot himself, Kitty! Is this why? Because of this baby? Is that why he shot himself?" She pats her pockets. "You're a bloody fool," she adds, pulling out her Lucifer matches and looking for her pipe. "A little whore!" she snaps, rattling her way about the place. She finds the gin and upends it straight into her mouth. There are a few good mouthfuls at least. "How will we feed three of us? Your own cousin, Kitty! I might have known a bloody Newton'd do this to you! But I thought you might have more sense!"

"More sense? Like you?" Mercy manages. She grimaces and struggles to her feet. "I hope that money of yours is still in the bank, for it is mine anyway, and it has more mouths to stretch to now." She takes up a piece of toast and bites into it defiantly. To her satisfaction, her mother flinches as she steps towards her.

Anne sniffs. "Didn't take you long to mention the money, did it?" She lights her pipe with a shaking hand. "Christ Kitty, a bloody baby out of wedlock, another bloody Newton. Quick little slut, aren't you?" she adds, as she stabs at the fire with the poker, keeping her voice too low for Mercy to hear, for she knows this comment will rile her to lose her temper, and for a pregnant Mercy to be all heated up and those veins in her forehead bulging would be an ugly thing indeed. Besides, she can still feel the sting of the slap Mercy dealt her on her return.

They somehow make ends meet. Anne takes in some mending to do and Mercy does some cleaning in the big house on the lane. One evening as they sit before the fire, Anne suddenly pipes up, "There should be a will, Kitty. Shouldn't there? Didn't your cousin James make a will? Won't it be read soon?"

Mercy stares into the flames. "I don't know anything about a will," she says. But her heart leaps a little. He knew she was with child. What sort of a man would leave his child and the mother of his child with nothing? "I will write to Mr Whitmore and ask," she says.

She takes three days to pen her enquiry, unable to shape her words into sentences that are not somehow poor and vulgar. But once she is satisfied with it, she reads it out to her mother, who agrees it will do well enough, and it is sent on to the Apley Estate.

It is summer now, and Mercy is so huge with the child that she can hardly move. She sits and feels the child, who is now so big that it does not move about so much any longer, but sometimes there is the pressure of a hand or a foot pressed up against the huge mound of her belly from the inside, and she wonders how it exists, cramped up in there. If it is a boy, and she is sure it will be, she will call it James. She is almost certain it is a boy, for what else could it be given the circumstances? Her mother gave birth to her in the summer after her father died. God surely could not see it happen the same, all over again. No, it will be a boy. It will look just like him, grow to be big and strong like him and take care of her in her dotage. As she nears the birth, she clings to that: he will look after her, he will take care of her once he's grown. If she clings to that, then she can get through this, for she is petrified. So many women die in childbirth. So many awful things can happen, and Mercy nor Anne can afford medical costs.

History and God, it seems, both see fit to play the same trick twice.

The birth, when it comes, is a torturous, twenty-hour long labour. Mercy has only her mother, Mrs Littleford and a woman from Bridgnorth called Sarah Lloyd by her side. Mrs Littleford recommends they send for Sarah since the labour is taking a good long while and the woman asks for a tenth of the money a doctor might charge to aid her in her labour. Mercy doesn't catch her words, nor does she care. The pain rips her in two. By the time this Sarah Lloyd arrives to help, Mercy is exhausted and ready to die. She had known it would be bad, but nothing could have prepared her for this agony. She has lost the energy to scream and each time she tries, no sound comes out. These three women tell her to do things, tell her when to push and when to wait, but she pays none of them heed. Her body is telling her what to do and she must not fight it; she *cannot* fight it. He will look after me when he is grown, she tells herself, and she clings to this as the baby tears her into pieces.

"Another Newton," says Sarah Lloyd darkly.

"It's a girl!" announces Mrs Littleford, as Mercy lies there, bleeding and empty.

"What?" she can barely raise her head, but she sees the bloody, clenched little fists sticking out of a blanket in the arms of her mother.

"Oh, Kitty, what a tiny little mite," her mother says and clucks at it. "She won't be a bother to us after all, will she?"

"A girl?" Mercy asks weakly, but it is, she knows it is, and she does not want it. "Take it away," she says and turns her face to the wall.

And so Mercy is delivered of a child, a little girl, five months after the death of the father, just as her mother was before her. The little girl is, once Mercy has got over the shock of her not being a boy, called Maria, a name chosen by Anne, for Mercy had no girls name in mind. Maria would have been the name Anne might have given a fourth daughter if her husband had lived long enough to give her one.

The one particular notion Mercy had conjured whilst carrying the child was to have her baptised at Stockton church, that her father might be there at least in spirit. Anne attends, head bowed. Since it takes place straight after the Sunday service, William Newton is in attendance. He has taken over as gamekeeper, is already married and lives now in the lodge house with his new wife. The Whitmores, and Edward, damned Edward Newton, who knows, surely, whose child he looks upon but blinks not an eye are present too. Maria will be overlooked, bastardised and unaccepted by the Newtons just the same as Mercy was.

Mercy gazes down at the child as she stands at the font, full of pity, and wonders that she has lived to be born through such sorrow. When the baptism is recorded there in the huge ledger right at the bottom of a page that carries the names of the parents, all married, all with a father and a mother, the curate registers her daughter as 'Maria, illegitimate daughter of Mercy Newton', even though word has got around and he knows, Mercy is sure, that this is the child of James Newton and he might very well put that in. But even as he writes, the babe stirs in her arms, raises two clenched fists and screws her face up into a scream that shakes the windows, her sympathy fades. She knows suddenly, how this child has survived, and she looks down on her and thinks, *You are a full-blooded Newton. Your wrath has brought you forth to continue the curse of this blood. You will be filled with darkness. Death will follow you.*

Now there are three mouths to feed at Batch Pool Lane, Anne will not give up the gin or her tobacco and grows meaner by the day. Mercy cannot stand the bawling of the baby, nor the blood that flows from her or the throbbing in her breast. Anne sees to the baby mostly; Mercy can hardly bear to look at it. It disturbs her sleep, pierces her ears with its shrill wails and sets her breasts leaking. She feeds it but with a sense of duty, and when she looks down at the little face suckling, it is the face of a parasite. The son she had dreamed of is gone and never will be. James Newton is dead.

One night Mercy wakes to cries, and groans and sits upright, but she knows instantly that the cries are not those of the baby. They are screams now, piercing screams: Anne's. She is down the narrow stairs quickly and the place is full of light. Anne is aflame. Quicker than anything she's done these past six months, Mercy is across the room and grabbing the bucket of water that sits by the door. Anne is shrieking, beating flames from her chest and her skirt is flaming. Mercy takes hold of the bucket and launches the contents at her, then pulls a coat from the door hook and smothers her with it, knocking Anne to the floor. They lie there in the water, Mercy on top of her mother panting. From the corner of the room in the little box they are using as a cot the baby is bawling now. Anne struggles to push the coat off her head.

"Kitty, I can't breathe!" she cries out hoarsely.

Mercy stares down at her. Then as the wails of the baby grow louder, she pushes herself off her mother and sits back. They are both wet, and Anne's charred, blackened clothes are ruined.

"What did you do?" she questions, but her mother is already over at the box shushing the baby with cooing noises.

"I can't pick her up, Kitty, she'll get wet," her mother says. "You take her."

Mercy's top half is relatively dry and she does as she is told, scooping the baby up and Anne, like a damp moth, flutters about, strips her damp clothes and pulls on dry ones from the chest beneath the table.

"Ruined," she tuts, buttoning her blouse, the pain from the livid burns on her skin lessened by the drink that is slurring her words.

"Had you been drinking?" Mercy asks, to which Anne snorts.

"Not much," she admits. "It was the fire, Kitty, too close I must have been. When it shifted, my skirt caught alight as I dozed in the chair, that's how it must've happened. Thought I had died and gone to hell, I did." Despite her fright, she casts a teasing eye towards her daughter. "Turns out I did, eh, Kitty?" And she laughs mightily, when she ought, Mercy thinks, to be wondering how to get by with a blouse, a skirt and a petticoat all taken by the flames. They lie in a wet heap now, browned and flimsy, and won't even do for making cushions.

"Are you hurt?" Mercy asks, but she's not sure now that she cares. Her mother had promised not to drink whilst she was around the baby, and now she's almost sent the place up in flames around them all.

"If my petticoat weren't so thick I reckon I'd have been roasted, and there's some sore points, Kitty, but you saved me," Anne replies, buttoning herself up slowly, for her fingers and eyes don't seem to work well together at the moment.

Mercy looks about her. Yes, there's the gin bottle by the side of the chair near the fire.

"Perhaps I'd have been better off if I'd let you burn," she replies caustically. "At least then I could have got my hands on my inheritance and it wouldn't be pissed down the drain."

Anne pauses. "You're an evil little bitch at times, Mercy," she says, shaking her head. Mercy can see her hand twitching. If this were fifteen years ago, that hand would have dealt Mercy a blow about the ears, but now it falters.

Mercy curls her lip and leans forward eyes flashing. "Maybe I should have let you roast," she hisses.

The baby begins to wail once more.

At last Mercy receives a missive from Thomas Whitmore. There is a will and it is to be read in a fortnight. If there is anything in it for her, he will be sure to inform her that she might attend.

Mercy is elated. There is not enough food for them, and she has to sell things, things that James bought her, in order to feed herself that she might feed her child: a pair of gloves, a pair of earrings, a vase and a shawl. She is running out of ways to survive.

And yet, when the time comes, Mercy is not invited to the reading of the will. In fact, out of the blue, she instead receives a visit in person by the Old Squire, Thomas Whitmore. He comes alone on horseback and tethers his horse to a tree outside the cottage, to rap upon the door smartly and take off his hat with the gentlemanly attitude she has come to expect from him. It is October, the leaves are browning off and everywhere is damp. His horse stands in the mire of the lane, and his boots, Mercy notes, are already thick with mud; she will be cleaning the floor for the next hour if she invites him in, but she knows she must if she is to hear of the will. She will make him tea and get out the fruitcake they have been saving and feeding for Christmas. All this she thinks before he has managed to get out a word.

"Miss Newton," he says with a charming smile, and her heart leaps. There must have been something left for her, some money or something she could sell. "I am come about the will."

"Come in, come in," she says, and her mother, who is jigging the baby, echoes, "Come in, come in."

He shakes his head. "I am, unfortunately, in a rush to get home," he tells her. "We have visitors waiting for my return. But I came out this way to speak to you personally. I felt that you ought to know. The will was read today."

"And?" comes Anne's sharp tone. She comes to stand behind Mercy with the baby.

"I'm sorry," Thomas Whitmore tells them. "You were not mentioned."

Anne's jaw drops. Mercy shakes her head. Her heart seems to have stopped. "What? Did he not get round to changing it?"

Thomas Whitmore shakes his head. "He made a new last will and testament on the 18th of March this year," he says. "It was up to date."

Mercy calculates. "When did he take time to do that?"

Then she remembers that day, when James had gone off on his horse without explaining, come home and taken a bottle upstairs to drink himself to sleep. How she had driven herself half-mad with thoughts of brothels and whores at the bottom of the Cartway. What day was that, she wonders. Was it the day he changed his will? Had he already decided that day, what he would do? That he would leave her and the baby with nothing?

"Oh God," she says and clutches the doorpost.

"I'm sorry, Miss Newton," Thomas says. "There were a few smaller bequests, but much of his assets were left to his brother Edward, and his nephew, William. You were not mentioned."

"Nothing, *nothing* for us?" she hears her words coming faintly.

"Bastard," breathes Anne beside her. "A bastard Newton to the end."

"Did he...know of the child?" Thomas asks, carefully.

Mercy nods. "He did."

"I cannot explain any of this, Miss Newton," he tells her. "Except to say that James Newton was not a well man. Miss Newton, you must know this, for I will ever be a man who speaks the truth. But James Newton tried to drown himself some twelve years back, and I was forced to have the man sent to Stafford Asylum for his own good. He came back to my employment afterwards with all the steadfastness we knew of him, but I believe he harboured a darkness within him, and this time, he did what he set out to do all those years ago." Mercy stares at him. That she should be given this information now, after all, is much to bear. Thomas Whitmore places his hat back on his head and turns away to go to his horse, then turns back again. "If ever you require references," he says. "Write to me for them. You took care of James and kept house well. I will be pleased to recommend you."

He mounts his horse, leaving Mercy staring after him, eyes burning and heart sore. It is as though she never existed. James Newton wiped her from his history. He had seen to it that no one knows explicitly of his shame, except those she apprises of it.

Their poverty must continue.

No son will ever save her.

No last piece of charity will come from beyond the grave.

She must toil on and will be ground into dust.

This evening, when her mother takes up the gin, so does Mercy.

They continue to scrape by, but now two of them need gin. Mercy sells things to make ends meet: her bonnet James bought her and her best boots for Sundays. She will soon run out of things to sell. Besides, when they drink together, neither mother nor daughter can keep a civil tongue in their head.

The baby lies in the corner, in a crib made from a vegetable box whilst Anne reaches for her gin. Mercy watches her hand miss the bottle. She snorts. The baby lets out a little snore.

"This is the last of it, Kitty," Anne says and upends the bottle.

Mercy leans over the baby and looks down upon her. "I thought you would be a son," she whispers.

"Don't take on so," Anne tells her. "Poor little thing, just like you with no father to fend for her."

"I can fend for her," Mercy states, although she must hold the table for support. "She doesn't need a father."

Anne chortles. "Last time you fended, you came back in the pudding club, Kitty." Then she laughs and cannot stop, and Mercy turns on her and the baby starts to cry.

"Shut up," Mercy slurs, snatches up the bottle and lets the last drips fall on her tongue.

"Last time you fended, you showed yourself for the slut you really are," Anne snaps and knocks the bottle from her hand. "Shut away in those hills, fraternising with your own kin when the cholera was raging. Didn't care to look in on your poor mother did you? Didn't send me any pennies did you? But now you're back with your bastard child and living off me again!" She bangs the table.

"You have five hundred pounds," Mercy snaps. "And that's your granddaughter." She points at the baby who is bawling now, little fists balled and eyes screwed tight shut.

"It always comes back to this, Kitty!" Anne is on her feet, swaying. "Always comes back to the money. Well let me tell you something, my girl, you don't deserve a penny of it! I'll live as long as I can to keep you from it!"

Mercy reaches down for the baby, who is red in the face now, high-pitched yowls coming forth from an angry mouth, and she bounces her a little but has to hold tight and put a hand to the table to steady herself.

"You've always hated me," she says, shushing the child whose wailing does not abate. "You've never shown me love. Not like I wanted to show Maria."

She glares at her mother, this woman who stands there clutching an empty gin bottle like a prize, swimming in her vision.

"And why might that be, Kitty? Eh?" Anne spits, setting down the bottle carefully and crossing her arms. "Might it be because each time I look at your lying, deceitful, ungrateful face,

I see your father looking back at me? Might it be that if you'd never been born, I might have married again, instead of raising an unwanted brat and festering here. I did my best with you, Kitty, but it's never been enough for you, girl."

The baby has settled in Mercy's arms. She looks down at her. She is perfect, so smooth, so small, James's daughter.

"What did you ever do for me other than embarrass me?" she snaps. The child is hungry, searching with her lips left and right. It needs her.

Anne is livid. "Ungrateful wench, I taught you to read and write, didn't I? I taught you your numbers! To sew! And for what? You spend more time living off my charity than you do earning a wage!" She lifts the bottle as though to hurl it at Mercy but stays her hand for the baby is there in her arms. "Just like your father, looking back at me, never good enough for him either, was I? Makes my flesh crawl just to look at you!"

Mercy stares down at the baby in her arms. James is there within her, looking back at her too. Suddenly, for the first time, she feels nothing but love for this child, no matter the inconvenience of her birth. She deserves better than this, she thinks.

"And here you are, waiting for me to die, and you'll end up just the same!" Anne spits. "You'll end up not good enough for her, Kitty, not good enough for the child you've borne, and you'll see her father in her, and you'll sink yourself in gin to be free of it, just the same, just the same as me, Kitty!" She draws near to Mercy and Maria and cranes herself over the baby. "You'll rot here," she breathes at them both.

Mercy feels suddenly sober. She can see it clearly now for herself. As detestable as Anne can be, she is right. If Mercy stays here and tries to bring up this child herself she will become just like Anne. Bitter, habitually drunk, and her daughter will hate her, as she hates Anne.

She steps away from her mother and holds her baby to her.

"Then I must work," she says. "I must make a life for her. And for me."

Anne stares at her. "And what will you do with the child?"

Mercy looks down at her daughter. In this instant, her mind is made up. "You must care for her until I can," she says through gritted teeth. "You and your five hundred pounds."

Anne laughs. She takes the child from Mercy and wraps her in her shawl. The child is snuffling, reaching out for something to suckle. Anne sticks the end of one grubby finger into her mouth. The child latches on.

"And you'll send money to pay for her keep?"

Mercy stares at her daughter. Her heart now could break. But she sees it as the only option; to work, provide for the child and leave her to Anne's devices until Mercy can make a home for her. Whatever the future might hold, Mercy knows only one thing: she cannot allow her relationship with Maria to end up like her own relationship with Anne. In this moment, her mind is made up. She wants more for her daughter than she has ever had herself.

She will look for a station somewhere and send money back to support them both. "I'll work," she tells Anne. "I'll make sure I can afford everything she needs."

Anne snorts. "You'll pay me for my services as your nanny," she tells Mercy. "And I want a good rate of pay."

Mercy eyes her sourly. She is sober now, as though all of her repugnance has chased the last vapours of gin from her body, yet her mother sways and slurs like a boatman up the Cartway on a Saturday night.

"Not that you deserve it," she tells her mother. "But this child will starve left to you."

"You won't go far, Kitty?" her mother asks. "You will take a day position so that you are here for the child in the evenings? I won't be left to raise her, not another little Newton brat."

Mercy sniffs. "Of course," she replies. She eyes the swaying wreck of a woman before her. "I don't trust you to look after her properly without me."

"Ever the ungrateful little slut, aren't you, Kitty?" her mother snaps. "The sooner the pair of you are out from under my roof, the better."

Mercy curls her lip. "I'll find myself a grand position. I won't end up like you," she tells her mother. "We will be gone soon enough."

Resolute, sobered and determined to avoid her mother's fate, Mercy writes to Thomas Whitmore again without mentioning the baby and the loss of James. Her request is entirely formal, despite his ready offer of a reference; she needs to prove to herself and the rest of the world that she is more than her mother, that she is more than this existence. She reminds him most formally then that she worked for his late gamekeeper as his housekeeper, and can expect no references from his account, and requests that Thomas Whitmore fulfil this duty in his stead. To her delight he replies quickly with excellent references, and with these she sets out to move herself out of Batch Pool Lane. She begins to hope that she might make something of herself yet. There are more places than the Apley Lodge House, grander houses that need attention, grander men with grander purses that need comfort and care. She pores over the newspapers, hoards the advertisements that ask for a housekeeper and sifts through them to find the best. She decides amongst other positions to apply to a Mr Dyer, whose name is familiar to her, for he is a burgess and a bailiff about Bridgnorth, and lives in a house she can only dream of.

Her application is posted in Bridgnorth on a day that bodes well, for the sun is shining and she is wearing the ribbon James bought her, now a little faded, about her neck. The cholera epidemic has all but ceased and sanitation is discussed now. New water pipes and waste pipes are being ordered and roads are being upheaved in places to affix them to different dwellings. The people of Bridgnorth are hopeful of their good health and are looking to the future, and so is she.

This is how she comes to send her references to Morville Hall, just outside Bridgnorth, on the Much Wenlock road, and how she comes to be accepted, for there are few other applicants. She leaves her baby daughter, Maria, behind, takes up her bags and escapes her mother's poverty alone.

Anne rails against her when she is told. "Damn you, Kitty, you said you'd take a position in town!" she yells, but none of the other jobs she has applied for has taken her on and Mercy has no choice.

"I will send money," she tells her mother. "I will come every Sunday!" The thought of leaving James's child with Anne is almost too much to bear, but it will not be forever, she promises herself. She will save her wages, as much as she can, to build them a life that is more than this. Besides, Anne is frail. She will not live forever. Five hundred pounds is a lot of money. They will be together soon enough.

"And I'm to raise your bastard child whilst you play lady of the manor!" Anne is drinking again. Mercy snatches the bottle from her.

"You won't need this if you are taking care of your granddaughter," she admonishes and hurls it into the lane. She kisses her daughter, who is sleeping in the corner, rests a hand against the sleeping child's cheek for a moment, and then steps out over the bottle that lies in the dirt, the contents glugging out into the muck. She walks away, leaving Anne scrabbling in the mud to pick it up and save the last few drops.

Morville Hall is inhabited by Mr John Dyer, a man with his finger in business and governance. His name is well-considered throughout Bridgnorth, and his huge house is modestly staffed. Mercy has been past it before, once when she and James went into Much Wenlock to the market, and once when they went to Morville for a fair in the summer gone by. She shrugs these memories away as she alights at the end of the driveway and takes up her bags. Mr John Dyer's name is in every newspaper, for he is the agent to Lord Sudbury and manages the sale of lots, the auction of items, the rental of plots and the management of his estates. He is a man to be reckoned with, and she wonders what he will be like to work for. She is sure that if she had not mentioned her references and had not explicitly noted on her application that they have been signed by Thomas Whitmore himself, she would not have been taken on. For this, she is thankful. She follows the driveway, which leads towards the three-storey mansion house, its two wings protruding from either side towering over a doorway that seems inconsistently meagre in proportion to the rest of the house. This house is Elizabethan, for everyone in the area knows it has stood here for the last four hundred or more years. It is set before a great grassy area, with a shallow haha, a dower house and church to one side and a mirroring estate office to the other.

It feels strange to be away from her daughter; her breasts ache. She harbours such doubts about her mother's capabilities to care for the infant, but there is no alternative that she can find. She is determined that Maria be shown a better life than she was. It is the right thing to do. She is filled with intentions now to earn, send a portion of the money to her mother for the keep of Maria and to have, at the end of it all, some savings of her own – oh, to have money of her own to save – and to make a way for herself and her child, that they might not wallow, but rise eventually above her mother's hovel in Batch Pool Lane.

Her boots crunch on the stones that litter the driveway. The wails of her mother are still mingled in her ears with the wails of the child, "I reared you, an unwanted, ungrateful brat, and now I'm to rear your bastard child? You're a selfish bitch, Mercy Newton, a selfish bitch!"

Like a crow, her mother's voice, piercing, unforgettable.

She hands over her references at the door, proud to show them off, but is given them straight back again and is taken into the study to meet John Dyer himself. He sits behind a desk which is orderly but mounded with ledgers, and to all sides of him are more. He nods to the manservant who sees her inside and beckons for her to sit in the chair on the opposite side of the desk to him. She nods in thanks to the manservant and takes her seat.

John Dyer waits until the door is closed.

"Miss Newton," he says. "Your references, I am assured, are from Thomas Whitmore himself?"

"Yes, sir," she replies and pulls them out, passing them toward him.

He takes them slowly, readjusts his spectacles and opens them onto the desk before him. She knows what is contained within those words and she knows that they are sound. She watches him confidently, and when he looks up she meets his gaze.

"Very good," he says. "These are excellent." He folds them

along the same lines as they were previously folded and passes them back to her. "You worked well for the Whitmores," he concedes. "And you will do well for me."

"I will do my very best," she tells him. "It is a beautiful house. I will see that it is taken care of, Mr Dyer, and will see to your comforts."

Mr Dyer takes his spectacles, folds them and sets them aside. "It is a small staff I have here, Miss Newton," he tells her. "I am growing older, my daughter is married and gone. I work all hours, all days, all seasons. I require little, but that the fires are lit at the correct hour, my meals are ready at the proper time and the place is kept clean and tidy."

"I will ensure that all this is done to your satisfaction, sir," she tells him, eyeing dust about the ledgers and soot ingrained into the rug.

He nods and indicates the door. "Call for Tipton to see you to your room," he tells her.

She finds herself standing almost involuntarily, as though his will is forcing her out of the room.

"Welcome to Morville Hall, Newton. I hope you will work hard and be happy here," he says as she reaches the door.

"Thank you, Mr Dyer, I shall," she replies, but he is already replacing his spectacles and reaching for a ledger.

Housekeeping at Morville Hall is altogether a different matter when compared with what Mercy is used to. This place is vast: three floors, cellars and attics, two huge wings, kitchen gardens, estate offices and grounds that extend out past the little church and into the countryside. She has a set of keys as big as her head, and it hangs from her waist clanking as she strides about the house seeing to her work. She exudes confidence but knows to her shame that she is underqualified for the post and must learn this position and all it entails quickly, for there are those that work here who expect from her what they have seen from other more experienced housekeepers. She is in charge of the accounts books, although Mr Dyer informs her that he will inspect them monthly. This is a new and frankly terrifying concept, but Mr Dyer is such a stickler that he spends an evening showing her exactly how he likes his ledgers to look – this pedanticism gives her the opportunity she needs to pick up what she must do. Mercy Newton has a sharp brain when she has need to apply it. The timetabling for cooking and laundry is already well-established, and she decides not to change it. There is a laundry-maid, two housemaids, the cook, and then for the grounds, a gardener and groom and his lad. Mr Dyer is alone here. His only daughter is married, his wife is dead and he runs this house on the fewest staff he can.

Mercy oversees the work of the staff, although the place is already running itself and she sees no need to change things at first. She enjoys making her rounds at different times of the day to ensure that the day's chores are properly done. The cook is a widow in her thirties who has worked here for the last three years and knows how Mr Dyer likes his meals. She keeps herself to herself, and Mercy likes her regimented approach to meal preparation. The housemaids, one a native of Morville village and the other a precocious young girl from Bridgnorth, however, are another matter. She catches them gossiping on the stairs at regular intervals and shoos them off. The Morville girl, Mary, capitulates easily enough, but the Bridgnorth-born girl is less easy. Mercy notes that this girl does not take direction as easily – her eyes narrow and her lips purse. One evening, as Mercy is counting through a delivery and marking it off, this girl, Lucy, sidles up to her.

"Mrs Newton," she says tonelessly as though the name is new to her. Mercy is going by 'Mrs' here as many housekeepers do, using the well-tried and tested reasoning that a married woman, a widowed woman, is more likely to garner respect from her subordinates than a perpetual 'Miss' might.

Mercy finishes counting the candles and marks the amount off in her ledger. The girl still lingers.

"Lucy, might I be of help?" she asks, curtly.

"That depends," comes the reply and Mercy notes a sly look transform this girl's face. "That depends entirely upon your ableness to talk Dyer into paying a better wage for me, doesn't it?"

Mercy puts down her pen. She stoppers her ink bottle with a cork and looks up at the girl, who is standing before her, leaning nonchalantly against the doorpost.

"I'll thank you to stand up straight when you are addressing your betters," Mercy tells her, but she is no fool. This girl knows something. She stands.

"I would," the girl continues. "If my betters were in the room. But it seems they're missing." She raises an eyebrow, in a most irritating way. Mercy gets to her feet.

"Are you drunk?" she snaps. "I can see no other reason why you would risk your job, talking to me like that!" She is dying to slap the girl, but she stays on her side of the desk, keeping it between them, for her hands are itching to get hold of her.

"I want a better wage," says the girl. "And in return, I won't tell everyone about you."

Mercy stares at her. "About what, precisely?" she asks. She must know what this girl knows.

"That you've a bastard by your cousin," the girl retorts. "That you're no Mrs, and your daughter was born out of wedlock."

And she stands there triumphant whilst Mercy leans upon the table, and she can hear her heart pumping in her temples, then adds, "It's a little bastard you've spawned."

Never has Mercy Newton felt the urge to take a poker to someone so violently before. That this chit, this vile girl, has the nerve to threaten her with this is beyond her patience. She grips the corner of the table.

At first, she considers denying it. She considers braining the hideous little thing. She considers telling her that she must pack her things and leave. Whatever she considers, every scenario she can conjure, they all end in her public shame, in Mr Dyer's dismissal of her.

"A pay rise?" she manages and the girl laughs. She actually laughs.

"I want three pounds more per annum," she says. "At least."

Now Mercy laughs, but it is dry and filled with dust. "He'll not pay that for a housemaid."

Lucy stares at her. She sets her face into a grimace. "Then you must add the remainder," she says.

Mercy stares at her. The girl's jaw is set, jutting out enough to make it a fine target. "I will see you get what's coming to you," she says.

"See that you do," the girl says and disappears away into the darkness in the corridor beyond.

Mercy is shaking. She sits as a wave of sickness washes over her. She cannot lose this position. She must stay here, she must earn this money, she must have this status. A room of her own, a separate dining space away from the lower ranks of staff. She is someone. She cannot be a nobody. Never again. Never again like her mother.

She takes a cloth and smudges some ashes about the grate in the drawing room and handles the silver. Then she opens up the room that Mr Dyer's wife once called her own. She takes a trinket, a brooch, from the dresser. As the rest of the staff sit down to supper, she goes to Lucy's room and places it beneath the pillow. Then she makes her way to John Dyer's study.

"Mr Dyer, sir, I have come to put to you an idea to save some money on the accounts," she says as he admits her to his study.

He gazes at her over his spectacles. "You have?"

She nods sternly. "It grieves me to say this, sir, and I do not like to speak ill of people, but I do think that if we were to let the two house-maids move on to other circumstances and hire one who is willing to do the job properly, then we might cover the work of the two with only one wage to be paid."

He steeples his hands and examines her. She hopes he can't see that her hands are shaking. She thrusts them behind her skirts.

"I have also, reason to believe that she might be..." she pauses. It won't do to sound too eager. "Taking things."

He raises an eyebrow at this. "What sort of things? Sugar? Spoons?"

"I believe she has been taking things from the late Mrs Dyer's room, sir," she says all in a rush, as though to get it out as quickly and as painlessly as possible.

At this he stands. "What gives you this impression?" he asks. "It's a serious accusation, Mrs Newton."

She nods and stands tall. "I know, sir," she says and hopes she sounds sincere. "And I have thought long and hard about the situation, but I cannot fathom it otherwise."

He crosses the room and stands by the fire. "What is missing?" he asks shortly.

Mercy stares at the back of him. She observes his shoulders tense. "On my rounds, I have been into Mrs Dyer's room to air the place, check the dusting is done, wipe the windows down and so on. There was a beautiful little brooch on the dresser; I remember it clearly, because the light from the window used to catch it. It has gone, sir."

He does not move. The fire crackles. It is growing dark outside. She waits.

"If she has stolen from me," he says, at length. "I want her out of here tonight."

"I can see to that, sir," she says.

He still does not move. She waits. The clock ticks.

"Show me what work is not done to your satisfaction," he says. "And then we will search rooms."

She whisks her way triumphantly through to the drawing room and he follows solemnly, and there she indicates the smeared grate and then shows him, in the dining room, the dirty silver all marked with fingerprints.

"Shoddy," he agrees, but his hackles, she can tell, are bristling for what is still to come. John Dyer is a man of principle, everyone in and around Bridgnorth knows him, has had dealings with him. Slovenliness is one thing and theft is another. Up the stairs they go. There is no one about. Supper is still taking place down in the kitchens.

"It's this one," Mercy announces and opens the door to the room.

"I will touch nothing," John Dyer announces. "You must look and I will witness."

She nods. It won't do to go too quickly to the bed. Instead she goes to the mantel and opens a tin box that sits upon it, but there is nothing but matches inside. She goes to the chest of drawers and opens each one, rifling through a petticoat, thick woollen socks, a shawl, handkerchiefs. She checks beneath the bed, pulls out the spare shoes beneath and checks inside each one. Then she runs a hand beneath the covers and throws them back and pulls the pillow away from the bed. She freezes.

The brooch is gone.

"What is going on here?" Lucy's voice comes from the doorway. Mercy spins around, the pillow still in her hand.

"Room search," John Dyer announces. "We will be looking through each room until the lost item is found."

"And what item might that be?" Lucy's eyes narrow. She glances at Mercy.

"The brooch from Mrs Dyer's dressing table," Mercy tells her shortly. The girl is amused Mercy can tell. Unnerved, she searches about her; it must be here somewhere. It must have fallen down between the bed and the wall. She sets forth, pulling at the under sheet.

"The blue one with the little diamonds around the edge?" Lucy asks. "Why, it was on the dressing table this evening when I closed the curtains," she says and Mercy turns to see that she is grinning. "Perhaps you are mistaken, Mrs Newton. Perhaps you require spectacles. You'll not find it in here."

And she stands there, hands on hips, encouraging, "Check the hems, Mrs Newton, the hems of the curtains in case there's something sewed inside. Check the pockets of my best jacket, Mrs Newton, check them deep! What about inside the ewer, there might be something down at the bottom, reach deep, reach deep!"

Mercy steps back at last defeated. "It is not here, sir," she admits, trounced by this damned girl. Mr Dyer frowns. He looks from Lucy to Mercy and back again.

"Perhaps we ought to search Mrs Newton's chamber?" Lucy pipes suddenly. "To be fair?"

Then Mercy realises; this girl has found the brooch. She's found it and she's hidden it in Mercy's room. She raises her eyes to meet the girl's gaze, which is black and trained upon her with such intensity that she has no doubt now: that brooch will be beneath her own pillow. And yet her door was left locked as it always is, for therein she keeps the petty cash tin.

"Wait," Mr Dyer says turning. "What is this beneath her jacket?"

Lucy's jacket, the pockets of which Mercy has already searched, hangs on a peg behind the door. The corner of something protrudes from beneath it. John Dyer reaches out and takes it down.

"You will look inside, Mrs Newton," he instructs.

Mercy's hands are again shaking, but she manages to take the bag and makes a play of setting it down on the bed to look inside, for the reality is that she does not trust the solidity of her grasp now and is afraid that she will drop it, the shaking is so pronounced. So instead, she upends it onto the bed and there, to her delight, out falls, between scraps of ribbon and lace, a pin cushion, reels and a pair of earrings. They sparkle in the shadows.

"What are these?" John Dyer steps forwards and takes them up. He holds them cupped in his hand, turns them slightly so that they catch what little light there is.

"They're mine," Lucy says, but her amusement is vanished.

"They're fine," John Dyer says. "I'd say they're worth upwards of ten pounds." He turns to Lucy. "From whence did these come?"

"They're mine," she says again, but she is faltering now. "A family heirloom," she tries, but John Dyer will have none of it.

"Have these come from the bedroom of my dead wife?" he asks calmly.

"No!" cries Lucy, "No, I would never take Mrs Dyer's things!"

"Do not speak her name," Mr Dyer says. He turns to Mercy and hands her the earrings. "See this young lady out," he tells her. Mercy nods, but Lucy is not to be undone so easily. As John Dyer walks away, she flies to the open door and calls after him,

"You know not what sort of woman you have working for you!" Mercy reaches out to take her by the scruff of her collar. "An inbreeder and a whore!" Mercy's fingers tighten on her collar and she begins to shake. The girl claws at her collar, but Mercy is strong and Mercy is angry. She shakes the girl by the neck until her teeth chatter.

"You are leaving this place, a thief and a liar," she growls and brings the stunned girl up straight. "You go tonight."

She walks Lucy herself through the house by the scruff of her neck. At first the girl struggles, but Mercy has a grip of iron, and every time she struggles Mercy shakes her all the harder. At last the struggling stops, and Mercy marches her through the place, past staff who freeze to take in the spectacle. The girl calls out to those in their path, but none will look her in the eye. All of them without a single exception slowly turn their backs to her. Profane and regale them with debauched tales of Mercy as she might, not a one of them will heed her.

"Those earrings were mine!" the girl whimpers, loose now in Mercy's grip. "They were left to me by my mother. The only thing left of my grandmother. Held for me! For me!"

Mercy is having none of it. "Liar," she hisses in the girl's ear.

But Lucy is sobbing now. "They were to be kept for my twilight years!" She can hardly catch her breath. "My...my mother gave them to me."

Mercy gives her words no mind. She cares nothing for where the earrings came from. They have served her purpose sufficiently, and this girl has threatened her authority and her position. There must be no mercy now. She does not stop at the kitchen door. She marches the girl out and up the lane to the road. Then out there in the darkness where there are just the two of them, Mercy makes herself known further. She takes hold of the girl's face, wet as it is now with tears of frustration and turns it towards her own blazing eyes. Right now, she thinks, Mr Dyer might well be searching her own room as the girl had suggested, and she is sure that the duplicitous little thing has somehow secreted beneath her very own pillow. She could strangle the little wretch. She must be quick.

"Never come back. Do not cause trouble for me or for my daughter," she tells her. "If you truly know anything at all about the Newtons, you'll know that when we are riled, we kill."

The girl nods. She turns, leaving the girl standing in the dark in the road and crunches her way back up the lane to the kitchen door. With every step she expects to hear the crunching of feet behind her, expects the girl to come running, to take some sort of last vengeance, but none comes. When she turns the corner she glances back and can see a faint white figure in the road. As soon as she is out of sight of the girl, she breaks into a run.

"Mr Dyer is asking for you," Cook says as she enters. "He's in the drawing room."

Mercy is there before she can worry further. She discovers her employer sipping something by the fire. She all but dives into the room, heart beating so hard that she feels she will choke on it. She pulls herself up, straightens her clothes, runs her hands over her bonneted hair and steps politely inside the room. No matter how many fires are lit in this house she is starting to understand that when the cold sets in, there is no fire on earth that can warm the place. He is wrapped in layers and wearing his velvet slippers.

"You asked for me, sir?"

"Ah, Newton," he sighs. "Come in, come in. We have matters to discuss."

She steps forth.

"Sit down," he indicates. "Drink?"

She shakes her head. "No, thank you, sir, I do not touch the stuff." This is truth indeed now that she is nowhere near her mother.

He eyes her, and in the shadows cast by the fire he seems old. Older. "Can we manage with only one housemaid?" he asks shortly.

Mercy nods. "If the girl pulls her weight," she says.

"You will supervise her work, I am sure," he states. He licks his lips. "Those earrings were not, I believe, the property of my wife," he tells her. "I doubt we will ever know where she stole them from, but I have no doubt in my mind whatever that they were indeed stolen. From somewhere. A girl like her has no cause to own jewellery so fine."

Mercy nods.

"You have served us well," he tells her. "I cannot have a thief in our midst."

"It is a relief not to carry the suspicion any longer, Mr Dyer," she tells him, and a relief it all is for she will hold this position a while more.

When she returns to her chamber, she finds the door is unlocked and the brooch is indeed beneath her pillow. The girl must have been a lock-picker, she thinks, and replaces the brooch before Mr Dyer finishes his drink and retires.

There is a pomposity about the inner rankings of the house-staff. Mercy eats with the butler, Mr Harding, and she wears the same black dress each day. They discuss the weather and never refer to each other by first names. Mercy ensures that bills are paid. On one occasion, there is a knock at the door and the local brazier is at the back door asking for his bill to be met.

She raises an eyebrow at him haughtily.

"Indeed?" she asks. "And for what item and for how much?"

"For a set of measuring jugs in brass," he tells her. "Two months hence. I'm come to have the bill settled." And he tips his cap, though he is a good thirty or so years older than she.

"That was before I took up my station here," she says. "I must consult the accounts books. Do come in, Mr...?"

"Edwards," he says. "George Edwards."

She strides away a few steps, leading him into the kitchen, that he might sit with Cook awhile whilst she checks her accounts, but stops suddenly.

"George Edwards?" she turns.

He has removed his cap and is holding it before him. "'S'right, madam," he says.

She knows the name. Not just that he is almost certainly a relation on her mother's side. She knows the name, for it is part of that Newton tale she cannot escape. She sniffs and tries not to show him any sort of overt display of recognition.

"Please come this way," she says, turns again, but now her hands are shaking, and she leads him forth into the kitchen, where he takes a chair at the table and greets Cook in a familiar manner. It is not until she has firmly closed the door upon them both that she feels she can breathe. This is the man who demanded his bill be paid at Severn Hall. This is the man who left Sarah Newton to the hands of her cousin John, knowing that he had determined to batter her. One hand flies to her throat, to protect it from the rope he would see wrapped about it. This is the man without whose visit her cousin John would not have swung at Shrewsbury Gaol, without whom he would have still lived, her cousin William might not have hanged himself for shame and her cousin James...she blinks tears from her eyes, wipes them on her sleeve. Perhaps James might have been able to live with her, marry her, had he not been blighted by the aftermath of this man's visit.

His presence here is surely filled with foreboding, she thinks.

She will never escape what happened at Severn Hall, she thinks. No matter her position or how she tries to better herself; it will always come down to this.

She steadies herself on the doorpost. She can hear George Edwards chattering away inside. He's clearly something of a regular; she will put a stop to that. No more orders to be sent out to him – there must be another brazier close by. There must be.

She returns within fifteen minutes and hands George Edwards his money. "Will that be all?" she asks haughtily.

He pockets it and rises. "Yes, madam, I believe the bill is settled then." He glances over to Cook for more chatter, but she is turned back to her work afraid of Mercy's disapproval.

"Then I will see you to the door," Mercy says with all formality. She sweeps onwards, sees him out and locks and bolts the door behind him. Morville Hall will never seek the services of George Edwards again while she is here.

Unlike her Sundays at Winscote Hills, Mercy does visit her mother most Sundays after church, for she is drawn there irresistibly to see the child. A clear resemblance to James has flowered, but each time she is disappointed by the conditions her mother is keeping about her daughter, and often her mother is worse for drink, nursing a bad head or a bruised arm where she has stumbled.

It is a fair haul from Morville to Batch Pool Lane, and she is lucky enough to be given a lift by a lad who drives a cart out from Morville to visit his own mother in Bridgnorth and who drops her off at the bridge. The walk from there is nearly two miles, but she is brisk and the basket she carries is at first always well received with what few items she delivers, although Anne Newton wants money more than goods. Maria is thin, unwashed and grows, over the first few months, less like James, beginning to resemble Anne Newton in her paucity.

"An Edwards through and through this girl is," declares Anne proudly, passing her to Mercy on her first visit. "She's got the look of my mother."

And a passing cadaverous wreck she must have been then, thinks Mercy as she takes the child in her arms. She could cry at the state of her. Maria is clad in ragged, thin things, with the smell of urine upon her skin. She weighs little but still has the wherewithal to bawl at the touch of this stranger, her mother. After a few bounces the noise does not abate, and Mercy far removed this last month from mothering hands her back.

"She needs more milk," she tells her mother. "She's as thin as a stick."

"I haven't had the money," Anne replies quickly. "You might see fit to give me some since she's your brat after all."

"You've five hundred pounds in the bank," Mercy tells her. "You've got money. Lay off the rum."

"Not this again, Kitty. The interest is a pittance as I've told you enough times," comes the reply. "I can't touch that sum of money you know full well, it's held for you."

"And when will I see it that's what I'd like to know," Mercy retorts sullenly. "Perhaps if you drank more I'd see it the sooner."

"You're better that I don't die, or you'd be back here raising this little one yerself on little but a few farthings a week," Anne grumbles. "And you'd not want to be torn away from your big house and your old man now would you?"

"She'd be a damn sight plumper if I was," Mercy tells her. "I wouldn't be pissing it all up the wall like you do." She eyes the gin bottle. “I wonder how often you’re passed out, drunk to the eyeballs and Maria cries herself to sleep. We’d both be better off without you.”

“You’re a cruel thing, Kitty, you are,” Anne tells her sharply in a whining tone that grates Mercy’s soul. “Leaving me here like this with your little one, and never a word of thanks.” Her voice is rising; the alcohol is still in her blood. “Whoring yourself out, are you? What will you do when this old fellow dies eh? Turn up on my doorstep with another fatherless babby for me to raise?”

Mercy’s blood is boiling, but she must keep Anne calm for the sake of the child. She stands, ignoring her, and unpacks the basket. She’s taken care to only put in things that will help with the baby: soap flakes, milk, some napkins and baby clothes she bought second-hand from Cook, whose daughter was selling them on telling her they were for a relative’s child. Nobody at Morville Hall knows she has an illegitimate child, and she intends to keep it that way.

“These’ll do for a while,” she tells her mother. “I’ll be hard pushed to come for another fortnight, and I’m paid quarterly in arrears, so I won’t have anything to give to you just yet awhile.”

“A couple of pints of milk and some old soap flakes aren’t enough to keep this baby going,” her mother says. “Don’t you have anything, Kitty? Nothing to pay for her?”

Mercy shakes her head. “Nothing,” she lies for of course, she could sell something – a bonnet perhaps. But she won’t because she knows very well that it’ll go on gin.

The following Sunday after church, Mercy walks out across the fields, over the little bridge that crosses the meandering, burbling Mor Brooke, up the hill overlooking the dower house garden and up to the ridge that looks down across the church and the house and the hall. There are a few houses here in Morville, but little else. Just fields, farms and green. She breathes in the air and sighs. For a while she allows herself to imagine James striding through the fields, the dogs scouting along before him, but there is no gamekeeper here, no need for a man like him. She will never find someone to love again, she knows, never fall into the arms of a man whose strength and kindness know no bounds. Never feel the heat of passion like that again. She sighs. She is twenty-four but these last twelve months have aged her beyond repair. Her thin lips are growing ever thinner, and when she catches sight of herself in a mirror she can see her mother glaring back.

Through the wood-panelled hall she stalks duster in hand, but stops at the sound of something, a scrabbling, a scraping. The rest of the staff are away now with family, and Mr Dyer will take a cold tea of ham and potatoes already prepared for him. He himself is away for the afternoon in Bridgnorth, to see his brother, Richard. Mercy is alone here in this house. She pauses. Through the open doors she can see the foot of the staircase, and the afternoon is already growing dark. This scraping is growing more and more agitated, and she listens, identifies its direction and steps quietly across the hall. She does not believe in ghosts, but her hands are starting to shake as she lifts a large candlestick from the mantel. Ghosts might not be real, but men are. She runs through a thousand scenarios in her head: men from Shrewsbury, Wolverhampton or Broseley coming to steal and plunder when they believe the place to be empty. She ought to hide, but she cannot let Mr Dyer's house be burgled and do nothing. She comes up close against the door to the morning room, from wherein comes a faint tap, tap, tapping now, and she reaches out her free, trembling hand to the knob. One deep breath, a twist and a rush inside, and there, flapping about, soot coming from its wings and its feet, is a jackdaw.

Black against white. It is marking the place, touching everything about it with flecks of soot from the chimney. It flaps about, leaving swathes of black across the walls, and she leaps towards it, arms spread, but it only flaps harder covering the place in ash.

"Stop! Stop!" she commands it, but it is afraid, panicking, fleeing from her, spreading a smell of charred fireplace about the room. Soon, she fears, the whole place will resemble a fireplace. No matter how hard she tries to catch the thing, it blackens everything it touches. At last, she steps back.

"Stupid bird," she berates it, although she is berating herself, for she does not know why she has spent so long now chasing this thing she cannot catch. No, she must let it free. Swiftly, she lifts the sash. "Go on, get out with you."

The creature goggles at her and then is gone, hopping up to the sill and taking flight, only to come down just yards away on the lawn and stand there, searching the sky for something. She slams the sash down, making it jump and hop, but still it stands and then slowly turns to look back at her.

She sets forth, pulling up the rug to be beaten and wiping down the walls to remove all marks from the bird before her master returns.

Each time Mercy claps eyes on her baby, the child is a little longer in length but still bone-thin, and by the time her wages come upon her she is anxious to ensure that the child will have enough to eat. Rather than hand money to her mother, she sees to it that there is a delivery of coal. Money in Anne's hands flows quicker away than water. Mercy has not touched spirits since leaving Batch Pool Lane, and she knows exactly how they affect Anne – she grows short of temper and handy with her blows. In fact, Mercy knows, she herself has become increasingly affected in much the same way since James's death. She dare not touch a drop now she has a good position, for she is sure it would be the ruin of her. She sees to it that there is milk and more soap flakes, and when she turns up and does not hand money over this time, her mother looks up from the cold brick floor with eyes as dark as night.

"Am I to raise this bastard of yours on nothing then?" she growls.

Mercy stares at her. "There will be coal," she says. "It'll be delivered on Tuesday. Enough to last. And milk from the farm, that'll come too. And here is soap. And here," she pulls out a loaf of bread. "To mix with the milk for pap," she says. "And I have paid the baker in Bridgnorth enough that you might take two loaves a week."

"Pap'll feed the child, but what of me?" Anne groans, rising skeletal from her chair. "What of me, Kitty, slaving away to keep this little wench of yours clean and fed at all hours? What am I gaining, looking after your bastard daughter whilst you are whoring away in Morville?"

Mercy's hand has struck her before her last word is out. Anne falls back, landing between her chair and the table. The bag of soap flakes topples and spills, like snow. Mercy stands over her, her face reddening, her blood pounding.

"You ought to die and leave me the five hundred pounds, and then *I'd* be able to live a life of idleness," she breathes and takes up the child, who is crying now, she can feel her ribs even through her layers. "And I'd not spend a penny of it on gin as you do."

"Oh, Kitty!" She rises from the bundle on the floor. "You struck me!"

"I'll strike you more," Mercy tells her, disgusted. "I'll strike you a hundred times if you show such ungratefulness again."

She looks down at the child who is still bawling in her arms. Her little fists are tight and her eyes are squeezed shut. She can see the little tongue and the toothless gums, rage issuing forth in waves of sound. There is little of herself in this creature and nothing of James, not now the poor little thing is so thin and ragged. She has been blighted by this time spent with Anne, warped into her little squawking shadow. Her heart is hollow. Things could have been so different, Mercy thinks, willing the child to quieten, but she does not. If James had married her, they would be at the lodge house, the three of them, perhaps with William in the attic room. She would have met James at the door each evening, the child plump and content in her arms and he would have greeted them both with a kiss. But now look at them. What a mess it all is. She feels her eyes prick. The touch of the child's own mother cannot soothe this baby, she sees now, for this child barely knows her. She knows only Anne, and Anne will be the ruin of her just as she's tried to be the ruin of Mercy. Anne will teach this child that there is no way forward but the gutter.

"Pass her to me, Kitty, and I'll see her quiet," says her mother, and although what Mercy would like to do is kick her in the ribs down there on the brick floor, she instead passes her the baby, for the crying is making the blood beat wildly in her temples and her head ache. Anne's thin hands grasp for the bundle and Mercy turns her back to the pair of them as the words, "Tush, little mite, don't cry, there, now," comes strangely soothing, and at length the crying stops.

"I'll see that you have credit at the butchers," Mercy says over her shoulder defeated, takes up her things and leaves Anne cradling Maria, who does not recognise her own mother, on the cold brick floor.

Mercy Newton holds the position at Morville Hall, in fact, for five years. Five years, during which time she hoards her wages, sending a little wood or coal and food, but never once does she put actual money into the hands of her mother, for the lot will go on drink. She hoards what she can, for she must have savings of her own and ensure that she can survive when this position is over – she does not expect anything to last forever. And not once in those years does she touch liquor for she cannot allow it to get the better of her, to ruin her, as it has done her mother.

Twice in those five years at Morville Hall, Anne Newton comes to the kitchen door unbidden and begging to see her daughter.

The first time, Cook calls for Mercy to come out of her room where she is totting up the petty cash, and there is Anne bold as brass, tarnished as a tramp, darkening the damned doorstep with her ghastly form which seems risen from the grave in the mist that has followed her.

"Kitty, let your mother in from the cold and bid her warm herself awhile," her whining voice comes, and Mercy steps back from this vision of despair upon the doorstep and knows not what to do. "Kitty," comes the voice once more. "Take pity on me; we're cold over in Batch and hungry."

"Is the girl here?" Mercy breathes, for she half-thinks the chid will be there somewhere, wrapped in her mother's skirts.

Anne shakes her head. "She's back at home with the Littlefords," she assures her. "It's just me."

Mercy glares at her. "Then you can go back the way you came all the easier," she snaps, striding forth and slamming the door in her mother's face. She stands behind the door for a moment, then pulls across the bolt. How will anyone here have any respect for her once word of the state of her mother does the rounds – she can do nothing to stop Cook from talking.

"Kitty!" her mother's voice is loud enough out there when all about this house is quiet. "Kitty! Take pity! Just a few shillings! Anything!"

"Be quiet!" she hisses, behind the door. "Go away!"

But Anne is having none of it. "Take pity on me, Kitty!" she calls, her voice rising like an old crow. "And on Maria, she's hungry! Your own little girl, starving!"

Mercy swears beneath her breath and unbolts the door. "Shut up and wait there," she hisses and closes it again. Past Cook who is scrubbing the kitchen table, ears always flapping, she goes, past the remaining housemaid who is laying fires ready for the morning. She goes to her room and takes out some of her savings, more than she had intended, just to be rid of her; she must ensure that this old demon does not arise again any time soon. Her hand shakes as she deposits the coins in her pocket. To come here unannounced and be seen by the cook, for everyone to know that this haggard, dreg of a woman is her mother could cost Mercy all the respect she has worked so hard to build. She grips the coins in her fist and imagines what it would be like to use that fist to knock her mother off the step and down to the ground. But she cannot, she cannot allow her anger to undo her, for think of the scandal then! Back, past the housemaid and past the cook she goes, opens the door and flings ten shillings on the ground, so that it rolls away in all directions at her mother's feet.

"Pick it up," she growls. "And don't ever come here again or you'll see no more money from me!"

She lingers for a while and watches her mother scrabble about gathering up the coins. Then slowly she closes the door on her and bolts it.

The second time Anne Newton turns up it is a Friday afternoon and Mr Dyer is in Bridgnorth taking a meal with his brother. Mercy is dusting in the morning room watching the birds through the window, imagining that she is the lady of the house. Then suddenly there is the form of Anne Newton, befouling the view through the morning room window, tramping up the drive past the haha, calling a salutation to the vicar who is just leaving the church.

Mercy almost drops the beeswax polish. The maid is helping with the laundry at the moment, and the cook will be busy in the kitchen. She only has to hide her from the gardener.

The groom and his lad have left a variety of equine accoutrements about the kitchen at various points, and she hastens there now, and takes up a horsewhip, then marches to the front door. As the bell rings, Mercy Newton swings it open, her blood boiling. How dare Anne come here? How dare she come here at all, but to the *front door*?

"Kitty, the child is hungry!" comes the plea. Mercy pulls her inside and slams the door.

"How dare you come here?" she hisses, prodding her mother in the chest with the end of the whip. "I thought I told you not to come here!"

Anne holds up her hands and bats the whip away. "Kitty, we're starving! We need more money!"

Mercy glares at her, standing there in her filthy skirt, the hem a foot deep in mud and muck stains, her very skin as filthy as though she has slept in a hedge for the night.

"You will get me fired," she growls. "You look like you live in the gutter. I told you not to come here, yet here you are – at the front door! – risking my future for a few pennies." She brings the whip down swiftly so that it sounds out in the air.

"A few pennies indeed, yet here you are, a great lady, whoring yourself out to the master of the house!" her mother is all venom, her lip curled, her eyes narrow. "Half a crown, Kitty, that'll see us right. You've opened your legs for less, no doubt! We need vittles, Kitty!"

"You want gin more like," Mercy replies, grabbing her mother's hand and holding it out to observe the shakes. "How dare you come here with your poison tongue? You'll be the ruin of me."

"The ruin of you?" her mother whines. "Why, you left me with your little fatherless brat, so who is the ruin of who? Couldn't keep your legs closed, could you? Now I'm paying for your sluttishness!" And she pushes Mercy with such a sudden force that Mercy falls into the mantel and knocks her shoulder against a vase that sits there, expensive and ornate. It wobbles, topples, but Mercy catches it in time with shaking hands and sets it straight, her heart in her mouth. She rounds upon her mother with the whip.

"You'll have me lose my job!" she hisses at her striking out, and Anne backs away, but despite her retreat she is taunting her daughter now, "You seduce your own cousin, my girl, and leave me with the mess! A Newton slut, that's who Kitty Newton is!"

Now Mercy is slashing the whip towards Anne to drive her away, panic rising within her. If Mr Dyer heard these words, or anyone else for that matter, this would be the last day she would spend beneath this roof. Mr Dyer is all for propriety. Anne will see her starving in Batch Pool Lane once more. She lashes out to send her mother backwards. Anne gropes for the door handle and pulls it open.

"Get you gone, go on!" she spits, swiping forth again, only

this time it catches Anne on the face and she yelps and turns away, stumbles down the step and falls over her skirts to land in a heap on the ground.

"Oh, stop, Kitty, stop!" she wails. "That my own daughter would use me so!"

Mercy stares down at her. She despises her and hates every bone in this woman's body.

"If I lose my position here, there will be no more coal, no more bread, no more deliveries from the farm, no more credit at the butchers," she growls. "I will be penniless. You will make it so unless you leave here and promise not to return. Do you understand?"

"Money, Kitty, money, for food!" Anne pleads, but Mercy shakes her head.

"Five hundred pounds in the bank, you have," she tells her. "And all the things I have set in place for the feeding and comfort of the child, and don't pretend it doesn't extend to you. That's plenty for anyone!" She slams the door upon her, but the slamming door and her stomping retreat do nothing to muffle her mother's final words that seem to echo about the place and ring in her ears for a long time afterwards, "I might be Newton by name, but you're Newton by nature, Kitty, and you'll be the death of me! And God help the child; she's Newton through and through!"

The First Trial: Spring Assizes

Recollections of Thomas Whitmore, MP

Apley Estate, Bridgnorth

17th of March 1849

Character Witness – Mr Newell

Mercy Catherine Newton stood motionless before the jury, and there were few indications to establish what emotions she was experiencing beneath her veiled bonnet.

Mr Justice Coltman was positioned to hear the case. A man of Miss Newton's ilk in that he appeared hard-faced and unsympathetic from the outset, a manner which must only go in our favour, I acknowledged. Lord Justice Coltman looked the sort of man who might enjoy a hanging.

Before the proceedings began, I noted a movement of the bonnet. Miss Newton was glancing towards her defence: a Mr Huddlestone and Mr Kettle. Both of these men appeared rather young and therefore were inexperienced to my mind. It seemed to me that only a miracle might save this woman's neck under their care.

"This most solemn inquiry upon which we prepare to embark," I announced as that black-clad ghoul sat motionless before the faces of the jury, "demands the utmost anxious and careful consideration of every man amongst you. This is the most atrocious of crimes," I noted, having researched and discussed this next pronouncement in order to give it credence. "So much so, that in times past ancient people conceived of no punishment for it; it was a crime so severe as to render it impossible to administer an adequate punishment."

A good firm introduction to the proceedings and the unexpected horrors would be put before this jury, emphasising the weight of the decision they must make, for a sentence such as this one must never be taken too lightly. I had given much thought to my wording, and wanted gravitas and severity to be the key message. The whole country knew now of this trial. The newspapers were full of it, and I had to ensure that the carnival created by the popular press would not pervade the courtroom.

"The disposition of any sane human mind," I told them, "is to shrink from deeming such a crime possible. If the prisoner standing before you at the bar..." Here I gesticulated towards Miss Newton whose head does not rise and whose form retains its unearthly stillness. "If her disposition was saturated with the customary emotions of love and compassion that generally exists in a child towards its parent, if the prisoner had persistently sought to prolong her mother's declining years and if indeed her character had been so moulded, it would have been a poorly executed thing indeed to have brought this case before a jury. However, it is my dire responsibility to demonstrate to you that the prisoner's conduct has been of a wholly distinct character."

J.E. Newell took to the stand. I knew him well – the ex-mayor of Bridgnorth.

"I was previously mayor and am currently a surgeon," he attested. "I have known Anne Newton, the deceased, some five or more years hence. I have been called upon more than once in those years to attend her in my capacity as surgeon concerning a violent altercation with Miss Mercy Newton."

"And in what state did you find her when attending upon her?" I began. "On these previous occasions?"

Mercy Newton did not lift her head.

Mr Newell took a breath. "I found her sorely beaten," he replied solemnly, as I knew he would. "From head to foot. So severely beaten, you must understand, that her flesh was cut from her arms. In consequence of this, I spoke with Miss Newton, the prisoner, and was told..."

Here I glanced at the prisoner again to see if some sort of response might arise from her veiled form, but there was nothing to indicate any emotion.

"She told me that she was very sorry that she had not finished her off," Mr Newell finished.

"In fact," I continued to press him, "this was not the only time you attended Anne Newton due to her daughter's battery, was it not?"

Mr Newell shook his head. "There were other instances," he agreed. "Once, when the deceased was at Skelding's Cottage, her daughter had injured the deceased's ankle so badly as to render walking impossible. Other instances occurred whereby the daughter beat her old mother until skin was hanging off."

"What was the reaction of the prisoner upon your intervention?" I asked him. "Did she admit that she had hurt her parent? Did she show remorse? I ask merely to gain an insight into their relationship, that we might understand it the better."

Mr Newell glanced at Miss Newton, then shook his head. "No, no remorse," he admitted solemnly. "On the contrary, she wished for worse to strike her mother down. This she has been heard to say on many occasions by those who visited the house."

"The house?" I asked. "Do you mean Anne Newton's house? This...Skelding's Cottage?"

Mr Newell nodded in an ungentlemanly fashion and continued, "I do not believe that Miss Newton had a care where her words were heard," he announced. "She would wish her mother dead wherever they were and to whoever would listen."

There was still no movement beneath the veil. Miss Newton may have shed a tear, but I could not ascertain any sort of rise within her chest that might account for a silent sob. She appeared utterly unabashed, her bonnet completely still, the folds of her veil impenetrable.

Perhaps, I mused, she was reliving those moments, moments where her temper had not crossed that irreparable boundary, where a chastisement from Mr Newell was all that might deter her from the next beating. Perhaps in her head she had gone back to the day Mr Newell had made his looming presence felt on the doorstep of The Watering.

Chapter Five

Mercy Newton

The Watering

1845

John Dyer died back in 1839 and although he left nothing in his will for Mercy, he did recommend her service to his brother, Richard Dyer, of The Watering, a big three-storey house next to the River Severn in Underhill Street, Bridgnorth.

Mercy lives here now, and as Richard Dyer grows ever more incapacitated, Mercy Newton grows ever more comfortable. Richard Dyer is an invalid, sixty-four years of age, the image of his brother and mostly bed-bound, a situation Mercy finds most convenient. She brings him breakfast, aids him in his toilette, reads to him in the mornings and then each day has three hours to herself whilst he naps. *Three whole hours*. Never at Morville Hall could she find three hours for her own leisure, except sometimes on a Sunday afternoon. Here she has found freedom in Richard Dyer's infirmity. It's not a bad life at all. This house is hers; Richard cannot leave his chamber without the utmost preparation, so all of these rooms, all of these floors, are hers. There is a study, a dining room, a drawing room, the kitchen, a morning room and the bedroom of her choice. Despite beginning here in a servant's room, she has eased her way into one of the better bedrooms next to Richard's that his hand bell might more easily rouse her, and now she has – oh luxury! – her own four-poster bed. Outside there is a washhouse and a brewhouse, and the garden which although small for a house this size is large enough for her to enjoy a constitutional down to look out over the river, thick as it is with industry. Her ambitions to save her money and provide Maria with a better life have not disappeared, but her mother still lives, the five hundred pounds is still not hers and her savings are not sufficient for her to set up home for herself and her daughter in anything other than poverty. Thus the girl grows and to Mercy's consternation, she remains in Anne's care. The longer she stays here in comfort, the more she is convinced that she could never exist again in the paucity of a hovel like the cottage in Batch Pool Lane.

Her afternoons involve the preparation and delivery of Richard Dyer's luncheon and the receiving of guests. He receives them in his chamber: his nephew most often, Mr Doughty, a self-important man; and sometimes his solicitor or doctor. She often absents herself from his presence in the afternoon, pleading for time to dust, black-lead the grates or bake bread. Sometimes she uses the brewhouse, but such is the bounty of Richard Dyer's purse that she need not brew unless she feels like it – there is money enough for wine, rum, whiskey and beer. Mercy touches it rarely, but she has allowed herself a dram of whiskey on a cold night or a finger of rum to soothe a cold. She is ever careful not to slip into Anne's ways however, for she knows that too much of the strong stuff in a person often causes fights and loosens tongues, purse strings and knicker elastic. She is mortally terrified of losing her position here with behaviour that is unfitting a housekeeper.

There are tasks she undertakes that are distasteful to her: she aids Richard's Dyer's use of the commode at all times of the day and night when he rings for her. She attends his fortnightly bath and aids in his undress, his drying and his redressing. She sees to his most intimate health needs. But she has this house and she is, moreso than she had ever hoped to be back at Morville Hall, the lady of it. She has a status of sorts. The only problem she has encountered is the proximity to her mother. The pair have never truly lived harmoniously, but as Mercy rises in status, she sees more and more starkly the foolish, petty, slovenly nature of her mother, and her inexplicable poverty when there are five hundred pounds in the bank for her to live on. The festering embarrassment and dislike of her parent has grown ever stronger these past years. No matter that the woman is bringing up Mercy's daughter for her. Mercy cannot stand the sight of her, the sound of her, nor the smell of her.

She comes to the house now more often – this place is much closer to her cottage at Batch Pool than Morville Hall was. No matter how many times Mercy turns her away, she returns at regular intervals asking for money. Now that Maria is nearly twelve and growing fast, she often brings her and sometimes to Mercy's disgust even sends the child in her stead, sending her traipsing through rain, hail and the hottest of days asking for money.

One Sunday after a week of particularly persistent badgering from her mother, she goes herself to the cottage, climbing the steep road out of Bridgnorth and over the brow to Batch Pool Lane.

In her cloth bag she carries an old dress, for Mr Dyer has told her that she may take any of the old dresses out of the wardrobes or from the attic at The Watering, as there are no ladies left in his life to give them to and he does not wish them to go to waste. Lodged amongst its folds are some candles, a jar of spiced apples and a small loaf. She is especially pleased with the dress, for with a little work it can be shortened, taken up at the hem, brought in at the waist and tucked at the sleeves, and it will give little Maria plenty of wear.

However, upon pulling out the thing and presenting it to Anne, she is met with a turn of the lip.

"That'll not fit the girl in a month of Sundays."

"It is for taking in," Mercy tells her. "Rather than cutting it, pull it up at the hem and so forth, and it can be let out as she grows."

"You'd see your own child looking like a sack of potatoes," Anne retorts, with a telltale slur. There is rum on the table close by the fire. "And a few apples I could easily pick from a tree and spice up myself, a loaf, some candles and raisin cake won't keep us alive here, Kitty," she goes on. "That's why I'm ever at your door; we are starving."

She opens up the spiced apples and takes the bread, hacks off a piece, drops it into a bowl and slops some of the apples on top. "Here, Maria, sweet girl, this is all the grub your ma has brought for you, no doubt to last the month," she says and drops it into the child's lap.

"Thank you, Mum," Maria pipes up. She is under the table on a bit of old sackcloth – a refuge she takes up each time her mother comes calling, for Anne is always fired up with drink and she knows that these meetings always end badly.

"That and an old dress that won't fit you for another five years," Anne adds and carelessly flings the dress over her chair. The arm of it swings out into the grate and suddenly it is aflame. The child beneath the table starts to scream. Anne flaps at it for a moment, then grabs her cup from the table and upends it over the dress. The flames spread across the garment now, for it was rum, not tea, in the mug after all. The child's screams are more and more fervent and the flames are growing in ferocity. Mercy grabs her mother by the shoulders and shakes her as the flames now catch hold of her own clothes, and by the time Mercy has wrestled her mother to the ground and smothered her with a blanket, both of the women are smouldering.

"You stupid bloody fool!" Mercy is seething. "No matter what I give you, it is never enough!"

Anne looks down at the singed rag and over to her empty cup lying on the brick floor. "Of course it's not enough, Kitty," she whines. "I'm raising your daughter for you, and it in't all roses, I can tell you. She's a nasty little thing when she wants to be, just like her mother. She'll end up a slut in trouble, just like you did."

Mercy cannot stop herself. She brings back her boot and lets it fly against her mother's ankle. As it connects, the old woman lets out a cry.

"You ungrateful old bitch," she hisses. "You have credit in half the shops in town, and yet still you ask for more. You are never satisfied with what I do. Each time I visit her, you ruin it."

"Oh! My ankle! My ankle, Kitty, it's broken!" yells her mother, but Mercy is trying to coax her daughter out from beneath the table.

"Come, Maria, let me see how tall you've grown," she calls to her, but the child has backed away right up to the wall and is shaking her head. "She didn't mean it, dear, you're a good girl. Come out and see me before I must go."

"Oh, Kitty, call a doctor!" Anne is shouting.

Mercy eyes her daughter; she can see the fear in the child's eyes, but she cannot tell if it is fear of Anne or herself. In despair, she sits back.

"You've hurt her," Maria says quietly. "I wish you wouldn't both be so angry."

"You know I make sure you have food, don't you, Maria?" Mercy asks for she fears that her mother has poisoned the child against her. "You know I do not let you starve?"

Maria nods but her eyes are unsure.

"Kitty, do not question her!" Anne howls. "Call for the

doctor; you've fairly broken my ankle!"

"How often does she drink spirits?" Mercy asks, crouching down to speak to Maria. "Rum, gin or brandy?"

"Oh, Kitty, leave the girl alone," Anne cries, struggling to her feet. "I can barely walk on it, Kitty!"

"Every day," Maria says. "We live off the credit you leave us. She spends the rest."

"Oh, the wench lies!" Anne hobbles to her chair and sits heavily. "Little liar, just like her mum."

Mercy nods at her daughter. "One day I'll take you away," she promises. "I'm saving up; we will have a home together." She glances at her mother, then stands. The old woman is paper-thin, her face a razor's edge, her eyes half-closed and her hands groping in her pockets for her matches to light her pipe.

"You've crippled me, Kitty," she moans, patting her pockets and pulling out her Lucifers. "Crippled me, you have!"

Mercy snorts. Whatever goods Mercy provides, Anne merely spends their worth on more spirits and tobacco. She despises her.

"It is your fault that you and Maria go hungry, not mine. If you would care to kill yourself, and I wish you would, I would give you the means to do it. You've kept me from that money long enough, don't you think?"

"Crippled, Kitty," Anne moans, sucking on her foul pipe and rocking to and fro.

Mercy takes hold of the door handle. "If only I'd killed you instead," she says and slams the door behind her.

In the spring, Richard Dyer summons her to his room whilst his physician is with him, and she is told, "Mr Dyer would do well to go to Buxton, to take the waters."

Richard nods. "Yes, Mercy, we could go to Buxton, could we not? You would like a little trip?"

She cannot suppress her smile. "Of course, it would be a pleasure to go to Buxton, sir," she replies. The doctor nods, and Richard Dyer beams.

"Very good," replies the doctor.

"I shall have my nephew arrange it all," Richard Dyer tells her. "There will be nothing more for you to do, other than accompany me, Mercy." And he beams again, takes her hands and wrings them in his own. "You're a good girl, Mercy, a good girl," he says, but all this excitement has tired him. By the time she has seen the doctor out and returns, he is still and quiet, conserving his energies. He sits there, his pillows plumped up behind him, with deep-set eyes looking at her from beneath their hooded lids and claw-like hands gripping the bedclothes. She smiles and curtseys. From deep in their sockets, his eyes are gleaming, she realises. He may have run out of energy but he is happy. She reads to him for a while until he starts to snore, then descends to the garden and stands watching the river for a while. Buxton. She hasn't ever been away from Shropshire. Buxton will be an adventure, but more than this, she thinks, there is more to this. She watches the water rushing by and hears the calls of the workers in the timber yard close by. A ship is being loaded at the port, and she hears the men swearing, singing and whistling. To have one of them, a docker or boatman for a husband would be to bring her back to nought. But what if Richard Dyer were to ask her to marry him? They live here together, just the two of them, as though they already were married. It would be nothing to him to marry her before he dies, but it would be everything to her.

She can make it happen.

She *will* make it happen.

They are to leave for Buxton in May and stay there for four weeks. Mercy sets about ensuring that Richard cannot conceive of life without her. She is all attention, warming his bed socks, putting salts in his bath water and sponging him down with extra care. No man could ignore the attention Mercy Newton takes when drying Richard Dyer once his bath is done. True, she must grit her teeth, but she pats him down most thoroughly now, leaving no crevice to damp. When he plaintively pleads with her to hold his limp member, she does not disappoint any longer, as she has since her arrival. No, Richard Dyer receives her full attention.

"Angel," he calls her and, "Nurse."

Once these things are done and he lies against his plumped-up pillows dead to the world, she looks in on him, calculates how long he might have left and smiles to herself. They are to Buxton soon and to her calculations he has but a few years left in him. Then she will be a most comfortable widow and she and Maria can be free of Anne. Imagine bringing the girl to live here, she thinks. Imagine the triumph they will feel, the hardships both will have overcome and the life of quality that will be theirs.

She is washing her arms up to the elbows with carbolic after one such bath-time encounter down in the kitchen one afternoon, when the back door knocks. She is expecting the coal man come to receive his payment, so she dries her arms, rolls down her sleeves and comes to the kitchen door. But when she pulls it open it is not the coalman, but her mother and her own thin, dreary little daughter, both standing bedraggled in a fine mist of rain, their moth-eaten shawls up about their ears.

"Oh," she says and stands in the doorway still fastening the buttons of her sleeves.

Anne pushes Maria forward. "Your daughter has come to see

you, Kitty," she says. "We are here to call on you, for we haven't seen you in a little while."

"Indeed," says Mercy and stands back to admit them.

Their presence here now dressed in greying tatters always embarrasses her. As much as she wants Maria to live with her, she wants the child dressed in good clothing first; she wants her to be a little lady and not to resemble a vagabond. Here the two of them come, the maiden and the crone, to illuminate her poor beginnings. To make her unweddable.

"There is stew," she says and sees them into the kitchen. "But eat it quick. If one of the Doughtys comes by and sees you eating, they'll say I'm taking advantage of Mr Dyer's good nature."

She sets them bowls, ladles them stew, takes out a loaf that is hardening and places it between them. "Eat fast," she repeats, and they set to devouring the tough loaf and the stew with such gusto she is sickened by it. Anne drips the gravy down her chin and wipes it up with a morsel of bread. She is missing some teeth now; no doubt the gin has rotted them away. Mercy cannot bear to look at her, nor listen to the repulsive slurping she makes as she spoons the stew into her gaping mouth. The child is little better. She turns her gaze away; they disgust her.

"Tell your mother you're to be a seamstress," Anne encourages the child upon observing Mercy's scowl.

At this Mercy brightens a little. "What is this?" she asks, for perhaps just once the old woman has come with news not to beg for money.

"Nanna has found me a position," Maria says. Her voice is reedy for her age – a mimic of the tone no doubt, Mercy thinks, from her grandmother, for she does not hear such a thin, weak tone in her own voice. James Newton was a fine, booming gentleman. She still finds herself watching the child for some likeness to him, yearns to see him in her brow as she did when the child was born but is always disappointed. This child is made more of Anne than anyone. Perhaps there is something about the eyes, she thinks, but overall Anne Newton has rubbed off on the child more than anyone could have wished.

"I'll be sewing buttons on to start," Maria says tentatively. "They'll teach me as I go. It's not much to take home, but it's something. When I'm thirteen they'll give me an extra thruppence a week if my sewing is good enough."

Mercy is pleased. A job will do the girl good and get her out from Anne's influence.

"This is good news," she says and goes to the pantry and takes out a little bottle. "We will celebrate. Just a small celebration."

Astounded by her own charity and pleased enough to wish for jollity between them, she pours a thimbleful of rum for Maria, who shrinks a little as she passes it to her, then takes it from her sheepishly in her skinny hand, and a larger draught for herself and Anne. She takes a little rum sometimes in the colder months now, for she believes it wards off the flu and the year is not yet as warm as it might be. Never though does she drink as her mother does.

"See how pleased your mother is," Anne says to the girl, nudging her all smiles as Maria sniffs the liquor then takes a tiny sip.

Mercy knocks hers back in a mouthful. But Anne is uncharacteristically lingering in her consumption.

"Kitty, we are short this month on the rent," she says, slowly. "Seven and six a week isn't enough for anyone to live off."

Mercy ignores her. She takes up their bowls, washes and dries them quickly, as is always the routine when they come – she is ever vigilant that nobody might accuse her of taking advantage of Mr Dyer, for over such trivial accusations are careers lost. And Mercy wants more from Richard Dyer than a career.

Mercy has plans for a future that is secure. Still, she can be more accommodating here, when the mood takes her, than ever she could be at Morville Hall. Here there is nobody to watch over her but still their spoons are taken up as soon as they are finished, washed and dried to hide all evidence that they have dined at Richard Dyer's expense. Anne helps herself to a little more rum 'to keep out the damp' and then she sets herself before the fire on the sofa and lights her pipe.

Mercy takes a seat at the table and asks her daughter more about the position she will take. The girl is formal with her mother; her replies are polite and contain just the facts for she lives in fear of her mother's temper. Mercy ascertains that she is to be apprenticed on the High Street. She is to first learn buttons, then move to hems. She is to supply her own needles and thread until she is good enough. She will be paid quarterly.

Then comes Anne from her seat by the fire. "Quarterly, Kitty, and we are short on the rent this month. Is there a pound you might spare? A guinea?"

At this the door is knocked, and Mercy goes to it; the coalman is there for his money. She has it ready in a little purse over the fire, which she takes down, and he sits with some rum whilst she counts it out and he makes her a receipt from his notebook. Anne is watching all the while; her sharp eyes miss nothing of the exchange. Once he is gone, Mercy replaces the purse and sits once more, Anne is ready.

"Is there more in that purse, Kitty? For we will be out on our ears if we cannot pay up next week."

Mercy has already had enough. Anne knows better than to think she can scrounge from the purse of a housekeeper; the money inside is not Mercy's to give.

"You'll not have a penny from that purse," she snaps and opens her mouth to say more, but there is a clanging at the front door, and she stops, straightens her apron and points a finger at her mother. "Don't move," she tells her. Up the stairs she goes and across the hall to the door. The layout of the house is such that the front door is directly next to the kitchen door, located one floor below and accessed via a ramp.

The front door reveals William Doughty here to see his uncle. She quickly examines his expression to check if he has observed her mother and daughter through the kitchen window for he disapproves of their visits.

"Good afternoon, Miss Newton," he says jovially enough for her to know that he has not, in fact, spotted them, and she takes his hat, coat and cane and ushers him in quickly, remarking on the weather.

"Yes, it might have been prudent were I to have carried an umbrella," he agrees, as she deposits his belongings in the coat stand.

"Your uncle has been sleeping, sir," she tells him. "If you wouldn't mind waiting, I will see that he is ready for company." She leaves William Doughty seating himself on a little sofa on the landing and knocks on Richard Dyer's door, then sees herself inside. Richard is awake but barely. His eyes are heavy and she can see that he might just as easily ask that his nephew come back tomorrow as see him now. She decides not to force his entry, for with her mother and daughter downstairs she would rather William Doughty leave as soon as possible.

"Mr Doughty is here to see you," she whispers, pokes the fire that he might feel cosy and snug and then covers him over with the coverlet which has slipped to one side. "I see that you are tired; I will tell him to come back tomorrow."

Richard coughs then, for the fire has spat out some smoke into the room, and Mercy curses inwardly. She helps him to sit, rubs his back as he hacks up whatever phlegm is residing in his tubes and passes him a handkerchief with which to wipe his lips afterwards.

"No, no," he manages once the coughing has rescinded. He gestures for Mercy to open the curtains and she does so reticently, hoping that perhaps Anne might have gone to sleep before the fire as she has done before, for she does not wish for William to clap eyes on her. "I will see him now. Please bring up a hot toddy for him; he must be perished."

Mercy grits her teeth; more to-ing and fro-ing will allow Anne to get up to mischief. She doesn't trust the old baggage as far as she can throw her, and Mercy knows full well that the money for the baker's boy is in that purse, as well as the money for the chandler. She admits William Doughty, who is all charm to his uncle and sees him seated.

William Doughty is a man of the town, a barge owner, confident and satisfied with life. He is in his thirties, married, self-content, with the rounded belly of a man who feeds when he desires and the furrowed brow of one who spends his time cogitating over his uncle's Last Will and Testament. He lives much too close to them for Mercy's liking, on Underhill Street, perhaps 150 yards from his uncle, and his presence is all too often beneath this roof. Mercy is under no illusion that this nephew is her rival for the fortune of Richard Dyer. She takes her leave of them both and hurries down to the kitchen to make a hot toddy, whereupon she discovers Anne with her hand in the purse.

"You thieving witch!" she hisses; already Maria is cowering in a corner. "I ought to know better than to leave you a minute!"

"It's for the rent, Kitty," Anne whines plaintively. "To keep a roof over your own child's head! Be charitable! Be kind, Kitty!"

But Mercy is already striding across the kitchen and delivers a blow to her mother with the back of her hand that sends Anne sprawling onto the sofa before the fire. "Kitty, don't!" Anne cries, but Mercy can see nothing but red, nothing but rage, her head pounding.

"When you've five hundred pounds in the bank and more I would wager!" Mercy cries, delirious with anger. "Still you see fit to risk my position!" Her own mother stealing from her employer. If William Doughty were to find out, Mercy would be out on her ear. She takes two steps towards the poker and grips it solidly.

"Charity, Kitty, charity!" her mother whines, but the thinness of her tone, the pitch and the whining does nothing but rile Mercy up all the more.

"There won't be any charity at all if you have me fired for your thievery," she growls and strikes once across her mother's arms, which are raised to protect her. The blow is a good one; Anne cries out, and a coin drops from her skirt pocket and spins round and round on the tiles. This is the final straw for Mercy; she knows very well the coin is from the purse, so she strikes again.

This time Maria cries out, "Stop!" Mercy turns on her for a moment, but she has no fury towards the child. It is Anne, the whimpering, thieving bundle of rags on the sofa who retains her wrath.

"You'll see me out on the streets!" Mercy brings the poker down once more, this time on her mother's legs, Maria leaps forward and grabs the poker to stop it falling again just as William Doughty appears in the kitchen doorway.

"What the devil is going on?" he cries and steps across the room, disarms Mercy and places himself between mother and daughter, and mother and daughter.

What is Mercy to do? Tell him that her own mother was caught thieving from Mr Dyer's purse? No, she cannot; she cannot bring upon herself the degradation.

"I think my mother will kill my grandmother one day," comes

the small voice of Maria Newton, and Mercy turns on her and glares her to silence.

"I rather think you ought to leave," William says to Anne, who rises trembling from the sofa a little bloodied, awkwardly takes up the penny that has dropped, and places it firmly on the table. Nobody speaks as Anne ties her shawl more firmly about her, wincing as the material tightens. Maria ties her bonnet back on and then the two of them open the door and step out into the cold, and it bangs shut behind them.

William turns to Mercy. "My uncle would prefer your mother not to call," he tells her. "It never ends well."

Mercy eyes the poker; he is still gripping it in his fist. "She is not welcome," she tells him. "She is a disgrace. She turns up with the child in tow. I cannot turn away my own child, Mr Doughty."

William eyes her for a moment. Then he replaces the poker. "I would suggest that next time, Miss Newton," he advises solemnly, "when you open the door and realise it is her, you instantly close and bolt it before she can gain entry." He eyes her solidly for a moment to signify that his suggestion is more actually a command. Then he turns. "I'll see myself out," he tells her over his shoulder.

When he is gone and the sound of the front door slamming has finished echoing about the place, Mercy sets the kitchen straight, places the penny back in the purse, tidies her hair and straightens her apron. Richard will be due his light tea soon and she must boil water for the pot. She sets his tray out and prepares his meal. She forces all thoughts of Anne and Maria down, and does not consider their slow, cold, wet trudge back over the bridge, up the other side of the valley and down the lanes back to Batch Pool. She is determined that their visit will not spoil her evening. She spares them not a single thought that night as she settles down to sleep. Nothing that is until the following day, when early in the afternoon Mr Newell announces himself with the clanging of the bell and she admits him presuming he is here to see her master, but is met with, "Now, Miss Newton, I am here about the condition in which I have found your mother."

Mercy takes a moment to allow his words to sink in. "Is she dead?" she jokes coldly. If only she were. Five hundred pounds would buy a pretty wedding dress.

"She is battered," says Mr Newell. "Badly so, so that skin is missing."

Mercy stares at him for a moment. He is exaggerating, she is convinced. "Will she recover?" she manages, her voice level, emitting a tone of sincerity, although she cannot conceive that he is being anything but overdramatic.

"She will," says Mr Newell, but he is glaring at her over his spectacles. "But she has been sorely used. If she were to press charges, her attacker might end up in custody. What say you to that, Miss Newton?"

Mercy curls her lip. She has never had much respect for authority unless she might make a few shillings out of it. "I say she's a thieving ingrate," she growls, stepping closer to the door and reaching out to open it. "And I say that it is nothing to do with you!" And with that she hustles Mr Newell back out into the street.

"She has been abused so badly that she requires medical help," Mr Newell is shouting as she slams the door in his face.

She can still hear him through the closed door as she leans her hot head against it.

"She cannot afford her own medical bill," he is saying. It is not enough that her mother sends the child here begging, now she sends Mr Newell after her money too!

Mercy Newton reaches into her pocket and pulls out sixpence of her own. Then she opens up the door, drops the coin at the man's feet and slams the door again, so hard that the whole house shakes.

Chapter Six

Mercy Newton

Buxton

1845

The journey to Buxton, when the day comes, is as difficult as it might be. Richard Dyer takes his sticks with which he can walk a couple of paces, but there is his bath chair to consider, along with their luggage. All of this is strapped to the carriage which will take them to Shrewsbury, from whence they will take a train, changing once to arrive at Ladmanstow and from there they will travel by carriage into Buxton. William Doughty has arranged it all fastidiously, but Mercy cannot help but feel there must be something closer to home that might prove just as beneficial to Richard's health. For a trip that is supposed to prove a tonic to Richard Dyer's health, the travelling arrangements might be rather less exhausting.

With consideration for Richard's health and comfort, the journey will take two full days, stopping at The Lion Hotel in Shrewsbury, before the train in the morning takes them north. Mercy coddles and cossets him, despite his constant grumbles. She has convinced herself that although this jaunt is under the guise of a health retreat, what Richard Dyer really wants, really *needs*, is a wife; she believes that he will propose to her in Buxton. She is all attention and reads to him as they traverse the countryside, out past Morville, where they both salute the grand house which was home to John Dyer. Mercy smiles fondly to recall those magnificent rooms, but still they were rooms that never could be hers. The Watering, that grand house, all those rooms, stand, she believes, within her reach. As she wipes the spittle from Richard Dyer's lips after he has finished eating a pork pie, lifts the crumbs from his lap on his napkin and throws them out of the window, she knows she has earned it.

They take a carriage from the station in Ladmanstow, and by the time Richard is settled inside, all their things are strapped to it. Once Mercy clambers in and tucks his blanket tight about his wasting legs, he begins to snore. She is glad to be able to look out at the hills in peace, for there is a mile or more to go yet and she savours this time to mull over the situation. She has packed her best dresses and her nicest bonnet. This is the furthest from home she has ever been, high up in the Peak Hills; she perceives already that the air is clearer up here. Here nobody knows the name Newton. Here nobody knows the history of her family. She can be free here; she breathes deeply and smiles. Buxton is pretty enough, grander in parts than Bridgnorth, which is filled with public houses and working men, whereas Buxton is more refined. Cleaner. The buildings seem less caked in coal dust and the people do too.

The cab stops at The Crescent, a marvel, that makes Mercy hold her breath. A perfect crescent-shaped building, the size of a palace, with archways spanning the ground floor and an array of breath-taking shop displays in all the lower windows. She has never seen a building like it. She lays a hand on Richard Dyer's sleeve to wake him and lets her hand linger there as he wakes.

"It's beautiful," she murmurs as he opens his eyes. "Look!"

But Richard Dyer is too busy harrumphing, snorting and clearing his phlegm to note with any sort of corresponding awe the elegance of The Crescent. His bathchair is taken from the roof and laid out for him. Out from somewhere in the hotel comes a boy clad in uniform, who takes their bags in his little hands and waits patiently for Richard to clamber into his chair before offering, "I could push the gentleman if the lady requires?"

Mercy smiles and imagines the furore that would ensue should the boy accidentally tip the bathchair with Richard in it.

"I rather think Mr Dyer would prefer it if I were to push him," she tells the boy, who nods politely.

"Yes, Mrs Dyer."

Mercy stares down at the child. "Mrs Dyer," she repeats.

It sounds well on her tongue.

William Doughty has arranged that they have adjoining rooms so that Mercy can tend to Richard at every moment day or night and never have a minute that is decidedly her own. This she is accustomed to, and although Richard can be fractious at irregular hours, she is dedicated to her purpose. He must not be able to imagine life without her. These days in Buxton, here in this finest of hotels, are spent together in the restaurant, up in Richard's room as she reads to him or dresses him, or with Mercy behind the bath chair crossing the road before the hotel to take the water at St Anne's Well together. Mercy quickly discovers that this habit is not to her taste. She is pleased to find that she has time to walk the town and explore, for Richard sends her to buy newspapers and sweets at intervals, and of course he must have his afternoon nap. So rather than frequent the shops on the ground floor of the hotel, she uses these times to wander the town. On one of these occasions, she discovers signage indicating a public attraction: Poole's Cavern, a marvel of a cave, nothing like the poky sandstone cave dwellings at home. She lines up with the other tourists outside the cave, pays her entry and follows a couple who are walking arm in arm, along with a well-dressed family, inside.

"Two million years old," the guide tells them, as he takes them further into the darkness. Reaching into his pocket he takes out matches and lights up a candelabra, then waits for the gasps of amazement, which neither Mercy nor any of her fellow company can quell. "The name – Poole's Cavern – comes from its use by an outlaw named Poole, who used to, they say, use the caves as his lair when robbing travellers," the guide says in a voice that echoes through the place.

"When was he active?" asks the father of the family, his hand protectively on his little daughter's shoulder.

"In the fourteen-hundreds, sir, not recently, not recent at all," says the guide, winking at the little girl. "We've no criminals amongst us now, little miss, never you fear."

No criminals, thinks Mercy, but if this were Bridgnorth all eyes would have turned inevitably to her, the cousin of the murderer, John Newton. Here nobody gives her mind at all.

She takes a pamphlet about the caves back to the hotel and shows it to Richard. "You might be interested in the history or the rocks," she tells him.

"The geology," he mutters dismissively. "Yes, very good, very good. But let us relax again tomorrow and take the water. I think perhaps it is starting to have an effect upon me."

And so each day, no matter what Mercy suggests, they do the same: breakfast, take the water, return to the rooms and Mercy reads to him a little until Richard falls asleep. Then she dons her bonnet and strides out to find newspapers and bonbons, and to explore the place before he awakes, ready for afternoon tea.

With each day that passes, Mercy grows more and more impatient – when will he ask her? When in this monotony of days, made it is true all the sweeter by the decadence of the hotel and the richness of the food, when, *when*, will he ask her to be his wife? She had convinced herself that it would happen, but each day that passes indicates that it will not.

It is on the final evening of their stay that Richard Dyer suggests they dress in their best to eat in the restaurant, and at last Mercy's pulse begins to race. She had almost given up hope that he might propose, but now she is sure it will happen whilst they are dressed in best. She sits before her mirror, shaping her ringlets with the curling tongs, whilst through the adjoining door she imagines Richard Dyer sitting, waiting, unable to take himself out of the room, reliant on her and unable to live without her. She is thirty-six years old, many would say an old maid. There are no romantic pretensions for Mercy; she has had her romance, her forbidden, misconceived bit of lovelorn tragedy, and now she wants Richard Dyer's money and house. Perhaps then if it were hers she might afford to keep her daughter better or even feel some sort of charity towards her mother. She mulls it over, sucking a burn on her finger from the curling tongs. If she had money, if she no longer needed to fear the grinding poverty that her mother inhabits, then maybe she could look kindlier upon her. *Yes*, she thinks, *when I am Mrs Dyer, it will not do to have poor, skinny, smoke-stained Anne Newton trudging about looking as though she sleeps beneath a bush.* She must be washed, brushed and placed either closer to hand that she may be governed and kept sober, or further away that she may be forgotten about. And Maria, well, Maria must continue to work, develop her sewing and perhaps one day she might run a shop of her own. Mercy smiles with pride to think of the name Newton above a shop on the High Street. Newton's – only the finest stitching for the finest customers. Yes, that would be a turn-up for the books. Newton, to be a name that people look for, not a name they shrink from.

When seven o'clock comes, she knocks upon the adjoining

door and is rather perturbed to find that Richard Dyer is napping in his bathchair, mouth open and dribbling somewhat; it glistens in the light of the fire. She shudders to think that if she is to be his wife, he might wish to put those thick, arthritic fingers upon her person, but she has endured much in her life and would, she has determined, endure this for the house and the money. From her years of nursing sick relatives, she calculates he only has a few years left in him at best. She takes his handkerchief from his pocket, wipes his mouth and calls softly to him, "It is seven and time for our supper." As he opens his eyes, briefly confused, and squints at her, she fixes him with the kindest, sweetest smile she can muster.

The restaurant at The Crescent is incandescent with candelabras, chandeliers and all manner of decoration. There are flowers upon the tables, huge great colourful hothouse flowers, and the walls glimmer with gold accents, the ceiling higher than any ceiling Mercy has ever encountered, and more decorated and fanciful than anything she could ever have imagined. She helps Richard Dyer move along – he is using his sticks this evening and has left his bathchair at the door of the restaurant, hidden behind one of the most ostentatious pot plants she has ever seen; another good sign, she thinks – he wishes her to know that he is still active, is still man enough for a wife. They are seated as equals, without his bathchair in sight, at a table with glasses and all manner of gleaming cutlery. Mercy wonders when he will propose: before the food or after. Either way she is ready with her answer; she will raise her eyebrows as though she is shocked, open her lips a little to emphasise her surprise, frown a little to convey confusion, then blink a few times and smile sweetly and say yes. She has practised it in the mirror enough to know that she will convince him; besides, his eyesight isn't sharp enough for him to catch the lacking details of her performance. They order a first course; Mercy is in her element. Of course, she knows her cutlery; no woman in charge of a place like Morville Hall can be ignorant of such things. The soup is certainly not the course for a proposal, she muses, as Richard slurps noisily and drops his spectacles in his bowl, sending a shower of droplets spattering up his napkin which she has tucked into his collar.

"Oh, oh dear, Mercy, might you...?" he fusses, but she has already risen – gracefully – and is all attention. She smiles indulgently, takes the corner of his napkin and pats his chin dry for him. No, he will wait for there to be solid food before a proposal, she is sure now, for no woman can be expected to accept a man whose spectacles are smeared with French onion soup and whose napkin is spattered like a Dalmatian. Solid food will be cleaner and much more appropriate. She flags the waiting staff for a new, clean napkin for him in preparation.

The wine is good and soon Mercy can feel it going to her head. Her cheeks flush, and she can feel her lips growing careless and silly words start trying to emerge. She fights them back down and thinks of her mother and this is enough to keep her on the straight and narrow.

"I feel that the waters here have given me a little more vitality," Richard Dyer confesses and reaches out to take up his wine. "Do you think so, Mercy, are my eyes a little brighter? I rather think my eyesight is improved." He squints at her happily; the wine seems to be affecting him too. He is enjoying himself, despite the smell of soup about his spectacles.

She smiles and takes the opportunity to look him full in the eyes.

"Yes, perhaps they are rather brighter," she smiles as she lies. "And your breathing too seems less laboured."

He smiles now, a sort of half-cracked grimace and takes a deep breath, puffing out his pigeon chest, and then splutters into his lamb. Mercy waits, glances about the place and sips her wine as he hacks up whatever remnants of his meal or internal blockages of phlegm are obstructing his passages. Well-dressed couples, women in hats the size of cart-wheels, men with shining pates and suits that cost more than a year of her wages, sparkling jewels and eyes that slant in their direction, and she can read those looks: the nurse hopes to wed the old man and the old fool will have nothing left if she gets her fingers into him.

She clears her throat.

"Perhaps we ought to celebrate your eyesight," she says and raises her glass. "To your renewed health."

Richard Dyer completes his coughing fit and sits gathering his breath for a moment. "To my health," he repeats out of breath, and then, "And to your continued and much-valued health, too." And he sips, replaces his glass and pats his lips with his napkin. "Mercy, there is something I want to speak with you about."

Her hands are shaking now, too much to leave them in his view. She thrusts them into her lap. This is it.

"You do everything, Mercy, everything about the house," he says. "I have relied on you these last six years, and I am only getting more and more of a burden." He looks at her over his wine.

"Not a burden, not at all," Mercy corrects him. "I love my position with you. It is a pleasure, Mr Dyer, it really is."

He shakes his head, coughs a little and says, "A pleasure to be woken in the middle of the night to help an old man empty his bladder; I think not."

Now she is concerned, for this does not sound at all like the opening to a proposal.

"I have always valued my position in your house, every moment, Mr Dyer. I would not wish to be elsewhere," she tells him earnestly, suddenly afraid that he plans to dismiss her and engage proper nurses for his care. Good God, is this what is coming? What will she do?

"But you cannot go on doing everything, Mercy," he tells her. "You cannot do all the cooking, all the cleaning, taking care of me night and day, it is too much for one person."

She stares at him. "But I *wish* it," she says, and now she feels that she is vying for survival, that perhaps he wishes to engage a proper nurse and she will be sent on into the unknown. She pats her lips stiffly with her napkin. "I wish it to remain so."

He takes a deep breath. "I would not have it that a woman so fine as yourself must toil every hour of every day," he tells her. "And with this in mind, Mercy, I am..." he watches her now for a reaction, and she steels herself for whichever direction the next part of his sentence takes them. "I am engaging a new maid," he tells her. "That you might share the burden of care for me."

Mercy stares at him. Is this it? Is this his grand gesture? To engage a third household member so that they are no longer alone? Someone to watch over her perhaps, to oversee her visitors, to spy on what she does when she is not wiping his arse?

"Through my nephew's inquiries, I have secured a local girl named Mary Corfield," he tells her. "She will start Monday week." He leans forwards, as far as his stiff body allows. "Let us discuss how she will take some of the burden from you," he tells her. "She might wait on me at night, that you might sleep well, and she might take on the brewhouse and some share of keeping the house tidy – the sweeping perhaps, to save your back. Like the rest of us, my dear, you are not getting any younger. It is to help you, I seek, Mercy. To make your life easier." He smiles at her indulgently.

Mercy stares back at him. "Is there anything more?" she asks slowly. One last opportunity for him to make a proposal she now suddenly believes will never come.

"She might bake perhaps, or be taught how to, and how to prepare some of the meals," he says. "Or help on washday."

Mercy Newton nods slowly. She picks up her napkin. "I rather thought we did well enough just the two of us," she says.

As she lays out her napkin, her hands are shaking. If he does not marry her, she will never inherit his money, and if she does not inherit money from her mother or him, then she and Maria will never be able to exist as mother and daughter. She will never have her chance to mother James's child.

"Might there be another option?" she asks steadily, firmly. "Might perhaps you wish a closer bond perhaps, with someone, a marriage?"

Richard Dyer looks confused. His face contorts for a moment, then of all things he laughs, splutters, the phlegm rising in him like lava.

"Good God, not in this lifetime," he breathes, and Mercy glares at his wet mouth, open like a wound and shudders.

She reaches for the wine and drinks it all back in one go.

Their return to Bridgnorth marks a decline in Richard Dyer's health and he takes to his bed. Mercy sends for the doctor, but she secretly hopes Richard does not surface quickly – this bout of illness serves him right, she concedes, for not proposing to her and for sticking his snout into that roulade in the piggish way that he did. It is once the doctor is called and Mercy is waiting for his arrival sitting in the kitchen alone at last, that she comes up with a new scheme. Quietly she slips upstairs to peer in at Richard Dyer. He is asleep, open-mouthed, snoring loudly, for his breathing is harsh and laboured. What if he were to die? Where would she be? His health is prone to ups and downs, but during their homeward journey, he has taken a sharp turn for the worse. If he were to remain abed, if he were to remain asleep, perhaps she might find another way to secure her place here, her hand in his purse and her feet in this house. When the lad comes back to tell her that the doctor will be with her within the hour, she passes him a coin in thanks and he replies, "Much obliged, Miss Newton."

"It's Mrs Dyer now," she tells him. "We married in Buxton."

The boy curls his lip but pockets the coin and pelts away with a "Much obliged, Mrs Dyer!"

She stands in the doorway and watches him go. He will tell all he meets, she knows. The lad is one of the river urchins who frequents Underhill Street, touting for any sort of little job someone from the docks might give him: he fetches ale for the workers from the pubs, takes messages about the town and holds horses for folk, anything to make a penny. These children know and talk to everyone and know not how to keep a secret. And who will know? If Richard dies, who will question her? Other than his nephew, he does not have a soul in the world. She must be convincing then, for William Doughty is no fool. When the doctor comes, however, Mercy does not apprise him of the happy lie. Not yet. She sees him up to Richard Dyer, leaves him there and returns to the kitchen to consider what to do next. She must choose quarters for this Mary Corfield and determine a schedule of jobs for her. She goes to the study, takes out paper and ink and begins to create Mary Corfield's weekly timetable. At length, the doctor returns from Richard's bedside and discovers her working.

"He is not a well man," he tells her. "His speech is much affected. He must take a little of this three times a day to alleviate his discomfort. Two drops upon the tongue, every eight hours."

Mercy takes the bottle from him. "Laudanum?" she asks.

The doctor nods. "He is in a state of some pain," he tells her. "I have given him two drops now and he is asleep. He will need more this evening."

"I will see to it that he has it," she tells him. "We are engaging a new maid soon and so the care of him will not fall solely upon me." She places the bottle down next to Mary Corfield's rota, which she has painstakingly copied out in pen and ink, and sees him to the door. "Will this visit be added to his bill?" she asks. The doctor affirms, and as she sees him out into the street, there stands a lad from the grocers, a delivery of vegetables in his hands.

"Vegetables, Mrs Dyer," says this lad, demonstrating the speed with which rumours spread in this town and the doctor raises an eyebrow but says nothing.

"Come to the kitchen door," Mercy tells the boy, savouring the moment, doing nothing to put him right. "You must be new."

"Yes, Mrs Dyer," says the boy and takes himself off to the next doorway.

The First Trial: Spring Assizes
The Prosecution

Recollections of Thomas Whitmore, MP

Apley Estate, Bridgnorth
17th of March 1849

Prior to the proceedings, I had ascertained from my mother of all people the links my family had with Miss Mercy Newton.

My mother was blessed with a good memory, and I had sought her company not only for the purposes of a succinct Newton history but also to ask her a question regarding the horses and dogs that my father amassed. A selection of these animals must be sold, for their number was excessive. I would rather retain only the number needed to run the park successfully and no more.

Therefore at her behest, I had taken tea with her a week before the trial and once the business concerning dogs and horses had been thoroughly discussed, she had named certain dogs and horses she would rather be kept and also named those she had always wished were gone due to a snapping or bolting nature, we had moved on to the history of the Newton family. My mother despised common gossip but her remembrance of the staff of Apley Estate was always second to none and I knew she would be able to dredge her memory of particulars surrounding the Newtons. Not without complaint, she applied herself to recall as much as she could but told me, in no uncertain terms, that she was most perturbed at my insistence. It appeared that my father, were he still alive, might have been put in a position of much difficulty had it fallen upon him to be working for the prosecution in my stead.

"Your father wrote that woman's references," she told me. "Upon the death of the gamekeeper, she was homeless, for her successor soon married and had never taken a liking to her in any case. The Newton woman went back to her mother, and she birthed a girl child, baptised at our church, and then looked straightaway for work. She applied to your father to write her references since, of course, she could get none from her dead cousin." She sighed at that and put down her plate. "Oh, Thomas, I despise all of this. These awful people and the misery they have cast upon themselves. Must you be embroiled in this trial? Our family has had enough of the dramatics that arise from these Newtons. First, the murder at Severn Hall – and that John Newton was a good tenant, always paid his rent on time, and he'd been our tenant for a good long while. All that business with his trial being fixed, and then his brother, our gamekeeper shooting himself. Another brother trussed himself up to hang. All so distasteful. Might we talk of something else?"

"Where did she take these references?" I asked her.

"To Mr John Dyer, of all people, the agent of the Right Honourable Lord Sudeley, who was living in Morville Hall. She took up a position there, I believe, and did very well by all accounts."

Indeed, I knew she had done exceedingly well out of her work for Mr Dyer. In fact, following his death, her employment had sleekly transferred to his brother, Richard Dyer, a man who prized her so greatly that after her arrest, his decline at the shock of her accusation had been so severe and quick that he was dead within a week.

Upon addressing the courtroom then, I found myself

wondering if Miss Newton was aware of the demise of her employer, that her actions had not only seen to it that she was standing here today but had exacerbated Mr Richard Dyer's frailty so keenly that his life was prematurely ended.

There were, of course, elements of the coroner's inquiry that I wished to give no heed to. The hitherto mentioned Reverend W.K. Marshall, for example, and his tale related before the coroner regarding his visit to The Watering on the 5th of September last. Absolutely and without question, his tale of the conversation he had with Anne Newton that day had a great deal to do with the jury's inability to come to an agreeance. His account of Anne Newton waiting for him in the parlour at Richard Dyer's house filled with troubled and unhappy thoughts of suicide most certainly played with the consciences of the jury. His final point, that he was convinced Miss Newton had only her mother's best interests at heart and had begged him to find her room at the asylum for her in Shrewsbury where she might be taken care of, had only gone to work in the brains of those jurors who could not perceive that a daughter might ultimately be guilty of the crime of which Miss Newton was accused. No, the Reverend W.K. Marshall would not be interviewed if I could help it.

Edward Edwards, however, was a witness most persuasive for the prosecution. Anne Newton's brother, the prisoner's maternal uncle, took to the stand most willingly for a character assassination that was made all the more powerful in that he was ripping the reputation of his own niece to shreds.

"What is your relation to the deceased?" Phillimore questioned him.

This man glowered, a pent-up storm raging within his skin. His eyes flitted again and again to the prisoner, his niece, then back to Lord Justice Coltman, as though he dared not look upon Miss Newton for fear of what he might do.

"She is... was... my sister," he begins. "And the way she was treated by her own daughter was despicable."

"To make clear, by 'her daughter', you refer to the prisoner, Miss Mercy Newton?" Mr Phillimore asked.

Edward Edwards nodded. "The prisoner. Mercy Catherine Newton," he clarified. He was a tall man, slight, but with clothes that appeared large enough on him yet well-maintained enough to indicate they were very old, rarely worn, and that he had shrunk in stature these past few years. "The deceased was my sister; she was 72 years of age, and her daughter, the prisoner, used her most sorely."

Phillimore nodded. "Can you tell me more about the situation between the two? Specifically, about the monetary situation, which as we will see throughout the trial, appeared to be a catalyst for Miss Newton's ire towards her mother?"

Edward Edwards took a deep breath. "I have here the probate of our father's will, which as you will see, left £500 directed to be invested upon government securities. The interest of which was to be paid to Anne for her lifetime. Upon her death, £200 is to be paid to Kitty, the prisoner, and the rest to remain invested, with the interest paid to her for life. Mercy knew of it, she'd always known of it, and she made reference to it whenever she beat her mother. She was always after that money."

Phillimore probed onwards. "Can you tell us how the prisoner abused the deceased?"

I glanced again at Miss Newton. To sit and hear her own uncle working towards her hanging was a thing indeed, but she had not flinched.

"She beat her badly with a broom and hit her about the legs with a poker. The last I spoke with her, it was about abusing her mother. This was about four months ago," he replied. "She said," he took a breath again – the whole thing was clearly wearing to one of such years – then narrowed his eyes with a passing resemblance to Miss Newton and imitated, "'She deserves worse. The accursed old bitch has lived too long and kept me away from my money and will continue to do so until the hairs on my head have gone quite grey; I should dearly love to see her cut up into quarters'." He added as Mr Phillimore nodded to maintain his momentum, "After our brother died, she was set to inherit £150 more."

"A whole £650 for the prisoner's inheritance!" Phillimore states. "Quite an amount!"

Edward Edwards licked his thin lips. "The daughter, Maria, was also concerned for the safety of Anne Newton," he added. "She stated such many times."

"Is the girl not available to come to court?" Phillimore has hit on a point. If the girl would stand against her own mother, we would have an impenetrable case.

"She is away, learning to be a seamstress," Edward Edwards tells the court. "Wolverhampton, I believe, although I might be wrong. There was talk of London for a while. I do not know her exact whereabouts."

A most useful witness, Mr Edwards. Miss Newton did not look up during his whole time in the stand, her head stock-still and her hands clenched in her lap.

I believe that Mr Edwards might have enjoyed the limelight for much longer, but his usefulness was wearing thin. Phillimore skilfully tied up his interview and then I came forth for my stint.

With confidence, I called the most useful witness I could to the stand.

Mary Corfield.

As I called her name, I observed a shift in the prisoner at last. A tensing, a movement of the head. She was watching from beneath that veil, scowling, no doubt filled with hatred.

Mary Corfield's deposition at the guildhall had betrayed intelligence and vigilance. The girl was, I must admit, a formidable and competent witness with a commendable ability to speak assuredly before her betters. Lord Justice Coltman cleared his throat as the girl came up to take her place. She held her head high, confidently placing herself before the jury, but I noticed made no effort to look towards the prisoner, whose bonnet had lifted and who was quite obviously staring in her direction. She stood smartly dressed and neatly coiffured, no doubt having borrowed a dress from someone. My own investigations regarding her person and her integrity as a witness had apprised me of the fact that she too, like Miss Newton, had an illegitimate child. There was nothing other than this child of Miss Corfield's to suggest that she might be considered an unreliable witness; a gratifying conclusion, for her testimony was paramount to the case for the prosecution. Yet I had no doubt, in other circumstances perhaps, if Miss Newton had been in possession of a sweeter nature, they might have been friends.

It was clear, however, from the onset that there was no love lost between the two. Mary Corfield and Mercy Newton were never destined to be other than at odds with one another.

Chapter Seven

Mercy Newton

The Watering

1845

Mary Corfield arrives with her bags dangling from her arms, fresh from service at some smaller abode where she did not live in. She is friendly enough to begin with, all chatter and excitement at her new position. It has been a long night, for Richard Dyer has spent much of it having to be sponged down and his sheets changed from under him, and Mercy has slept but a little. She has taken a little rum to give her strength, forgetting that the new maid would arrive today. And yet here she is.

Mercy sees her to her room – a poky little servant's room up at the top of the house, sparse and dark, in stark contrast to her own, which is furnished elegantly and which only she retains the key to. Mary is young – perhaps twenty-three or twenty-four, to Mercy's thirty-six years – and she is filled with the precociousness of youth.

"Been here long?" she asks, as Mercy leaves the room, and as Mercy turns, she narrows her eyes. "You're a Newton, aren't you? My mum says there's history round these parts with the Newtons."

Mercy turns on her. The rum is warm in her belly. She clenches her fists. Before she can bite back her tongue, the lie has sprung from her lips, for how dare this girl denounce her family name.

"You may call me Mrs Dyer, since we wed just this month in Buxton."

Mary steps back. "Oh, I did not realise..." She bobs a little curtsey.

Mercy hates her already. She does not respond, closing the door as calmly as she can, and makes her way back down the stairs, grinding her teeth; her blood is up. As Mary sets out her brush and comb and puts her few belongings away in her room, down in the kitchen Mercy knocks back a little more rum to calm her nerves. Then she takes out the timetable she has drawn up for the girl and in spaces where lenient jobs have been assigned, she scores out the words and adds more distasteful tasks: wash Mr Dyer's underclothes – those are always soiled, empty and wash chamber-pots and see to Mr Dyer's bath. Anything Mercy must grit her teeth whilst doing is assigned to Mary Corfield from now on. Was that not what the old man wanted anyway?

The damned girl doesn't bat an eyelid when handed her list. She merely casts an eye across it, rolls up her sleeves and says, "Much as I'd expected, Mrs Dyer, with an invalid in the house."

And so this interloper makes a third in the house, and Mercy does the lightest of work and soon loses any regrets she might have had from perpetuation her lie with such brazen front, whilst Mary is put to it at all hours.

It is a joyful existence being the lady of a nice, big house like this with a maid. Better than Mercy had expected. She finds time now to read, relaxing in the drawing room in the evenings with a book whilst Mary feeds Richard upstairs and brings her tea. She has time to think. With Richard invalid, Maria could come here and finally live with her. What stands in her way now of being a mother to her daughter?

There is only one obstacle that she can ascertain – William Doughty.

Doughty stands to inherit from Richard's death. He will be the one to try to refute this. She tops up her tea with whiskey when Mary leaves the tea at her hand.

Every time a delivery boy comes to the door, she feeds them with a snippet more about her 'wedding',

"A beautiful church it was, up in Buxton," she tells one. "And the wedding cake at the hotel was the tallest cake I've ever seen!"

"My bouquet was all hothouse flowers," she tells another. "Great big blooms as big as your head!"

"Such a wonderful choir, there was, at our wedding," she muses, when the church choir practice at St Mary's rings down. "Brought a tear to my eye, they did."

Word spreads and Mercy must steel herself, for Mr Doughty, Richard's nephew, will hear these rumours soon and Mercy must be ready for his wrath. And then Anne comes knocking.

Mercy spies her through the window, tramping through the gates with her pipe hanging out of the corner of her mouth, Maria following behind. Mary is upstairs with Richard, and Mercy flings down her sewing and dives towards the kitchen to shoo her away before Mary sees her. After all, the lady of such a fine house as this ought not to be plagued with a vagabond of a mother before the serving staff.

As she pulls open the door, her face set in a scowl, Anne holds out flowers and Maria is smiling.

"Good Lord above, Kitty," Anne says, before she can speak. "And the happiest of congratulations to you, for I heard it off the lad who came to drop off my meat from the butchers not three days ago, that you were wed at last!" She thrusts the flowers at her daughter and bustles past before Mercy can concoct a scheme to be rid of her. Maria stands on the doorstep, her hands clasped to her heart. Anne's voice, harsh and loud, carries, "Now I'll put the kettle on and make you tea, for it is the least I can do for my daughter, the lady of a good house like this one!"

"Who is this?" Mary's voice rises from the hallway. She is standing, carrying a bowl and a towel across her arm. "Do we have a cook now?"

Mercy opens her mouth, but nothing comes out. Maria is still standing on the doorstep meekly. Mercy turns her back to her and glares at Mary. To admit to Mary that this is her mother, to take ownership of this woman who is dressed in tatters and stinks of tobacco, is to reveal the true, humble nature of her origins and to confirm Mary's initial suspicions: that she is one of the Newtons who has history round here.

"And who is this?" Anne asks, so celebratory in her pride in her daughter that she has not registered the look of contempt on Mary's face, blatant as it is. "Do you have a maid now, Kitty? Oh, that my daughter has her own maid! Come on in, Maria, and look at your mother's maid!"

"Mother?" Mary stands and stares from one to the other. "Daughter?"

"Not that it is any of your business," Mercy says turning to her. "Get back to work."

Mary hesitates a moment; Mercy can see the amusement in her eyes. Maria comes inside, closes the door gently and passes Mary to take a seat at the table. Mary observes her movements. At length she crosses to the table and puts down the bowl. Maria observes her in return. Anne is talking ten to the dozen.

"And Maria is proud as punch," Anne is clattering with cups and spoons. "And we was wondering if she would be continuing to live on with me, or if she would be coming to live here now?"

Mary's head rises listening. Mercy licks her lips. She must make the best of this. She opens her mouth to speak, but suddenly Maria is talking.

"Whether I live here or whether I don't," she says, pointedly looking up at Mary, "it is uncommonly rude to stare."

Anne stifles a laugh. Mercy bites her lip.

"Mary, the sheets must be dry on the line by now," she says, and Mary casts an eye back and forth one last time, nods, takes up the peg bag and the basket from the corner and leaves them alone.

"Oh, Kitty," says Anne, setting down a cup of tea on the kitchen table, then hesitating. "Is it right for me to put your tea here, now you are married?" she asks. "Ought you to have it in the drawing room instead?"

Mercy nods. "Yes, let us go to the drawing room," she concedes, for at least in there they will have some privacy. Anne insists upon taking all the cups, tripping over her skirts, her pipe left on the table, still smouldering. Maria follows behind.

At least in here with the door closed Mercy can think properly. She smiles at Maria and gestures for her to sit on the big chair near the fireplace. Anne places her cup on a little table at the side of the sofa and seats herself primly. Her eyes dart about the room – Mercy has never let her this far into the house before.

"A great many comforts you will have now, Kitty, all deserved, all deserved," she says. "And my five hundred pounds won't seem nearly as grand now, will it?"

"What want will you have for five hundred, when you must have, oh! – a few thousand at least!" Maria gasps and rises to take hold of an ornament on the mantlepiece.

"Oh, it is quite the right time for your luck to rise, Kitty," Anne says, feigning a more proper accent, a more fitting persona, as the mother of Mrs Richard Dyer of The Watering. She nods toward Maria. "She has been learning a trade, has your Maria, she's been doing a bit of stitching and a bit of cleaning at the big house at Batch Pool Lane; they've taken quite a shine to her. She will be free again on Sunday after church and she will be delighted to celebrate; perhaps you might have cake on Sunday?"

Her words seem strangely eloquent. Mercy narrows her eyes suspiciously. "Are you sober?" she asks.

Anne takes up her tea. "As sober as I must, until pay day," she winks, but now Mercy sees her hand is shaking.

"We are come to the end of our pennies once more," Maria says, putting down the ornament. "Nan doesn't see any of her money until Monday, and I won't be paid until the end of September for my work at the big house." She turns, and Mercy sees her as though for the first time. The girl has grown. When she was spindly and slight like Anne before, in these last months she has broadened. She has hips now and her face has widened, her jaw squared. She looks, Mercy thinks, for the first time like her father.

"Twelve years old," she breathes. "Twelve years we've been apart, you and I."

Maria nods. "Needs must, but not forever," she says, and for a moment Mercy thinks these could be James's words. Not forever. They will be together once more, in a better place than this, one day. She glances at her mother. Anne is doing her best to drink the tea, but Mercy can tell without a dram of whiskey in it she is struggling.

"Not forever," she tells her daughter. "Something must give. Soon."

There comes a knock on the front door. Mercy passes to the window, then draws back.

"It is Mr Doughty," she says. Her heart is racing.

"Come, no doubt, to give his congratulations to his uncle and his new aunt," says Anne, unsteadily setting down her tea.

Mercy feels sick. She thinks fast. Down to the kitchen she hurries, to Mary who is folding washing. "When did Mr Dyer last have his laudanum?" she snaps.

"About an hour and a half ago," Mary tells her. "He will be

asleep, I shouldn't wonder."

The bell is ringing now, jarring and resounding through the house. Mary sets down her washing.

"Don't stop, I will open it," Mercy tells her. An hour and a half. Richard Dyer will be nonsensical, and unable to deride her little tale of their wedding. She flings open the door.

"Mr Doughty," she says, stepping back, customarily welcoming, but today she holds her chin a little higher than she was wont to do.

"Miss Newton," he says, stepping inside most formally, and removing his hat, eyes narrowed. "Or ought I call you something different now?" His tone is careful, clipped, displeased.

Mercy closes the door, takes his hat and places it on the sideboard. "That is your prerogative," she replies. "You know your way up."

She waits to hear his tread on the stairs before she returns, heart fit to burst, to the drawing room. Maria is sitting on the sofa now, next to her grandmother. Mercy stares at them both. If Mr Doughty is to lose his temper, to denounce her, she would rather neither of them saw it. She fumbles in her pockets and takes out a couple of shillings.

"This is all I have at my disposal," she tells them both. "See that you make it last." Then she gestures to the door. They rise. Anne pockets the money swiftly. Then she leads them back to the kitchen.

"Ought we not come and go by the front door now, Kitty, now that you are married to Mr Dyer, us being family and all?" Anne asks. Mercy pauses. Upstairs, William Doughty will be attempting to grill his unconscious uncle. He will not see.

"Of course," she says, and takes them forth hurriedly through the hall. The front door and the kitchen door both lead out of the same side of the house, but the kitchen door is set down the ramp, on the floor below. It is through the lofty, arched portal of the formal front door she quickly speeds their departure, before closing it quietly behind them.

William Doughty is soon back down the stairs. "He is asleep," he says accusatorially. He brushes his hand through his hair. "I must ask you, Miss Newton, that is to say..." He is really, Mercy notes, most agitated. "Rumour has reached me that an event took place whilst you and my uncle were..." he snorts. "It seems ridiculous, to say it... there are rumours that you were married, in Buxton."

Mercy puts a hand on one hip. "You'd best ask your uncle about that," she says most definitely. "It's not for me to join in with the gossips of Bridgnorth. I'll not say a word on the matter." And she pulls open the front door and waits there for him to depart.

William Doughty opens his mouth. Then he closes it again.

"I hope to God it's not true," he tells her. "Or there'll be questions asked about how a man goes off to Buxton single, and comes back married, bed-ridden and without the ability to speak."

She slams the door once he is gone.

She must, she realises, find out how much Richard Dyer can remember, and see if he can function when the laudanum is out of his system, for he will not be on it constantly for much longer. And so she tells Mary she will sit with him awhile whilst Mary prepares the evening meal. She sits and she waits.

By morning she has ascertained that Richard Dyer remembers everything, although he cannot, it is true, speak more than a few words. Only "Yes," "No," and "Mary," come from his lips. This is, she realises, enough to condemn her lie.

She has a choice. She must either keep him drugged up on the laudanum or come clean. This time she has not had rum nor whiskey, and she can see what will happen. By the time the doctor says Richard Dyer must come off the laudanum, unless he dies in the meantime, she must give up her lie and Maria will not be able to come and live in this house after all.

Mercy Newton must steel herself. Richard Dyer does not improve by much but she is instructed to lessen his dosage, and once his laudanum runs out she is to see to his care without it. As the doctor leaves he calls her 'Mrs Dyer'.

Yet she knows it is over.

Mercy has never overtly told William Doughty that she had married his uncle, and so when next he comes to the house she makes a deal of taking him to one side to refute the rumours once and for all.

Doughty is incredulous. "I asked you days and days ago whether the rumours were true," he snaps at her. "You refused to talk on the issue."

"I did not wish to be dragged into the gutters of the gossips of this neighbourhood," she tells him. "However, I fear they have gone too far now."

"All the delivery boys in a three-mile radius have been referring to you as Mrs Dyer for full on a month," Doughty tells her. "Why only yesterday, before my very eyes, Mary Corfield called you Mrs Dyer to your face!"

Mercy eyes him haughtily. "If the stupid girl wanted to take up with the local gossiping populace perhaps we would do better to relieve her of her services," she suggests. "It was that very moment when I realised how ridiculous these rumours had become."

William Doughty scratches his head and heaves a sigh, Mercy recognises, of relief. He is, she has noticed, quite pink about the cheeks and she guesses he has just come from his gentleman's club. Perhaps the drink in his veins has helped to soften his reaction.

"I'd all but come to terms with the fact that I might have to start calling you aunt, Miss Newton," he says, his natural bluster forced to the fore.

Mercy nods. "That will certainly not be necessary, sir," she tells him.

When he leaves, Mary Corfield reveals herself from behind the drawing room door a duster in her hand. "So you aren't Mrs Dyer, after all?" she breathes.

Mercy stares at her. "Whatever I am, it's more than whatever you are," she tells her. "And don't you forget it."

But now Mary is everywhere, butting her nose into Mercy's business, asking questions about the bills, suggesting a different recipe for a cake Mercy makes, casting judgment and telling the delivery boys, "That's not Mrs Dyer; there isn't one. That's Mercy Newton. Now be off with you!"

Within a week Mary has seen off anyone whose lips bear the name of Mrs Dyer, and Mercy is back to plain old spinsterly Mercy Newton once more. The girl's words spread quickly like cholera, until everyone is purged of the idea that there ever was a Mrs Dyer.

Expecting her mother to come knocking, Mercy takes up more of a share of the housework. She would find a way to dismiss Mary Corfield if she could, but now that Richard Dyer's laudanum is run out, the two times she has mentioned letting her go, his lips form the word, "No," quite succinctly.

Then one Sunday afternoon, when Mary is off visiting her

own mother, Maria lets herself in by the kitchen door.

Mercy is sitting with a book at the kitchen table as the door opens. She gasps, jumps as the door handle turns and is on her feet before the girl has stepped inside.

"Maria!" is all she can say.

"You lied," Maria says. She is shivering; the year is drawing to a close and her shawl is thin. "You never were Mrs Dyer."

Mercy holds out her arms. "I did it for you, Maria. I just wanted..."

"You wanted his money," Maria says. She pulls her shawl about her. "Just like you want Nan's money."

"For you!" Mercy cries. She comes towards her, arms outstretched. "I couldn't be a mother to you because your father was dead and someone had to pay for you! I thought I could give you a home here if I were married."

"All you've ever cared about is money," Maria says coldly. Her face is set, suddenly more like James than Mercy has ever seen her. "You never cared about me."

"That's not true," Mercy cries, grabbing her daughter by the arms. All these months she's plotted so that Maria could come and live in this house and be safe and warm, far from the starvation and deprivation of Batch Pool Lane. And it has all come to nought. "I wanted to be your mother, I wanted us to be a family!"

"Not enough," says Maria, and her eyes are James's eyes, and despite her twelve years, she looks thirty. And starving.

Mercy bids her sit and gives her biscuits from a tin. The girl crams them into her mouth, thin, long fingers grasping at them as though they are the stuff of life itself. Mercy watches her, thinks of her poor savings and wishes she had put more of them towards feeding this girl. Only Anne would have seen it go on gin before the child got a crumb of it.

"You must believe me," Mercy tells her and now she is fighting back tears. "I wanted us to be a family, you, me, and your father. I loved him so much, Maria. So much."

Maria swallows her biscuits. "Nan says he was cursed. She says we are all cursed, all us Newtons, and I'd better be careful because I have the blood of two of them in my veins." She eyes the biscuits again. "Am I cursed? Are you?"

Mercy stares at her for a moment, then reaches out for her hand. She thinks of James, of how he killed himself rather than father a child by her.

"I'd say we might well be," she says slowly. "For little seems to go well for us, in truth. And if I lied, it was to try to benefit us, Maria, to try to give you the home I wish you had. Though it has all come to nought and was my own folly."

That day she gives Maria a sovereign into her hand and bids her not to tell Anne about it. "It is for you, for what you need, and not for *her*," she tells her.

Maria nods and pockets it quickly. She steps towards the kitchen door but turns before she leaves. "She will not be kind, now she knows you aren't Mrs Dyer," she warns her mother.

Mercy nods. "I know."

Two days later, Mercy is feeding Richard, spooning his stew into his mouth slowly as he splutters and dribbles it back down his chin. After she eventually leaves him with a cleansed face and a full belly, she treads down the stairs and hears voices rising from the kitchen.

She can tell without trying that one is her mother's voice. Her harsh, thin tones rise up from the kitchen, accompanied by laughter. She knows it is that damned Mary Corfield down there, plying her with tea or even beer, all the while fuelling her mother's fire. She treads silently forward to listen to them.

"Taken in, I was," Anne's voice comes whining. "A bare-faced liar, that's all she's ever been." Mercy can tell by her tone that she is half-soaked; her words jumble together and her consonants are slurred. "It was scandal enough when she birthed her cousin's child, and he didn't want her, did he? Shot himself in the head to get away, that's what he did. Couldn't stick her in the end, and no wonder, the lying, conniving little madam."

Mercy sets down the bowl and spoon silently. She is shaking so much she is afraid she will drop them.

"Well, I never heard the like!" Mary's voice states firmly. "I was calling her Mrs Dyer for weeks when first I came. Serving her tea and doing her work for her, and all the time she wasn't no more important than me."

"As if a rich man like him would wed a miserable wench like her!" squawks Anne, and the two of them laugh heartily together, as though they had known each other their whole lives.

Neither knows Mercy is standing there behind the door listening, cheeks burning. She backs away from the kitchen up the corridor, temples throbbing. She had been so sure that Richard Dyer would ask her to marry him, so sure that she could secure both her own and Maria's futures. Now that she knows she will never be the true mistress of this house, this mocking interchange sends shivers of sickness and rage through her veins. To think of how she has nursed that man night and day, sponged his arse and patted his rancid little manhood dry, dried between his toes and wiped up his spittle. To think of the money she has handed over to that ungrateful mother of hers, the bags and bags of food and deliveries she has arranged for her mother, and here she sits telling Mary Corfield all of Mercy's past, her darkest moment now revealed. She leans against the doorpost to the drawing room and listens to Mary and her mother hooting down in the kitchen and has to restrain herself from bursting back in and throttling the pair of them. There is a decanter of whiskey in there. She goes over to it and takes some in a glass.

At length, Mary Corfield must return to her chores, and Mercy hovers, drinking in the drawing room until she hears her clank up the stairs with a bucket and cloth to wash the inside of the windows. Then she puts down her glass, the whiskey hot in her veins, and descends upon her mother who is still chortling to herself. She stinks of rum and raises her head with a slurred and jovial, "If it isn't Mrs Dyer, back from Buxton, lady of the house. Oh, but wait, but where's the ring?" Here she cackles and raises herself to her feet. "Let's hope this one doesn't shoot himself, eh, Kitty?"

At this Mercy cracks. Her mother sees the glint in her eye and gets behind the table as Mercy charges for her. Anne is flighty for all her years and she is around the table, out of the door and through to the parlour quick as a flash with Mercy on her heels.

"This place is no sanctuary for you, old woman!" Mercy growls and sends her mother backwards into a chair with a blow from her hand. Anne falls into a chair, and Mercy is on top of her, pulling out her handkerchief. "See if you talk and laugh about me so easily now," she hisses and starts to ram the kerchief down her mother's throat. The old woman scrabbles at her, eyes bulging, but Mercy is bigger and stronger, and she grabs her hands and kneels on them on the old woman's lap, and shoves in the handkerchief. Somewhere behind her there is shouting and the sound of the door slamming and then,

"Stop! Stop it!" Mary blasted Corfield is there, pulling Mercy off her mother. "You'll kill her!"

Mercy pushes her away, but her onslaught is corrupted. She turns on the girl, but Mary Corfield is as bold as brass and she does not flinch when Mercy raises her hand towards her. Her head is swimming.

"You'll kill her," Mary says again. "Let her go!"

Mercy curls her lip. She stays her hand, the blood pumping in her temples. How cruel the pair of them are, this Mary Corfield and her own mother, laughing about the death of James, laughing about her own frustrated ambitions. She is shaking now and the taste of the whiskey rises in her throat. She cannot lose such face before Mary; the girl will become anarchistic. She must retain her gravity and claw back some semblance of authority.

"Best she goes sooner," she growls. "She's lived too long on my five hundred pounds."

She climbs off her mother, who is gagging and rasping, and pulling the kerchief from her mouth, yelping and fussing. Mary pushes past Mercy to help Anne.

"There now," she says to her, an arm about her shoulders. "Will you come to the kitchen with me? I'll fetch you water."

In strides Mr Doughty and behind him through the kitchen door peeks one of the local street boys. Doughty flips him a coin and the boy scampers away. Mercy stands watching Mary gently guiding Anne by the elbow. Anne is sobbing, and Mary is holding the handkerchief, which is stained with blood.

"Miss Newton, what has happened to your mother?" Mr Doughty asks sharply.

"'Tis nothing, nothing!" Anne wails, but her whole body is racked with sobbing and striving for breath, her nose is running and her whole form is shaking. "Nothing, Mr Doughty, it was all my fault. Don't take on with Kitty!"

Mary is pouring her tea now and mopping at her face with a cloth. "She was almost suffocated, Mr Doughty," she says glancing towards Mercy. "I do think that this ought to be a criminal case. She was like an animal!"

Mercy scowls. This girl knows nothing of how it is between mother and daughter.

"Mrs Newton?" Mr Doughty asks, kneeling by her side. "Ought we speak to the magistrate?"

Anne stares up at Mercy in the doorway. "Not for my Kitty," she says limply. "It was an accident. I was sharp-tongued. She was pushed to it, sir!"

"She is just shaken," says Mercy, arms folded. "A canon ball couldn't knock her down."

"I will talk to my uncle," says Doughty, and he points at Mercy. "I am seriously concerned that a situation between the two of you could end very badly. Do not lay another finger on your mother whilst I am gone."

He leaves the kitchen. Anne looks up at Kitty. "Are we straight, Kitty?" she chokes, tears running down her cheeks. "I oughtn't to have said what I did. I shouldn't have mentioned James Newton. I'm sorry for it."

Mercy stands broiling in her own emotions. Her passion came from not only James's name, but from her own mother laughing with this upstart about her disappointment and how readily her mother could belittle her before another rather than offer her comfort. Her heart is broken, pounding and fit to burst all at the same time, and though her anger is fading, she cannot bring forth the words to explain to her mother how she behaved badly – emotions are not discussed readily between the two of them. She eyes the razor, which lies waiting to be sharpened for Mr Dyer's shave.

"I ought to cut your tongue out," she says, knowing full well that this will make Anne understand better than any emotional plea. Sometimes, to communicate with an animal, it is necessary to speak its language, she thinks. "That'd stop you laughing at me, you old witch."

Mary, brow wrinkled, filled with panic anew, seizes the thing and runs out of the door, up the ramp and into the yard, down the garden and hurls it into the river. It ought to be funny, this reaction so exaggerated in its execution, but Mercy cannot laugh. Enough is enough. The passion is gone, the whiskey is dulling within her, and now Mercy looks upon her mother, sees her shaking and is sorry for it. She wonders what Mr Doughty is saying to Richard Dyer upstairs.

She sighs. "You're living on my property and keeping me out of it," she tells her mother, and they all know she's referring to the five hundred pounds again, for there never is an end to her obsession with it. "You'll keep me out of it until my hair is quite grey." Anne is trembling, but not so much that she cannot put her hands around her tea now, take a swig and request a snip of sugar from Mary.

The sound of Mr Doughty's feet pound down the stairs. "I'll fetch Mr Newell now," he says and goes for the doctor, and Mercy's heart sinks further.

When Mr Newell arrives and looks into Anne's mouth and ear, he requests that they all leave him alone with her for a short moment. Mary says she will check on Mr Dyer whilst Mercy and William Doughty wait in the parlour. There is silence for a while, just the ticking of the clock and the sounds from the street outside the window.

"I don't want her here," she tells him, the words catching in her throat. "She turns up and I do shut the door on her, I do. But this time, that Mary let her in. I didn't even know she was here until I came down from seeing to your uncle. And there they were at the table, laughing, drinking too, I'd wager. That Mary oughtn't to have let her in." She doesn't tell him that her mother has tried to steal from this house. She doesn't tell him that her mother turns up hungry, having spent all her money on liquor, and demands food. She doesn't tell him that her mother has an evil tongue and can rip out her heart in just a few words.

William opens his mouth to say more, but Mr Newell is calling to them to come to the kitchen. Mercy wipes her hands on her apron and follows Mr Doughty along the passage.

"Your mother will not press charges against you," Mr Newell tells her. "She says she will not put her daughter before a jury."

She nods and looks down at her hands. It was just a scuffle, she thinks, when all is said and done. Of course her mother will not press charges against her. These men are so pumped up with importance that they are making a deal out of little. Yet to assuage them now, she will act penitently.

"When the passion is upon me, I act in ways I oughtn't, Mr Newell," she says, eyes cast down. "But when the passion is over, I see what I have done wrong. I am shamed, sir, I know I am. It won't happen again." And she is sorry, she knows, for her mother is shaken, but the sting of the laughter has scarred her and deepened the rift that already parted mother from daughter.

Mr Newell looks at her quizzically. "You remember your relation at Severn Hall was hanged for killing his wife, and if you kill your mother you will be the second hanged in your family." He frowns at her and sees that she appears truly sorrowful. He nods at Mr Doughty, satisfied that he has affected peace. "I shall see myself out, Mr Doughty. Please apprise your uncle of my visit and tell him that were I he, I would see to it that Mrs Newton no longer frequents this house for her own safety."

William Doughty arranges for a cab to take Anne Newton back to Batch Pool Lane. He waits until the cab arrives and hands Anne a bundle of bread and cheese as she clambers up into the seat, the horse snorting. He pays the driver in advance and watches it depart towards the bridge. After tipping his hat to Mary, he frowns at Mercy and stomps off down to the river port.

Mary Corfield closes the front door of The Watering and turns to Mercy. As she turns, Mercy makes out the corner of the handkerchief, the one she had tried to ram down Anne's throat, sticking out of her pocket; there is a bright red speckle on it.

"Best get yourself back to those windows," Mercy tells her coldly, determining to go through the girl's pockets as soon as she finds opportunity. "They won't wash themselves."

Chapter Eight

Maria Newton

Bridgnorth

1846

Maria Newton is thirteen years old, quick, slight and good with her needle, and she has a hankering for freedom. She has outgrown her grandmother's slurred and sharp-tongued company and is tired of waiting for her mother to fulfil her promises. She has worked hard, learning a trade, sewing on buttons at first, then progressing until now she can do seams and buttonholes and cut and put together an apron and a simple shirt. She is learning, ever learning, and ambitious too. Her nan has taught her to read and write a little, as she taught her mother before her, for her nan came from a good, prosperous farming family in Chelmarsh, and despite her drinking, knows her letters well.

Many a night Maria reads to her old nan, as Anne lets her head swim in gin or cheap rum with her eyes closed. The girl reads out stories from the newspapers that come wrapped around the candles or from the Bible, the only book they have, which was Anne's mother's. Maria knows that her nan drinks more than she should and she knows her mother hates to see it, that her mother despises drinkers for the most part, for they grow quickly weak of character and doltish of brain; Anne grows cruel of tongue.

"A bastard wench," she has called Maria countless times. "Daughter of cursed blood."

She detests Batch Pool Lane. The poverty, the cold, the

hunger. Perhaps, she often thinks, this is her curse: to remain half-rotting here with Anne. Her mother lives in a grand house, works there and once promised that it would become home for Maria too, but it all came to nothing, as everything in her life does. Maria has lost faith that her mother will ever give her the home she has promised. Her mother is running out of time, for Maria is growing and will soon be a woman in her own right. No, Maria knows that Mercy Newton will not pull her out of poverty, except with this sovereign which she has hidden away so that her grandmother does not buy liquor with it. With this she will make her way to Wolverhampton, for she has applied to work there, learn more and *be* more.

The day the letter arrives inviting her to begin a new job on the first of September, Anne is astonished. In fact, having waited all day for Maria to return from her work, Anne has opened the envelope, but her eyesight is not what it was and she has not been able to focus on the writing to read the message within.

"What now, is there a letter for little Maria?" Anne crows, as the girl shows her the paper. Maria has made it no secret that she is looking to find work, but she has not told her grandmother she has looked so far afield as Wolverhampton.

"Don't you remember I applied for a good few positions?" she asks, but Anne had been glugging rum at the time and has no recollection of her granddaughter's toils.

"Well, blow me down, Wolverhampton?" she expostulates, quite bemused, then, "You'll send your old nan a penny or two when you're earning money in the city, eh, child?"

Maria tucks the letter away into a pocket. "I will go into town and tell Mum," she says. "I shan't wait for the other jobs to reply to me – this is the one I want."

"Ask your mother for a few shillings to get us by until the end of the week!" Anne calls after her. "She might give them if you ask!"

She throws on her shawl for it is early evening and it will be dark and cold by the time she returns. The walk into Bridgnorth is pleasant enough, and Mercy only lives just over the bridge on Underhill Street. Maria slips in through the gate and down the ramp to the kitchen door, and slides in unseen closing it quickly behind her, for her mother hates the neighbours to observe the comings and goings of the rag-tag pair from Batch Pool Lane. Maria is still wearing her work dress which is smart enough, but she is ever afeared to embarrass her mother with her attire, this being the finest house Maria can imagine.

There is nobody in the kitchen, and Maria stands awhile listening, but she cannot hear any voices. Setting her shawl down on the sofa before the fire, she makes her way through the kitchen and up into the hallway. She has never ventured forth into the house before and her heart is pounding, but she is struck with the possibility that if things had only been slightly different she might have come to live here, and now she wants to see what she has been missing.

This place is vast. The hallway covers more floorspace than the one main room of the cottage at Batch Pool Lane. She treads as lightly as she can listening the whole while for voices or footsteps, but none come. Into a study she pokes her head. It is cold in here and the place is filled with books and dust, and she wants to sneeze so pulls her head out directly. There is a dining room and a drawing room. Each contains finer things than she has ever laid her hands on before. She fingers the tablecloth upon the dining table, the tableware, picks up a glass next to a whiskey decanter in the drawing room and holds it up to the light, watching the glittering of the waning light through the window upon the cut glass. She slips off her boots and creeps to the foot of the stairs. To look up them and see those high ceilings and the bannister as it disappears above makes her dizzy. The soft carpet that leads upwards pulls her towards the first floor. What manner of luxury must her mother sleep in? Not a cold, dank pallet on a brick floor, like Maria, she is sure. She must see, she must know, what wonders might have been hers. Up she goes, ever vigilant, up to the first floor to a landing where more of the thick, green carpet leads to the left and right, room after room, it seems to her. She treads carefully, hardly daring to breathe. One door is ajar and a light shines within for it is dusk now; the glow of a fire and the light of a lamp create a warm, yellow stripe across the dark green of the carpet. She can hear her mother's voice now, authoritative in tone but not loud. She slips into a different doorway and slowly, carefully closes the door behind her. This room has a bed so large she cannot contain herself. She lies upon it and stares up at the ceiling. Imagine waking each morning lying here, knowing that this whole house is hers. She thrusts her hand into her pocket and it closes around her offer of employment. Then she closes her eyes for a moment.

When she wakes, it is light. She recognises it instantly: the cold, white light of morning. She gasps, sits up and realises that someone has placed a blanket over her as she slept. There are no sounds within the house that she can make out, and she suddenly realises that not only has she spent the night here uninvited, but she has no idea of the time and could already be late for work. She throws off the blanket. Her thick woollen socks pad across the floor, past a watercolour of the river and a mirror that makes her pause. Her hair is plastered to her face, a nest of tangles. She cannot go to work looking like this. A quick search of the room provides her with a hairbrush and she rakes it quickly through her locks standing there before the mirror watching her own reflection become neater, tidier. She must hurry and yet now she is wondering what might be hanging in the wardrobe and whether it might fit her. She pulls it open, but only suits hang therein. A key turns in the lock and the door handle turns.

"Come down for some breakfast before Mary gets up," Mercy's voice whispers. "You've time before work."

As if in a dream, Maria steps out onto the landing. Her mother is there waiting on the panelled landing, finger to her lips. She follows her down the stairs through this house which is her mother's domain and might have been for the both of them but for the misdirection of an old man's intentions. The house is silent save for the swish of their skirts as they make their way down the hallway.

"Mary will rise in half an hour," her mother tells her as they enter the kitchen and close the door upon themselves. "Time enough for you to breakfast and to appear to have come calling on your way to work." She crosses the room, opens a cupboard and pulls out Maria's boots and shawl.

Maria is bashful as she takes them from the hands of her mother. "I didn't mean to," she tells her. "I honestly didn't mean to sneak around like that, I just wanted to see..."

Her mother nods, tight-lipped. "I think I understand," she says, indicating for Maria to sit at the table. The smell of porridge is heavy in the air, and Maria does as she is bidden gladly. "You wanted to see what might have been," Mercy states.

Maria nods. "I only closed my eyes for a moment," she says. As her mother ladles porridge into a bowl before her, she pulls out her offer of employment. "I'm going away," she tells her.

Her mother's hand stays. "What?"

Maria's body is moving by itself now; no matter the gravity of her news her stomach must be filled. She picks up the spoon that lies beside her bowl. "To Wolverhampton. To work."

Without speaking, Mercy replaces the porridge pot over the fire. She takes the piece of paper from Maria's grip and reads it slowly three times, as her daughter shovels porridge into her mouth like a starving orphan.

"Then I've failed," she says tightly and passes the paper back. "I've run out of time, haven't I?"

Maria gulps down a particularly chewy mouthful. "I can't live with her any longer," she says bluntly. "She's too hurtful and she's too drunk."

Her mother nods. "I know." She reaches out and takes her daughter's free hand. "I'm sorry," she says, and to Maria's astonishment, wipes a tear from her cheek. "I wanted so hard to be able to look after you in a way that was better than my own childhood. But this is a hard world for a fatherless child and a husbandless mother, and all I did was condemn you to a life that was the same as my own."

Maria puts down her spoon. She does not know what to do. Her mother never shows emotion like this. She is hardened, as they all are, to this life they live.

"You had to work so that we had meat," she says. "I know that."

Mercy shakes her head and wipes her eyes on her sleeve. "I wanted more for you." She gestures to the room around them. "I wanted this for you."

Maria takes up her letter, folds it carefully and replaces it in her pocket, then picks up her spoon. "I am going to Wolverhampton," she tells her mother firmly. "I'll make my own way, like you did."

Mercy Newton looks deep into her daughter's eyes. "Don't follow my footsteps," she tells her intently. "Make your own and make them better, and do not be fooled into carrying a child before wedlock or without the proper arrangements in a man's will to provide, for two generations now have suffered from this and you must not let history repeat itself again."

Maria pats her mother's hand. "I won't be foolish," she tells her. "I will make my own history."

When Mary Corfield awakes, Maria is sitting at the table, shawl about her shoulders as though newly arrived. All evidence of porridge is cleared away.

"She's off to Wolverhampton for work," Mercy tells Mary proudly. "My girl, off to the city to become a seamstress."

"Good morning, Mary," Maria says smiling, "I popped in to tell the good news on my way to work, would you like to see?"

Mary Corfield takes the paper from her and reads it over. "Then perhaps we ought to celebrate," she suggests. "I believe there's a bit of bacon left over that might not be missed, perhaps we ought to get a good breakfast down you, if that's to your mother's liking?"

Thus Maria Newton steps out that morning having spent the night in a grand bed, with two breakfasts in her belly, an offer of employment in her pocket and a sovereign to her name. Ever present in her mind is the threat of the Curse of the Newtons, but she knows she is pure of heart, kind of character and hard-working. She is not waiting for an inheritance that will never come. She is escaping the lash of her grandmother's tongue and the broken promises of her mother, and she is moving as far as she can imagine is possible. She will make her own history, she promises herself, and it will be nothing like anything her family has ever seen before. She will escape the curse and live a good and free life, and she only prays that it does not reap its havoc upon her mother and her grandmother in return.

Chapter Nine

Mercy Newton

The Watering
4th of December 1848

The river has flooded its banks so high that it rushes through the bottom end of the small grounds that extend out from The Watering. Brown water, powerful, alive. It sweeps away whatever it touches and lines its wake with scum. And the rain! Such rain flows in rivers of its own, down the steps from High Town, down the Cartway, and Underhill Street is flooded right up the steps to the doors of the houses.

Mr Richard Dyer is abed. So frail is he now after an apoplexy that he can utter only very few words: 'Mary' (which can stand for either Mary or Mercy, and neither is sure he can tell the difference anymore), 'aye' and 'no'. Mary Corfield spends her nights in his room sleeping on a little bed in the corner so that Mercy might be spared the hardship, although Mercy has kept her good room next to his with its four-poster bed.

The relationship between Mercy and Mary is often one of cool indifference, sometimes one of convivial drinking, but usually they are wary each of other. Mary knows the violence Mercy is capable of, and Mercy knows that Mary is not afraid to stand up for herself.

The nights are fast drawing in, and under such an onslaught from the heavens and such a chill that rises from the river, it is dark early and damp. There are fires lit about The Watering, one in Mr Dyer's room, one in the kitchen, a little one in Mercy's room to keep out the chill, another in Mary's minute grate and another in the drawing room that is dying down now that the day is done. The curtains are drawn to keep out the cold, and Mr. Dyer's hot milk has been supped with help from Mary who has been in charge of wiping his dribbles since Mercy's administrations came to nothing matrimonially speaking. The two women have settled in the kitchen at the end of their chores and are, this night at least, on hospitable terms, for there has been a current of peace recently that has washed through this house, much as the river is now washing through the bottom of the garden. It is nine o'clock, as the clock on the mantel testifies. Late enough for them to relax now their day is done.

"If it grows any higher it'll be up to the house," Mary says bolting the door. "Might be only the steps by morning that keep the water out. The cellar will likely flood."

Mercy pokes the fire and yawns. "It must surely stop soon," she says. "And there's nothing worth worrying for in the cellar just now. Old bits of furniture; not much else."

Mary moves to find food for them, but there is a banging on the door.

"Whoever would be out in this weather?" she asks and opens the door to find Mr Bell standing on the doorstep in the rain. "Why, Mr Bell, whatever brings you here in this weather?" Mary cries. "Come in and warm by the fire."

"I'll just heat my bones and then I'll be gone," he accedes, following her through to the kitchen and nods towards Mercy who is hacking at a loaf of bread with the knife. "It's Miss Newton I'm here to see."

"This knife's blunt," Mercy complains and sets it down. "Not paid her rent then, Mr Bell? I suppose she's sent you here to try to get it from me?"

Mr Bell shakes his head. "No, not the rent, Miss Newton," he says. "But your mother has nothing to eat. Nothing to eat, but tobacco enough to lie smoking in her bed with a candle in a pint mug on the blanket." He shudders and moves closer to the fire. "I've had to speak to her already on that account and she's not been lodging with me a fortnight. I'll not have her setting fire to my house and burning to death in her sleep. But now it seems she also has no food and says she won't have more for days as she's waiting for her interest to come in. So I thought I'd best come and let you know. I can't see her starve, Miss Newton, but I have only food enough for myself and my family you understand. Times are hard enough."

Mercy looks down at the bread knife, then over at the fire warming Mr Bell's backside.

"You'd best tell her to come down here then, Mr Bell," she says slowly.

Mr Bell nods, more towards the loaf than to Mercy, for her eyes are narrowed and her jaw is set and it is not a face that will relish a nodding.

"I'll tell her just that, Miss Newton," he agrees, and Mary sees him out. She returns to find Mercy hacking away with the bread knife again.

"Best make sure there's bread enough for three," Mercy breathes.

"It's a harsh night for Mr Bell to come here; he must truly believe her to be starving," Mary suggests softly, though there is always the possibility that Anne might have taken a drink and when she is half cut there is always a fall out between mother and daughter. But then if the old woman cannot afford food perhaps her cup runneth dry of gin also. Mary is charitable and likes Anne, or at least pities her. "Mr Dyer won't know she's here, there's no harm in it," she adds.

Mercy shrugs and carries on hacking away. Crumbs amass as the knife saws bluntly through the loaf. Mary tidies away some things, then goes to check on Richard Dyer. He is dozing, so she leaves him and returns to the kitchen, whereupon the door knocks once more. Anne Newton is standing there in the yard soaking up the flood water with her skirts, shivering, a basket hanging off her elbow.

"I've come to see Kitty," she says breathlessly, the rain spattering off her cloth bonnet and dripping off the end of her nose, the hems of her skirts wet up to about six inches.

"Are you sober?" asks Mary warily. It is always her first question now, for she's learned that Anne's mouth cannot be trusted if she's had a drink before she arrives, and this is what always begins the trouble.

"As a judge," says Anne shivering in words that are shaped enough to belie that she is telling the truth. "Do let me in, Mary. These skirts are chafing round my ankles. I might have swum here if I'd known how."

Mary stands back to admit her, and in Anne limps, complaining of her ankle. "It is still weak," she mutters but says nothing of the beating she took from Mercy months before that made it so, instead heading to the sofa next to the fire. "Evening, Kitty."

"Did anyone see you come here?" Mercy asks from the table. She does not get up. "Doughty?"

Anne shakes her head. "I was quite, quite sure I was unobserved," she says, removing her bonnet and setting it to dry by the range. "I don't want to go getting you in trouble now, do I, Kitty?"

She sets down her basket, takes off her boots and seats herself so that she may hold her feet out to the fire for her boots are soaked, then pulls out the little bottle of liniment she carries and applies some to her ankle.

"Have you heard from Maria?" she asks hopefully.

Mercy nods. The mention of her daughter's name enhances the hole she has felt since the child left. She goes to a little box on the mantle, takes out two pieces of paper and hands them to her mother.

"Two letters in all. It appears she is settled, has made friends with some of the other girls and is happy enough."

Anne humphs, taking them and squinting at Maria's hand. "Well, she hasn't written to me," she complains. "And you didn't mention it last time I saw you."

Mercy takes the letters from her. "She says here that I am to pass on her regards to you," she reads. "No doubt she knows how your eyesight is not what it was and if she were to write you'd not be able to read it well." Placatory words, yet Mercy is glad the child has not written to Anne; a small triumph, that she is first in the girl's affections after all. A small triumph indeed but now the child is gone, and she will never be a true mother to her.

Anne tuts to herself. "That girl needs to remember who raised her," and she eyes Mercy, rubbing the liniment into her ankle to see if the comment has riled her or not. "She is doing well, no doubt? Saving her pennies? She ought to send some in this direction, to repay the cost of her upbringing, to my mind. What say you, Kitty?"

Mercy sighs. "Well enough by her account. Yet ever in my mind is the thought that she's a Newton," she says. "Each letter that comes I shake to open it in case it bears news that she has been hurt or has hurt someone else. We are cursed, and yet with Maria's good fortune, your new lodgings and me here, I feel blessed. It cannot last. This life has never been happy for long. Perhaps the most we can wish for is that she doesn't kill anyone." She stares for a moment into the fire. "Or herself," she adds bleakly. She remembers James's words, 'We've all got a touch of the morbs deep in our veins, us Newtons. Can you feel it too sometimes?'

This feeling she has had since Maria left, this feeling of loss and failure, this darkness inside her, perhaps this is what he meant, she thinks, and it seems unshakeable.

Meanwhile Anne is reaching into her basket. She pulls out a card. "Kitty, here is a card with the Lord's prayer on it," she says. "We ought to say it and wish for Maria to have peace." She holds it out to Mercy. "And perhaps He might see to it that I get my daily bread," she adds with a glint in her eye. Mercy sighs, reaches out for the card, snatches it and tosses it into the fire.

"That will not feed you," she tells her mother, who cries out and starts towards the fire, but the card is already ablaze and she cannot rescue it. "Pray all you like; I'm the one that'll put food in your belly this night."

She goes to the pantry, brings out cheese and beer and adds it to the table. The three of them sit and eat and drink quite jovially. At length, Mercy announces that it would be nice to have some rum to finish off the evening. She turns to Mary, who knows she will have no choice but to head out across the road to one of the public houses. So, after a quick assessment of the atmosphere to ensure that no fighting will ensue the moment her back is turned, Mary Corfield puts on boots and a coat, ties a bonnet to her head, hoists her skirts up and wades off out of the door, up the ramp and down the road for it, leaving Mercy and her mother alone.

The First Trial: Spring Assizes

Recollections of Thomas Whitmore, MP

Apley Estate. Bridgnorth

17th of March 1849

Character Witness – Mary Corfield

Mary Corfield stood before Lord Justice Coltman and the gentlemen of the jury, and her eyes were clear and bright, bold and defamatory.

"Not long after I arrived at The Watering," Mary related most confidently, "Miss Newton beat her mother with a whip until the skin hung from her. I do not believe that this was the first time she had attacked her in this way. When I intervened and pleaded with her to stop, she said..." Here she faltered and looked about the room. I could tell she was seeking permission and remembered that foul language had been part of her experience with Miss Newton. She was seeking permission to use the obscene words of the prisoner's lexicon.

"Go on," I reassured her. "The language she used will not shock us on your account. But please use the words she did, that we know the true state of affairs."

Mary nodded. "She said," she stated in faltering words, her cheeks rising in colour, "'Fuck her, let the old bitch die'."

There was a whispering about the room, which Lord Justice Coltman brushed away with a sweep of his hand. Mary continued.

"About five months ago she beat her with a whip again, and this time when I interfered she threatened to do the same to me."

"Do you think she would ever have used the whip against you?" Mr Phillimore joined me.

Mary Corfield did not deliberate. "I do not believe so, in my heart," she replied charitably. "I believe Kitty's anger, I mean, Miss Newton's anger, was towards her mother. She always said Mrs Newton had lived too long and kept her out of her money."

At this, I noted, the prisoner's shoulders rose slowly, then sank. She had sighed at this; I imagined she was tired of hearing the details of her ire related yet again.

"She often said," Mary continued, "that her mother would send her to her end; I believe she meant that one day, she believed she would hang for her murder. She had terrible thoughts, did Kitty; she would wish her mother's legs cut off at the knees, and she said that when Mrs Newton was finally dead she would drive a stake through her heart. One time she tried to choke her, to force a handkerchief down her throat. I sent for Mr Doughty that time, and I kept the handkerchief all this time, for I was sure it might be used as evidence one day." And here the clever little thing pulled out a handkerchief from her pocket, one which we knew nothing of, which she had kept for just such a moment. She straightened it out and held it up all speckled with old brown blood, and all about the room people gasped in horror.

"Objection; the sighting of a bloodied handkerchief is nothing to this case," retaliated Mr Kettle for the defence quickly. "It might have come from your own nosebleed. Let us remain focused on the facts."

Lord Justice Coltman reiterated this stance, and the handkerchief disappeared back into the pocket of Mary Corfield, but the mark of it was still imprinted in the minds of the gentlemen present in the jury despite her rapid, apologetic curtsey.

"Please," Mr Phillimore remonstrated, "continue to tell the courtroom anything more that might attest to the relationship between mother and daughter."

"There was a thunderstorm, on a Sunday I remember, last year in the summer," Mary continued, her remembrances coming naturally to her, it seemed. "It was raging, and I said to her, 'Kitty, a thunderbolt has fallen somewhere'. To which she replied, 'Yes, and I pray it has fallen right on that old devil'. And once her mother came starving to our door and asked for food as she was feeling very faint, and Miss Newton answered, 'That fucking old bitch, she can clem to death'."

"'Clem' meaning?" I asked for clarification.

"To starve, sir," replied Mary most clearly.

"When Miss Newton abused her mother," I pursued, "however did you stop her?"

"I often sent for Mr Doughty, Mr William Doughty, sir," Mary replied. "Mr Dyer's nephew, he lived not 200 yards from us. I'd shout out the door for a lad to go, or if I could I'd run myself. Sometimes the things she did required me to stay and get between them, and other times I could leave them whilst I fetched him."

"Can you give an example?" asked Phillimore. "What sort of treatment did her mother meet with at the hands of the prisoner?"

Mary nodded. "Once she threw a bucket of water all over her mother as she stood in the yard, and when I said to give her dry clothes, Miss Newton wouldn't allow it. She said, 'Let her bide in her wet; let us hope that by the morning, she will be dead'. Anne Newton never came across as a saint, mind you. She was a drinker and her words could sting. And she smoked like a chimney. She had set herself alight before now, smoking on the sofa in the kitchen at Mr Dyer's; Miss Newton would let her sleep over in front of the fire. And she'd burned her dress before, and on another occasion her apron, from being too close to the flames. When she lived at Skelding's Cottage she had also set fire to herself. She wasn't capable really of taking care of herself, being so extravagant in her ways and always so cold. Always cold she was, so she liked it by the fire..." her words trailed away. The courtroom was silent for a heavy moment whilst we all imagined the smoke. Then I knew I must forge onwards.

"Was there ever remorse shown by the prisoner?" I asked.

"Sometimes," Mary conceded. "She always said, once the passion had faded, so too did her anger. Sometimes she was regretful afterwards, but other times she would say she ought to have finished her off."

"In the time leading up to the incident on the 4th of December," Mr Phillimore asked, "what were relations between the mother and the daughter like?"

At this, most apparently, Miss Newton raised her head.

"They were more peaceful," Mary admitted, and here the prisoner appeared to give a little nod. "In the week before the incident they certainly were. Anne Newton had just moved into new lodgings a week prior with a Mr Ball in the Lower Churchway. She'd been in and out of lodgings since Miss Maria left to learn to be a dressmaker, but Anne Newton always struggled to pay the rent wherever she landed up. Kitty, Miss Newton that is, had helped her find this new lodging. They seemed more content with each other then. It seemed to be to both their liking, and they had been planning on making it nice for her; Kitty had talked to Mr Ball of papering the room for her and all. Miss Newton's daughter, Miss Maria, having gone away to work, Anne was lonely, you see, so me and Kitty were all she had. They were close, Anne Newton and Kitty's daughter,

Maria. That girl was afraid of her mother though. I heard Maria say that she was afeared her mother would kill her grandmother. It was always a fear, for all of us."

"Tell me about Anne Newton and her smoking," Mr Phillimore coaxed. "Did she carry her smoking paraphernalia in her pocket?"

"She smoked a pipe," Mary said. "She lit it with her Lucifer matches. She'd leave them on a chair, I believe, at her bedside. She smoked in bed, Kitty said, with a candle in a tin mug on her lap to see by. In fact, Mr Ball complained of it as soon as she moved in. She carried the pipe and the matches in a basket with her when she came to see us. I never did see her carry it in a pocket, but perhaps the matches might have been carried in her bosom at times. She'd set herself alight at least twice before, once at Skelding's Cottage and another time. She burned the corner of the sofa cushion at Mr Richard Dyer's too, once before."

"And on the night of the 4th of December last year, in the year of our Lord 1848," I came to the point, for this girl was the most crucial witness to the whole case. "Can you tell me, in your own words, from your own recollection, exactly what happened?"

Chapter Ten
The Death of Anne Newton

Mercy Newton

The Watering
4th of December 1848

Underhill Street is calf-deep in the freezing, stinking brown water that has run down St Mary's Steps, down the Cartway and cannot find its way past the buildings on either side of the road down to the lower ground, picking up the dross from the gutter on its way. Mary wades through it quickly, knowing that to leave those two alone might spell disaster, and dreading to think what turds and muck are in that water bumping against her ankles. The closest public house is only about a hundred yards away, a grotto of a place that sells cheap rum and whose landlord is delighted to see a customer on a night such as this, for those brave or foolish enough to venture out tonight are frequenting public houses on higher ground this evening where their boots won't get wet. Mary tarries not and does not dally with small talk at the bar. She cannot risk leaving the two Newtons together longer than she must. She is half-expecting to have to break up a fight, as she sloshes back across Underhill Street, through the yard and down the ramp, past the door to the brewhouse and into the kitchen, her skirts waterlogged and heavy, pushing the door open tentatively. The two Newtons are sitting companionably, a mug of beer and an empty plate for each, discussing the best way to bake a potato using Anne's tiny grate. Mary plonks down the rum, but before she can say a word a sneezing fit is upon her, and Mercy grips the bottle, telling her mother,

"This is not for you. But, Mary, you must have one for that cold you are festering with requires a little warmth." She turns to her mother with a shake of her head. "Beer is enough for you," she tells her, pouring her own portion of the drink into a tin mug. "For myself, it'll take this much to warm me; I'm feeling the damp this evening."

Anne says nothing in Mary's presence about the rum. She meekly takes her beer in hand and mutters her thanks, and the habitual pleading and begging that both have come to expect from her does not surface. Mary catches Mercy's gaze. Both are shocked by the change that has come over her recently. Mary cups her rum and sips slowly, a sneeze here or there, unbuttoning her boots and taking a seat on the sofa to warm her damp skirts. At length, Mercy goes to the pantry and returns with a butter boat full of dripping. There is still bread and cheese on the table. Anne takes another slice of it, slaps on a bit of dripping and munches, and Mercy, Mary notices, takes a swig from the rum bottle. Soon Mary is feeling sleepy, and when Anne Newton takes a place beside her on the sofa, still chewing some cheese, and reaches for her basket to take out her pipe for a smoke, she starts to think of bed. Anne is chattering to her as she fusses with her pipe, lights up a Lucifer and puffs her stinking smoke so that Mary's eyes sting. Certainly, by half past nine, Mary is tired and choking enough to make her excuses and retire, satisfied that there will be no squabbling this evening. Mother and daughter are now relaxing most sociably, and Mercy is preparing to undress for the evening. She often undresses here before the big fire and throws on her house robe for warmth. Anne, it seems, will be spending the night on the sofa before the fire, as she has done many times before.

Mary shuts the kitchen door on the pair of them and listens for a moment, and once she is completely satisfied that they are calm and all is well, she mounts the stairs. She undresses and, in her nightgown, slips inside Richard Dyer's room. He is sleeping soundly, gurgling a little, and she climbs into her little bed made up on a sofa in the corner and settles down. The fire in the grate is burning low, sending a flickering, orange light about the room. Mary is used to this place by now, used to this room and the sounds, snores and otherwise that rise from her master's bed. She has nothing to fear from Richard Dyer – he has been confined to his bed now since his apoplexy, and she is confident to fall asleep in his room, although she sleeps lightly in case he needs her. However, tonight, no matter how she tries, she cannot sleep. The rain is battering the windowpanes and no matter the thickness of the curtains, it is loud and fearful, so strong that she imagines it could break the glass. After a while, she hears the thud of the kitchen door closing. It is never normally closed, she thinks, but perhaps there is a draught – it is an unholy night after all. She lies there, her bedcovers up about her ears, thinking of the river water and how it will rush beneath the buttresses of the bridge sucking detritus with it. Suddenly there is a little shriek downstairs. She is up in an instant, out onto the landing and down the stairs, but as she reaches the kitchen door, she realises it was perhaps a shriek of laughter for the mother and daughter are talking in there, and she presses her ear to the door to listen. Their voices hold no malice. More – there is merriment. Mercy has taken more rum, Mary thinks, and only hopes that she has kept her resolve to keep her mother from it. She listens a while longer but is soon placated that nothing is amiss and resolves not to disturb them when they are getting along so well. Satisfied, Mary retires once more, slips back into her little sofa bed and closes her eyes. Just once more she hears a noise from downstairs as her eyes close, just once, the words, "Don't, Kitty, don't!" but Mary's eyes are already closing in that irresistible way they do when sleep is coming, and so she sleeps.

Mary knows nothing more until she is woken by the spluttering cries of Richard Dyer. She rouses herself, takes her blanket from over her face and breathes in smoke. At first, she presumes there has been a backdraft down the chimney and goes to the fire to make sure there is no ash about the place, but it is all clean and burning low, yet the whole room is somehow filled with smoke. Richard Dyer is coughing now, eyes bulging. Her own eyes are watering too; the air is too coarse to breathe well. She sees to it that he has water, quickly opens the window so that he might take air, pulls his blanket up about him so that the chill of night will not cause him harm and promises him she will look into the matter. Heart pounding, she almost trips as she descends the stairs, her nightgown bunched up so that she might move all the quicker, and out of the window in the yard she sees a light. The whole house is smoky, the air is thick with it; she bursts into the kitchen and stops for the place is too filled with smoke to be able to enter. She cannot see the room, it is so dense, and yet her feet are splashing, splashing in water as though the river has risen like never before and come inside. She slams the door and runs for Mr Doughty. The rain and the wind drive her back, the water is as high as her knees and all the buildings she can see are in darkness. She yells Mr Doughty's name before she even reaches his door, all down the street through that thick water, the cold wetness of it seeping quickly up her clothes until she is freezing and shaking, yet all she can feel is the hot sweat of panic. At last she reaches his door and brings her fists down upon it as she shouts to him. Hammering, desperately hammering.

"The house is on fire, Mr Doughty! Mr Doughty!"

At last a pale face can be seen at a window, and then after a moment the door opens and she is admitted, pulled in out of the water that has soaked her nightdress, and in she goes to be warmed and coddled by Mrs Doughty.

"Whatever is it, Miss Corfield?" she asks, as Mr Doughty, who appears half-sozzled, his hair bedraggled as though he has not long got in from the rain himself, pulls on his jacket. "Will, whatever can have happened?"

"Fire!" Mary sobs, shaking and shivering now. "You'd better come now, Mr Doughty, or your uncle is likely to be burned to death!"

Mrs Doughty wraps a shawl around her soaking shoulders as Mr Doughty, who seems to have become sober very quickly, strides forth into the beating rain, and Mary and his wife scurry after him.

The water reaches almost up to his boots in places, but Mr Doughty reaches the house quickly as the two women rush to keep up with him. As they turn into the gates, Mercy is out near the kitchen door next to the brewhouse, but before she notices them, she flits back into the house and slams the door.

"She must be fetching a bucket of water from the barrel in the brewhouse to douse the fire!" Mary yells through the rain.

There is the stink of smoke in the air but no glow, no flickering of an inferno. Nevertheless, Mr William Doughty declares they must wake anyone who might hear so that they may assist. He is certain Mr Ridley might come out to their aid.

"Fire!" he calls out, and Mary and Mrs Doughty join him in his cries.

Once satisfied that the alarm has been given to the neighbours, Mr Doughty goes first to the front door but it is, of course, locked, so he goes down the ramp and finds the kitchen door locked too, bangs upon it but nobody comes. Mary and Mrs Doughty cling to each other in the rain as he attempts ingress. Back he goes through the dark, through the rain, back up the ramp and the steps to the front door, bangs ferociously, then sets his shoulder to it but to no avail, until at last Mercy Newton opens it and Mary can smell the rum on her. She stands glaring, holding on to the doorpost for support, but Mr Doughty pushes past her and Mary does too. They take the stairs as quickly as they can, although Mary's skirts are heavy with rain and Mr Doughty is much quicker. Up the stairs he goes two at a time to attend to his uncle and Mary follows. They find Richard Dyer cold with the window wide and half the room soaked with rain. Mary busies herself to close the window whilst Mr Doughty takes his uncle by the hand.

"Fire?" he asks. "Was there fire?"

The invalid stares up at him, eyes boggling. "Aye," is his reply. Then, "Mary."

This is of little use. Richard refers to both Mercy and Mary as Mary. Nevertheless, William nods.

"I will make sure the place is safe for you," he promises his uncle. "Mary is here, look. Miss Newton is downstairs – it was she who let me in. All are accounted for. Do not fear, Uncle." He holds water to Richard's lips, wipes his chin and then leaves him, indicating for Mary to come with him and to tell him what has unfolded this evening. Mary cannot conceal the truth.

"Anne Newton was here," she tells him. "They drank rum."

"The old baggage must have set herself alight again with her damned pipe," he returns, as they reach the foot of the stairs. They repair to the kitchen where they find Mercy standing swaying in the doorway. He tuts.

"Here is Miss Newton, drunk. Her mother, no doubt, is as drunk as she is and has set fire to the house again." He is triumphant in his hypothesis, but Mercy will not have it.

"It is not *I* that is drunk," she returns unsteadily. "Look to yourself."

William Doughty looks her up and down. "But I can stand, whereas you cannot," he retorts, at which she snorts, and Mary looks past her to see that the sofa is indeed burning dimly, rising smoke. She goes to it and realises that beneath her feet, water is sloshing. Mr Doughty smothers this small blaze with a cloth from the grate, as Mercy, in words awash with drink, asks his wife, "Do you remember when she set fire to herself before?"

Mrs Doughty replies, eyeing her with the sort of canny observance she is capable of. "I do, but that was an accident. This seems wilful to me."

Mary takes the cloth he has used to smother the smouldering couch from Mr Doughty and replaces it near the range and there, she notes, sit an empty butter boat, which was full when she went to bed, and an oil bottle, which she knows full well was topped up the previous day and now is empty. She looks about for Anne Newton, but she is certainly not here. Her basket, however, sits in the water on the floor, and the sofa, which is where she must have settled herself to sleep, is wet all through the seat. There is, most oddly, a stocking hanging on the iron fastening before the crevice in the shutters blotting out the darkness.

"You and your mother have been near to burning Mr Dyer in his bed," Mr Doughty remonstrates, but Mercy is unperturbed.

"What have *I* to do with my mother?" she asks sharply, and goes to a cupboard, unlocks it and pulls out a rum bottle, half empty. "Rum?"

"I won't drink with a wretch like you," he replies, at which Mercy glares at him, takes the bottleneck in her hand and swigs straight from it, staring him down with her rolling eyes the whole while. Mary feels a rising panic now, for the old woman.

"Look at you, you can hardly stand," Mr Doughty,

remonstrating, tells her, and Mercy replies that she is not drunk, but lies down on the wet sofa nevertheless.

"I will look for Anne," Mary declares.

"You'll not find her here," Mercy's words rise from the sofa. Mr Doughty passes by her and out into the hallway to begin the search for the old woman, and Mary passes out of the door into the yard, back out into the rain and the darkness, whereupon through the open door of the kitchen she hears Mercy cry from her stupor, "Oh passion! Passion! Yet when the passion is over, I forgive sincerely!"

The rain is unforgiving, almost deafening in its onslaught, and the light from the kitchen is obstructed by the form of Mrs Doughty, who comes forth to follow Mary but lingers there in the doorway behind her, and her words ring out amidst the beating of the rain, "Passion may compel people to undertake sinful things."

It is dark here, and Mary steps forth towards the brewhouse, for Mary has determined that if she were alight upon a sofa, she would get herself to that barrel of water that sits within and douse herself. Too dark to see, she steps upwards, feeling her way, but something in the torrential blackness touches her foot. Something is obstructing her. She stares down at a pair of feet in their stockings. Her eyes adjust, and the smell now of roasted flesh comes up to meet her nostrils. She falls backwards, back down the steps, gagging. She must get to the light, she must get to Mr Doughty and his wife. As she reaches the doorway, she emits a scream.

"Good God, the old woman is dead! She is burnt to death!"

Mr Doughty streaks past her, as Mary staggers back into the kitchen, one hand over her mouth, the other clutching her heart. The door shuts behind him. Mrs Doughty clutches at the table. There is no movement from the sofa. In comes William Doughty, his face as pale as a sheet. Mary cannot move. The vision of what she has seen is emblazoned behind her eyelids. She stares down at Mercy lying there, rum-soaked on the sofa, and knows not if she ought to feel pity or fury towards her. Mr Doughty steps gravely forward and stands before Mercy Newton, who opens one eye to take him in.

"You wretch," he chokes, his face wet and red. "You have murdered the old woman at last."

The First Trial: Spring Assizes

Recollections of Thomas Whitmore, MP

Apley Estate, Bridgnorth

17th of March 1849

Witness Statements – Mary Corfield and Police Constable Evans

Mary Corfield had already related this night at the coroner's inquiry. Despite the three months that had passed between the crime and the spring assizes, she was visibly shaken at telling of it again. Her tears became her; her sweet charitable nature towards the deceased did her credit. As a witness she seemed faultless.

"She was lying on the brewhouse steps, her legs sticking out to the yard," she told the courtroom. "Lying on her front. There were sheets near her feet, the ones she'd have used to cover her on the sofa, I think. And her little bag was there, that she used to fold up and use as a pillow and there was blood upon it. There was water everywhere, all over the steps, all inside the brewhouse, and Anne, erm, the deceased, she was soaked too."

"It had been raining, had it not?" I pressed. "Would you say the water was due to the rain?"

Mary paused. Her reply to any question was never hurried, never a quick, unconsidered answer.

"It was raining like the heavens were coming down. But I would say that the amount of water on the brewhouse floor was not normal for any amount of rain," she assessed solidly. "I would say that rain doesn't get in there like that. It was like it had been splashed all over her, like a bucket or more had been emptied over her, there was such a quantity of it."

"And what was the prisoner doing whilst the body of her mother was discovered?" Mr Phillimore asked her. The courtroom had descended into the sort of silence that overtakes the human race when a tragedy of incomprehensible import has occurred.

"She was on the sofa," Mary described. "Lying there as though asleep, but she wasn't; her eyes opened and closed whenever she was listening. And when Mr Doughty said it was a good thing that I'd fetched him, she looked at me and she smiled in such a peculiar way. And she said, 'It was you then, who fetched him. You have begun something now'."

At this I observed the prisoner make a surreptitious movement. Her veiled face did not adjust its set, but her hands, her gloved fingers, balled into fists. One must admit Mary's retelling of that night was just as accusatory in its detail as it had been in the guildhall. Miss Newton must have been furious beneath all those layers of black cloth.

"Mr and Mrs Ridley from one of the nearby houses came," Mary went on. "Mrs Doughty had sent for a policeman. Mrs Ridley came into the kitchen, and Kitty, I mean, the prisoner, Miss Newton here, beckoned her over and put her arms around her neck as if to kiss her, but asked her, 'Is she dead?' And Mrs Ridley said she was. And then Miss Newton said, 'Get her hence into the parlour'. Then she put a cushion over her face, let out such a moan and said, 'I do not want to see anything'."

"In your opinion," I inquired, "was the prisoner drunk at this point?"

"Very much," Mary Corfield replied. "Drunk as I've ever seen her. Oh and then," she paused, struck, no doubt, with the horror of it all once more. "She sat up dead straight and said that she was so happy she might be in heaven, and then she lay back down and closed her eyes. And then, after a little while, when a little crowd had gathered in the yard, for none of us had been quiet about it thinking the place was on fire and we had roused half the people in the street including my brother, William Corfield, she came up from the sofa and was standing next to him, and she flung her arms about him and tried to kiss him!" At this there was a murmur from the spectators that such a notion might have taken place in Miss Newton's head whilst her mother lay dead not thirty yards away. Mary, however, did not allow the unrest to swerve her. "And not once did she go to see where her poor mother lay."

At this point of the trial I would have given much to have the veil removed from the bonnet of Miss Mercy Newton. It hid too much. Her reactions might have been priceless in swaying the jury one way or the other but they were too easily hidden by the drape of the material. I hoped, and here I may appear callous, but I hoped that she was seething, that she was riling in some form of earthly torment for her behaviour.

"There is something else," Mary told the court suddenly. "About a week or so later, after the..." she floundered for a moment, "death of the deceased," she managed, and I noted she did not label it as 'murder', "when I mopped the kitchen, it became evident that there were footprints. Oiled, bare footprints on the floor that had been hidden in all the muck and water. Three footprints and a handprint. That night, someone in bare feet walked and touched that floor, and touched that floor and their feet and hand were oily."

There was a silence about the courtroom. To a man they must have been running the evidence that Mary Corfield had furnished them with through their imaginations. Either, one must postulate, they were imagining a burning woman, pushing herself up to a standing position with her oiled hand and her oily feet, stumbling toward the brewhouse; or they were imagining a murderous daughter, barefoot and having poured oil over her mother, bending down perhaps to see if her mother is awake, placing an oily hand upon the flagstones to listen for a moment before striking a match and letting it fall.

This most heinous image was left to inhabit the minds of the jury. Her initial statement completed, Mary was removed from the stand to be replaced by Police Constable Richard Evans. Still that veiled face remained hidden from sight. Her bonnet dipped low, the brim wide, her face obscured. If Huddlestone and Kettle had, as I would have done were I working in her defence, advised their client to appear penitent, there was nothing to denote this in her form.

PC Evans swore his oath and stood, hands clasped behind his back, chest puffed out, filled with the gravity of the matter before him. Without question, this moment in his career must have been the most momentous for the police constable thus far; other than drunkenness and the odd case of battery, Bridgnorth has always been a place of small concerns. This man would indubitably talk of this moment for the rest of his days, and his children and grandchildren would talk of it too. A defining moment indeed. His fame, however, would be nothing to the infamy of the woman in the black veil; her name and the name of all her kin, Newton, will outlast us all. Long after she swings.

Chapter Eleven

Maria Newton

Wolverhampton

1848-1849

Maria Newton is fifteen years old, accomplished enough in her trade now for a girl of her age and has made a name for herself as a hard worker. She lodges with a family called the Biddles, whose son, Edward, is three years her senior and learning carpentry with a patient master and is attentive. There is talk that perhaps when she is old enough they might make a good match. She is unsure of him as kind as he is, for she is still certain that the world might have more to offer her than the graft of a working-class wife. She hankers to see more of the country, to work in London perhaps, that she might escape further from the shackles both Batch Pool Lane and her grandmother's drinking habits had imposed upon her.

It will soon be Christmas, and she has mastered the use of a Singer sewing machine to produce finer items than she has ever made before. She will, she has determined, take money home at Christmas, money for Anne, though she knows it will be squandered and one of her beautifully embroidered handkerchiefs for her mother that she might admire her daughter's skills.

Wolverhampton is bigger than she had ever imagined, and in the evenings and her Sunday afternoons she explores with Edward Biddle, his brother and other girls who work with her. Together they are a merry bunch, and the world seems, for her at least, that there might be opportunity.

Then she is accosted by the cries of a newspaper boy and her world ends.

"Matricide in Bridgnorth!" comes the cry. "Murderess in custody!"

Something within her stays her tread. Her heart falls.

"Go on without me," she tells the others.

The girls carry on their way without question, but Edward lingers. She waves him on but cannot speak now for her heart is pounding and she is fumbling for a coin. With shaking hands she takes a newspaper and there before her is her mother's name.

"Oh God!" She falls to her knees there in the street, in the mire. Edward is at her elbow.

"You know them?" He has not read the print. He steers her to a low wall where she may rest. "Who is it?"

Maria is crying and retching now. Her tears fall as she reads and devours this lie, for a lie it must be – how can this have happened?

Edward is reading now, leaning over and he turns to her, speechless.

"We are cursed, us Newtons," she tells him. "And it has caught them both."

The newspaper falls from her grip. Edward's arm is around her and she must lean on him, for if she cannot lean on anything she will fall to the ground.

"Curses are not real," Edward tells her fervently. "You are not cursed. Marry me, Maria, and I will take care of you."

She turns to him and smiles. "I'm too young, and it would be better for you if you didn't," she tells him. She scrabbles at the newspaper, gathers it up and reads again. A coroner's inquest at Bridgnorth in the guildhall has been indecisive. Her mother will go to trial at the March assizes in Shrewsbury. "I have to go," she tells him. "I will hand in my notice. I must go to Shrewsbury."

Nothing Edward can do or say will deter her. Eventually the most he can do is secure lodging for her with a friend, William Ellis, and his new wife over in Shrewsbury. Maria is grateful, but she cannot reciprocate any feelings he has, for she is wrestling with such loss that nothing he says or does can redirect her thoughts. She hands in her notice and goes about her daily work like a little ghost, pale and broken, until the day comes when she must set off to Shrewsbury on the train. She is handed references for future employment, and she packs these away amongst the newspaper cuttings she has amassed, so that she might piece together what has happened. Edward Biddle comes with her to the station, but his presence only serves to annoy her.

"I will be waiting for you," he tells her, as her train draws in. "I love you."

She stares at him for a moment. How selfish, she thinks, that he wants to deter her and draw her from her purpose with these words. They do not work on her. She is immune to them. A mother ought to love her daughter, and a daughter ought to love her mother, and look at how that turns out. No, love is a lie.

"Goodbye, Edward," she says and takes her bags from his hand. "Do not wait for me. Newtons bring nothing but sorrow. I am sure that you are better off without me."

"That's not true," he tells her. "And one day when you need me, I will be here."

She nods. Numbly she alights the train and dutifully waves to him as it draws out of the station. She hopes to God she never does need him, for she is sure that Edward Biddle would be better off without her. One so kind and devoted as he ought not be tied to someone like her, whose blood runs thick with a curse so heavy that it sucks the life from those it is closest to.

She determines never to speak to Edward Biddle again. To

keep him safe. To protect him. That is how one can show love, or at least, friendship, she tells herself. And she allows herself tears now, for she knows that once she is in Shrewsbury, she must prepare herself, ready herself, buttress herself, to watch her mother hang.

The First Trial: Spring Assizes
The Coroner's Findings

Recollections of Thomas Whitmore, MP

17th of March 1849

The Murder Act of 1751 had been the abiding deterrent for murder in this country for many a year, and as such, when Miss Newton's cousin, John Newton, was hanged for the murder of his wife in 1823, he knew the penalty full well. This Act sought to deter murderers further, not just using the threat of hanging as a deterrent, but also with an abhorrent penalty post-mortem, that is, the murderer would be denied a Christian burial, instead having the corpse gibbeted or else given up for medical dissection. *Lex talionis* – the punishment resembles the crime. This would have been the fate of the unhappy prisoner's cousin's corpse following his hanging in 1823. Since then the law had changed – Miss Newton would not be subject to dissection. Of this, I am sure, the gentlemen of the defence would have apprised her.

Of course, the miserable wretch had heard the findings of the coroner before and the details of her mother's post-mortem. She knew well herself what had occurred on the night of the 4th of December. Her conscience, one might hope, must have been tested sorely in hearing details of her mother's demise in such cold and clinical terms laid bare, as it was before a room full of strangers. Coley and Newell, the surgeons tasked with the initial post-mortem and delivery of coronary evidence, took to their feet.

Miss Newton sat motionless as the findings were announced.

Mr Coley began. "Anne Newton was found face down, her skin burned, bare footed, her legs on the brewhouse steps and the rest of her lying inside the brewhouse, drenched and lying there in water."

For the purposes of the uninitiated reader, British law states that a cause of death must be found in order to find a murderer guilty. At the initial inquest at the guildhall, no such agreement upon cause of death had been made due to the inability of the medical men to agree. Therefore, the jury were intent upon the words now iterated, for their decision must be made clearly from these coroner's findings.

"The deceased was on her belly face down, her hands linked across the upper breast. Her nose, obvious in life, was compressed down, now not rising over an eighth of an inch from the face. The surface of the whole body was burned, charred. From just above the knees almost up to the throat, the thighs and body at the front, the lips and tip of the tongue were burned. About the outside of the mouth was swollen and livid. One toe had been bruised, as though trodden upon; there was no blood or redness upon it. The first examiner presumed that burning had been the cause of death."

Here now was the rub: would the medical gentlemen involved in the coroner's delivery of evidence make much of the disagreement regarding the cause of death?

"The burn marks on the sofa were the width of a person's shoulders, the evidence states, as though the deceased had been sitting up at the end. The butter boat which had been, in the words of Mary Corfield, 'full of dripping', was empty, and a pint bottle of lamp oil that had been almost full when Mary Corfield went to bed was found empty. There were marks of grease and oil on the pillowcase, the sofa and the sheets found near the body.

The butter boat was found upon the hob slightly singed."

Here many of the jury I noted, glanced again at the prisoner. Indeed, I myself could not banish from my imagination an image of this devilish form dousing her sleeping mother in oil and lard before a raging fire.

Lord Justice Coltman asked Dr Samuel Wright, a professor of clinical medicine at Queen's College, Birmingham, to step forward.

"Dr Wright is an authority in the sphere of asphyxia and devised a prize-winning paper on asphyxia by submersion," was his introduction. Also, a Mr David Bolton, lecturer on clinical anatomy, also at Queen's College. "Gentlemen, your opinions on the evidence please."

Dr Samuel Wright stroked his substantial whiskers, a habit that conveyed his solemnity and fastidious nature, I thought. "It is our joint opinion, having examined the evidence, that without the application of oil or dripping, the body would not have burned so substantially; oil or dripping would have intensified the burns to the manner which were seen upon the body," he told the court, and a wave of gasps abounded the place. Here I found myself nodding. He waited until all was settled again before he continued. "It appeared, initially, that the deceased had burned to death, however, further investigation refuted this."

The court was all aflutter once more, and I exchanged a knowing look with Mr Phillimore. Had evidence suggested Anne Newton burned to death, the jury might well cling to the opinion that she set herself alight as she was wont to do accidentally with her pipe. Here an esteemed medical man was justifying our prosecution most scientifically.

Mr Bolton adjusted his glasses and took on the delivery of evidence. "One small blister containing a straw-coloured fluid on the inner right leg," he maintained gruffly, checking his notes carefully for the details. "Four inches below the knee, far below the place where the burning started. There were no blisters on the body. No redness where the injured and uninjured tissues touched, nor around that one blister on the leg."

Mr Coley nodded and here interjected. "Taylor, in his Medical Jurisprudence, says that in the absence of signs, there is no data whereon to decide whether burning took place either before or after death."

Drat his caution.

The other medical men rumbled. Dr Wright added, "The absence of marks evidently signifies that burning took place postmortem."

Mr Bolton, "Of course, the colour of the blood in the lungs proves this."

"In your opinion, gentlemen, the burning occurred after death?" Justice Coltman pushed, requiring clarification.

The responses given were most strongly in favour of the burning having occurred after death; no screams were heard, which would undoubtedly have been the case had the woman awoke on fire and dragged herself out to the brewhouse.

"On further investigation," Mr Bolton continued, "during internal examination, a congestion of the lungs, heart and brain was discovered. This proves without doubt that death was due to suffocation."

"Yet no marks were found upon the neck," said Mr Newell. "No signs of strangulation."

This was a course of confusion and disagreement which must be averted. I rapidly posited the prosecution's theory, "We propose that the prisoner put something over the mouth and nose of the deceased, say a cushion, pressing it down forcibly enough that it broke her nose, flattening it in the aforementioned manner, thereby smothering her. Then once dead the prisoner set fire to her, dragging her out of the kitchen and leaving her to burn on the steps of the brewhouse."

The prisoner, I warranted, had little memory of what happened. It was well-known that she had imbibed a quantity of rum that night, enough to unseat even the heartiest of gentlemen, but perhaps she had flashes of remembrance as some drunks do. I wondered if she had a recollection of the smell of burning flesh. Her mother's burning flesh. How it must have stayed in the nasal passages afterwards, perhaps still she was tormented by it. Perhaps a remembrance of smoke all around, the room spinning, the heat of the fire and the stinging as her own flesh was caught by the heat. Her mother's corpse, a hellish furnace. But I digress; all of this conjecture was my own. In actuality, the prisoner sat as unrepentantly motionless as ever.

Mr Huddlestone set forth a short summary of the defence, "Anne Newton smoked when she was abed and had set herself alight on more than one occasion. On the night of December the 4th, or the early hours of the 5th, she set herself on fire once more. Shocked and terrified, she ran into the brewhouse but was overcome with flames. She suffocated the death lying on the steps, the smoke preventing the ingress of air. This would," he addressed the jury specifically here, "instantly induce suffocation by what is medically termed a spasm of the glottis. A noxious vapour, indeed any irritant, can cause this, can it not, gentlemen?"

Mr Coley nodded. "It is feasible that suffocation can occur should flames inhibit the ingress of air," he admitted.

Mr Thursfield, that irritant of the case, then took the opportunity to disagree most loudly. "I cannot conceive," he expostulated forcefully, "that in this case the deceased was suffocated by the flames."

"I agree with Thursfield," came Mr Newell's response, one which surprised me, for back at the guildhall, he had been unable to agree with Thursfield. "This means of suffocation might be possible were the body entirely surrounded by flames, but in this case only one side of the body was on fire."

Mr Bolton added, "If the flames were reoriented by mechanical means and the body was already insensible, this may have occurred, if not, I deem it implausible."

Good God, I thought, now we have four men unable to agree. However in this case, their confusion appeared to lend credence to the prosecution. Namely, that Anne would not have suffocated from an accidental fire caused by her lackadaisical use of tobacco, but that the flames were caused by a dousing of oil. Mr Phillimore, I thought, winked at me, but my mind was ill at ease. This disagreement could mean the difference between a hanging and the woman walking away unpunished.

Suddenly a voice unheard before, unsure and quavering, rose up from the jury. "Your honour, after all we have heard, I have some evidence which I believe is important."

What new fresh evidence hitherto unknown would rise from this interjection? Even the silent prisoner cocked her head beneath her bonnet, and for a moment her razor-sharp lips could be observed open slightly in surprise, as I accede, were mine. One of the jury was standing, adjusting his waistcoat.

"My name is John Whatmore," he said clearly, although his voice was shaking. "And I live near The Watering, in Bridgnorth. On the night of the murder or the death, whichever way you think it, on the 4th of December, I was close by the house and I observed Mary Corfield at half past ten in the evening outside talking to a man I did not know. And yet she said that she went to bed at half past nine."

The room was silent. Justice Coltman stroked his beard for a moment. "Can you be sure it was Mary Corfield?" he asked slowly.

John Whatmore nodded. "I could see her plainly by the lights that were lit," he answered earnestly. "The reflection from the gas lamp on the bridge, the lamp post at Hop Pole and the lights near the Wesleyan chapel. There was enough light to know her by."

Mr Justice Coltman considered a moment. "How close would you say you came to her?"

I found my mouth was dry. This man was making a mockery of our best witness and her statement regarding the whole evening. This man was making a liar out of Mary Corfield.

"Within a few feet as I passed by," John Whatmore told the courtroom. "So when she says she went to bed at half past nine, she has chosen to withhold something."

Mr Justice Coltman eyed him and mulled it over for a while. I turned to Phillimore. Almost imperceptibly, he shook his head and took a breath. Whatever considerations Coltman was making it could upturn the whole proceeding. Mary Corfield's credibility had been questioned. I glanced at the prisoner and remembered that when her cousin stood trial for murder, he and the coroner had attempted to interfere with the jury – could this Whatmore have been paid to perjure himself? My suspicions aroused, I watched Miss Newton for any sign, anything that might give herself away. Yet I knew that all her money in the world had been taken from her to pay for her defence; with what could she bribe this man to make this accusation?

"Does she have friends we do not know about?" I whispered to Phillimore. "Could he have been paid to speak out against Corfield?" Yet neither of us knew the answer to this. I resolved to find out.

At last, Coltman turned to the jury. "The full case for the defence will be heard at nine o'clock on Thursday morning," he announced in a definite tone. "For now, gentlemen of the jury, ensure that you are fully apprised of the facts for the prosecution and ensure that you do not discuss the proceedings out of this court."

I watched Miss Newton as she was taken away for another night of uncertainty, alone in a cell.

I wondered what sort of toll it must take upon a person to hear the hellish detail of their crime picked apart again and again.

What sleep might she have, perchance to dream betwixt now and Thursday that would not be pricked with night terrors of smoke, burning, hellish heat and the stench of her own mother's roasting flesh?

The First Trial: Spring Assizes
The Defence

Recollections of Thomas Whitmore, MP

22nd of March 1849

The defence of the unhappy prisoner fell to Mr Huddlestone and Mr Kettle; the forty-three pounds of Miss Newton's worldly goods perhaps not stretching to a defence of more venerable lawmen.

Having dissected the case from all quarters, Phillimore and I were prepared for a poor argument in the woman's defence.

"This is the day, Whitmore," Phillimore greeted me as we made our way into the courtroom that fine morning. "Let the medical men drive the jury into our hands with their confusion and contradictions, and we shall see her hanged on Monday."

We settled ourselves in the courtroom to await the arrival of the prisoner and the farce we anticipated from the defence team.

The initial defence in the coroner's inquiry back in Bridgnorth had implied that Anne Newton may have taken her own life and they had brought forth a witness to corroborate this. When this did not appear to stick, they had pushed for the medical evidence to prove that she burned herself to death with her pipe. They asked Mr Thursfield for a second autopsy, a move that only blighted the inquiry with confusion, and I was anticipating more of the same.

"Mark my words," I whispered to Phillimore as the prisoner

appeared and every voice twittered into silence, "the suggestion of suicide will not be brought back into it. It did not stand before and it will not stand now. They will suggest she set herself alight. There are enough people to corroborate that she had done that at least twice before."

I was sure that this would be the case. Thursfield's second autopsy had caused him to disagree with Mr Coley, asserting that he now believed Anne Newton had died by strangulation (either by force or from the fumes of the flames that had been exacerbated by oil on the clothing), and that the burning had been a subsequent event. This had sent the jury into turmoil. The disagreement between the two had ensured that the majority of the jury had shied away from a verdict of 'wilful murder'. Thursfield's suggestion that the smoke from the fire might have suffocated her was enough to rattle their consciences. Indeed, nine had averred that 'found burnt' was a more accurate verdict as none could be sure now of the cause of death.

Thursfield's alteration in his stance was, in my opinion, the largest reason that Miss Newton had not already taken her last breath. This then was the argument Phillimore and I were waiting to tear apart. The medical men who would put forward their opinions today must agree as a matter of urgency on the cause of death, or else this other jury would be put into such turmoil once more.

I observed the prisoner glance about the courtroom upon entry on this occasion, as though she sought sight of someone in particular, but soon her head returned to that bowed position she had taken on previous days.

Lord Justice Coltman was seated, and young Mr Huddlestone set himself to talk to the jury.

"Never have I felt so burdensome a task," he told them confidently but with a sympathetic tone that I judged did well to portray a gravity to the matter of his argument. The man might have made a wondrous actor, but I was unconvinced from the outset that he might be so naive as to consider his client innocent. "So burdensome a task necessitated upon me than this. I have spent a sleepless night weighing every aspect of this case. And if I feel such an obligation, what must you, the jury, judges of the life and death of this prisoner, feel?"

At this all eyes about the courtroom flitted to Miss Newton, whose hands were now deviously clasped as though in prayer and whose bonnet was dipped lower than must have been comfortable to penitently take in her boots.

"I entreat you," Huddleston continued, "dismiss from your thoughts all the representations introduced into this case by the prosecution evincing the emotions of the unhappy prisoner at the bar towards her ailing old parent. Disregard gossip and statements inclined against the prisoner. The press has, to my utter disbelief, given exposure to such rumour, none of which is apposite to the case. Empty your thoughts of it now, for this will bias you when you must be clear. This is a matter of life and death."

Here I observed the prisoner noticeably shudder and a movement of the bonnet to the side sharply to crack her neck. One eye flashed towards me as the veil moved synchronously with the bonnet, and that eye was filled with darkness.

Mr Huddlestone wove a tale of the death of Anne Newton for the jury, much as a storyteller relates folklore to children; the darkest details ignored. As I had predicted, the defence was insisting that Anne Newton suffocated from the flames that she herself had occasioned when she fell asleep smoking by the fire. They argued that when she fell forwards onto the wet brew house floor, her nose may have flattened, or perhaps it was an unrelated injury from a previous mishap. Phillimore and I exchanged glances throughout his delivery more than once.

"Entirely accidental," was his summary. "An unhappy, miserable and awful accident, of which the unfortunate woman before you is innocent. Gentlemen," he said turning to Lord Justice Coltman and then to the jury once more, "my duty over, yours, the more significant one, commences after the summing up of My Lord." He genteelly gesticulated, implying perhaps a penchant for amateur dramatics, I thought, towards Coltman. "In your hands you hold the destiny, life and death of a fellow being. If she be accountable and hangs, you are her executors; if she be innocent and hangs, her murderers."

A powerful ending I had to admit. One that must only bring to mind her infamous cousin, John Newton, who, it was said, begged for his life in this very dock.

"Weigh well every consideration," Mr Huddlestone continued solemnly, his voice deep for one of his years and fatherly, his demeanour advisory. "And I predict with certainty that your decision will be one of justice and that it will be a verdict of not guilty."

Here as though practised, Miss Newton's head rose from her boots and the veil fell back to reveal a face that might have ninety years to it for all its lines, eyes black and rimmed with red. Ringlets about the ears, a mouth downturned, thin lips, a slender nose. She did not look at me, and for this I found that I was relieved. Instead, she turned her eyes upwards as though praying to the Almighty. So fervent she seemed in her prayers that I was caught for a moment in a remembrance of our church in Stockton, and I was back there on a Sunday morning then. As a lad, I would frequent the church and there in the pews, side by side with her cousin, James Newton, our gamekeeper, Miss Newton sat, god-fearing and prayerful, and utterly ignorant of the twists and turns that life was soon to take upon her. Back then she had appeared grateful, content, happy. Could that pleasant young lady, just a few years my junior, really have strangled her mother to death and burned the corpse?

Lord Justice Coltman began his summary, and I watched Miss Newton sedately turn her red-rimmed gaze upon the jury and her face was the visage of someone who has known hell. Ragged, worn, exhausted and bitter, and I shook all sentiment from my soul once more. Her eyes roved across the jury. I believed her to be eyeing their measure. Did they appear to be against her? Were they scowling at her? Did they appear God-fearing? Would all question of their morality be immaterial were they the sort of people who love a gossip and a sensationalised newspaper print? I allowed myself to indulge in her musings for a moment and observed them in the same manner as she herself did. John Whatmore, who spoke against the validity of Mary Corfield, was still amongst them although he did not meet my gaze. I knew full well that we had not asked him to speak up. Under whose authority had he raised his head? Was it truth or fiction? These irregularities annoyed me and could prove antagonistic to our case, no matter that his words would appear to work in our favour. As her prosecution, why had he not made his information known to us? Whatever his purpose, he had been ignored for now, although to bring the jury to doubt the word of Mary Corfield could well have aided our case. I determined to seek him out and speak with him as soon as I could to ascertain for my own mind if what he had said bore validity. For now we had done with him. Lord Justice Coltman addressed the jury.

"I ask you, as did the defence," Coltman requested these earnest men. "Set aside the vile words previously asserted to have been exercised by the prisoner towards her mother. The only matter you need to establish an answer to is whether the prisoner is guilty of murder? There are ten prospective circumstances which might have resulted in murder: 1: death was induced by a cord around the mouth; 2: by imposing a cushion on the throat and nostrils of the deceased; 3: by the prisoner placing her hands around the neck and throat of the deceased; 4: death by burning; 5: death by igniting her clothes and restricting her breathing with them; 6: death by suffocation from the smoke; 7: death by burning and smothering; 8: suffocation by means unknown; 9: suffocation by forcing a handkerchief on the mouth, or 10: death by constricting her throat with the hands and smothering her mouth and nose with a cushion and handkerchief. It is not essential in my view to determine by what means suffocation occurred. Unless you are utterly convinced that Anne Newton, the deceased, died of suffocation, you must acquit the prisoner. Otherwise she must be blamed for the offence."

Ten potential murder methods, and these men only had to say that she had done it, not by what means. It was time for the jury to be incarcerated until a verdict was found. Voices rose in the courtroom: conflicting cries of "Guilty!", "Set her free!", "She's lost her mother!" and "Murderer!" I observed Miss Newton reach for the sleeve of the first officer who stepped forward to escort her back to her gaol cell, and also observed him shake her off.

Anticipating a rapid conclusion to the proceedings following the jury's departure from court, Phillimore and I repaired to the inn where we were staying, took port together and proceeded to analyse the case for the defence and its chances of swaying the jury to make the wrong decision.

"There is no case for the defence," Phillimore stated quite accurately. "Their argument largely hangs on the old woman's past misadventures with her pipe and her bedding. However it cannot account for the oil. It is incomprehensible that she might douse herself with oil, clothing and all, before settling down to sleep by the fire. Laughable."

"The case of the juror who averred to have seen Miss Corfield at the garden gate after she said she had gone to bed appears to have made little difference to the hearing thus far," I stated. "But one must question if it has impacted upon the minds of the jury – indeed, Mr Whatmore himself must make a decision as part of the jury, and he is compromised. To remove him from the jury at the late stage in which he spoke up and replace him would be impossible, however."

"If it comes to the matter of his statement," Phillimore returned, and we took more port for it seemed a good enough moment to refill our glasses. "Then he might be discussing whether Mary Corfield is a credible witness as we speak. His assertion might well cause reasonable doubt in her character, if she not only lied in court about her whereabouts after nine o'clock, but also about meeting a man in the dark in the garden. All that work you did to find out how credible she was, and here – what coincidence – a man randomly chosen for the jury has reason to doubt her on the very date of the crime which he is sitting in judgement of." He shook his head. "It is a coincidence too extraordinary to believe."

"To my mind," I told him. "The biggest problem is that there are ten possibilities to explain the old woman's death. Although Coltman requires just a judgement that suffocation was the cause, how can a jury sift through so many possibilities whilst hearing the professional medical men involved in the trial disagreeing?"

We sat mulling for a while, sombre. "If she is not found guilty," I said finally, "it will be a travesty of the British legal system. All evidence, I believe, points to her guilt. I would not work for the prosecution on a case where I believed the prisoner innocent of the crime."

Phillimore agreed most heartedly.

Late into the evening we sat, growing increasingly morose as the port took effect, until we received word from the court: The jury had nothing to tell before the morning. They could not agree and they wished to retire. The trial would reconvene in the morning.

"Dear God," I breathed turning to Phillimore. "What is there to consider? Unless we have utterly missed a crucial piece of evidence, a possibility that is as ridiculous as it is improbable, there cannot be any question of her innocence. Surely?"

However my hand still shook as I laid down my empty glass and when I took my leave from Phillimore neither of us smiled.

We repaired to our rooms, but sleep did not come easily to me that night. I found myself awake, listening to the sounds of the place being locked and barred for the night. In 1828, The Offences Against the Person Act stipulated that a murderer must be executed on the day next but one after the sentence is passed, unless of course that might be a Sunday, in which case, the execution must occur on the Monday. This being Thursday and the verdict being proclaimed in the morning, a Friday, that would mean in this case Sunday would be the day but one after the verdict. Therefore should my prosecution prevail, which if God be on the side of right it would, Miss Newton would hang on Monday.

The next morning was grey. The courtroom was grey too, as were the faces of the jury and the visage of Lord Justice Coltman. We, none of us, had slept well.

The prisoner stood ready for the verdict, and Huddlestone and Kettle stood by too, dark about the eyes, waiting for the foreman of the jury to speak. I noted the prisoner's gloved hands gripping the rail and was brought to mind the tale of her cousin once more, being manually prised from the dock with a cry of 'Dunna kill me! Dunna kill me!' What would be Miss Newton's response?

"We cannot agree," came the voice of the foreman. "Certainly not so early at eight o'clock in the morning. We cannot come to an agreement, no matter how we try."

Never have I stood in such disbelief.

Justice Coltman eyed them wearily over his spectacles. "No verdict?" he asked wearily.

"No verdict," was the reply.

Huddlestone turned to Kettle, I noted, with a brief smile and then back to Miss Newton with a barely noticeable wink. All this I saw, before turning to Phillimore, who was raking his hands through his hair.

"Then you will be discharged," said Lord Justice Coltman wearily, scanning the jury members, his tone severe yet with a faltering gait that implied his astonishment at this outcome. "Without a verdict." He pinched his temples with his thumbs. "The prisoner," he nodded at Miss Newton. "To be detained to the custody of the keeper of the gaol, upon my order, to be there incarcerated until the summer assizes, when she will again be put on trial for this most dreadful tragedy."

And with that he rose rigidly, and so did everyone else. All his movements were tired and awkward, the stiffness of an older man who had slept badly in a bed that was not his own. Voices rose about the courtroom, taunts of "Murderer!" and "Have mercy!" All about us the people rose to their feet, all mouths gaping, the courtroom a cacophony of indignation.

I leaned towards Phillimore. "It cannot be! A second trial?"

He nodded. "Legal history, surely?" he whispered back. "Has this ever occurred in the history of Britain? A murderer tried more than once?"

I stood then, though the weight of this trial bore down upon me with such a force that my legs seemed to struggle to bear my weight.

"I believe only once before," I replied. "Only once."

"I will appeal," I overheard Huddlestone say into Miss Newton's ear. "The judge has no right to discharge them like this. It is all for the good anyhow. They cannot decide that you are guilty, therefore, you will be found innocent, mark my words."

The man was incorrigible. Why he might wish for this fiend to walk the streets once more was incomprehensible.

I watched her go, the murderer, Mercy Newton, with a small look of triumph on her face, out of that room filled with people, some calling for her to hang, others calling for her to walk free. A fight broke out at the back of the room, and policemen were discharged to set it right. We rode a tidal wave of bodies to discharge ourselves from that pell-mell of indignation until we reached the street where another fight had broken out. I looked Phillimore in the eye and said, "Port?"

He shook his head. "I'm sorry, Whitmore, I find I do not have the stomach for it now."

Sadly, I recognised a similar reaction in my own gullet. "Then I will bid you goodnight," I said sombrely, and we walked our separate ways.

Chapter Twelve

Maria Newton

Shrewsbury – Cardiff

22nd of March 1849

The people pile out of the court, and Maria Newton waits in the street. A fight has started, but she cannot make out why. A torrent of suspicion, hatred, guilt and terror has sent her shaking from her lodgings to be here outside the court – for what? A glimpse of her mother as she is taken away? To gloat if she is found guilty? To weep? Maria does not know what to think or what to hope for. If her mother is found innocent and inherits Anne's £500 as she always wanted, then so be it, but Maria knows in her heart that it is unlikely; the beatings she witnessed Mercy mete out to Anne were undeniably horrifying.

She stands, staring at the current of people as they wash about her, jostling, clutching hats and canes, voices upon voices, but none of the words tell her what she needs to know.

"What happened?" she asks, but nobody stops. "What was the verdict?"

But she is left there standing alone as the people pass by, as those who have spent the past hours with her mother flow away into the town, each and every one of them disgruntled, leaving her ignorantly staring at the building which houses the woman she believes murdered her grandmother.

She turns and follows those who have left her in their wake and finds a couple of young men who have stopped to light their cigarettes in an alleyway.

"What was the verdict?" she asks, but they look at her with confusion.

"Verdict?" one spits. "I'll give you a verdict."

Maria backs away. "I… I'm sorry. I thought perhaps you were at the trial."

The other snorts. She can see now that these two have certainly not been in court. Their faces are blackened with sweat and dirt. They've been toiling all day, and now they are looking for sport.

"Ah," the snorter emits. "The trial, that woman who killed her mother, today, was it?"

"Interested in murder, are you?" The first comes closer grimacing, but Maria is backing, backing away, and as he reaches out to grab her, she flees out into the street, where a horse and carriage almost runs her over, but a pair of hands pulls her back in time.

"Slow down, little rabbit," a voice says in her ear, and she turns to find a gentleman, older, tired-looking, a little familiar. She shakes her shoulder free.

"I… there was a man, he frightened me," she tells him.

"No need to be afraid, Maria," says the man, and she blanches and almost falls in front of the next horse and carriage, but he grabs her again.

"How do you know my name?" she asks, as he sets her firmly on the pavement. She is crying now, sobbing, like a child.

"Come with me," says this man, but she is backing away from him too. "You are fatigued. Let me buy you something to eat and drink." She shakes her head, for Lord only knows what horrors he might expect in return, until he tells her, "I'm your father's brother, Edward Newton." She stares at him blankly. "I'm your uncle," he tries again.

At this, her mouth drops open. She gawps at him and points

back towards the court. "Were you...?"

"I was in the courtroom," he tells her. "I saw your mother, but I don't think she saw me."

Maria wipes her eyes and nose with her sleeve. "Will you get me something to eat?" she asks, dizzy with it all.

Edward Newton takes her to a public house just below the prison. He buys her beer and stew for them both. Maria watches him, observes his face, the lines upon it, his receding hairline and the strength of his hands.

"Do you look like my father?" she asks.

Edward sets down his beer and shrugs. "I was born the year after him," he tells her. "I'm the closest to him there is in this world."

"What was the verdict?" she asks him, gripping her beer.

He eyes her and swigs his. "What would you like it to be?"

Her very heart hurts. She cannot meet his gaze for a while, but he waits patiently, expectantly, for an answer. At last, she lifts her head to him and says,

"Cursed as we are, I believe that one less Newton might not be a bad thing for others."

Her uncle nods. "Us Newtons are certainly not long for this earth," he says. He sniffs. "But today, there was no verdict. She'll be held 'til the summer assizes."

Maria slams her beer down so hard that it splashes across the table. "So the trial is not over?"

Her soup sits growing cold before her. Edward Newton rips up some bread and dunks it into his. "She will have a second trial," he restates. "Then it will be up to the jury to decide."

She stares at him, dripping soup from his chunk of bread as he shoves it heartily into his mouth.

"Do you think she will hang?" she asks.

He sucks the vegetables from between his teeth. "Seems to

be the way a number of Newtons make their peace," he says. He eats another hunk of bread and then asks, "Are you staying round here for the trial?"

Maria Newton shakes her head. "I can't stay here any longer," she tells him. "I was working in Wolverhampton, but when I heard about the trial I had to come here. The people I'm staying with, the Ellises, they're newly married and they want me gone. I can't wait until there is an ending to this – whether she hangs or not. But I have no money, nothing to afford a roof over my head. And who would house a Newton after all this?" She can feel her tears coming again, but she wishes they wouldn't. She does not want him to think she is weak. She does not want his pity.

"Here," he says gruffly, and passes her a fistful of coins. "What will you do with it?"

She considers telling him that she wasn't begging, but what will become of her if she doesn't take his money? So she opens up her hands and he tips the coins in and she thrusts them all down deep into her pockets. If her mother is hanged, she could come back to accept her inheritance, she thinks.

"I'll go to London," she tells him. "I'll get on the train. I'll go to London or, or Manchester, and I'll find a job there. It'll be easier there, won't it? Far, far away from all of this!"

He nods. "You'll read about your mother in the papers soon enough," he says. "You'll know if she goes the Newton way."

And he makes a gesture of a noose.

Maria Newton eats the soup and drinks the beer. She is afraid of this gruff, insensitive man. She is afraid of her mother and what might happen to her mother. There is nothing here for her. She will get on a train after all. She will go anywhere, as far away as possible. She will run away from the curse of the Newtons.

As she stands alone first thing in the morning with a little parcel of belongings on the platform, she knows there is no way back, not unless her mother hangs. Around her more people wait, some with proper luggage. She is not used to trains, nor stations of this magnitude. The world is very big for a poor girl from Bridgnorth. When it arrives, the train is vast. Carriages upon carriages, and the huge great engine belching out smoke. It is a beast, rumbling to a standstill, and the people who alight are quick and nimble footed, jumping the gap from doorway to platform without a thought. She climbs aboard and finds a seat, heart beating wildly. She has, of course, only paid for the cheapest seat she can find, for the other coins Edward Newton gave her are to be used for lodgings until she finds work. She's caught the train before, from Wolverhampton to Shrewsbury, of course, but this is altogether a different sort of adventure.

She watches the station slowly start to move, and grips her seat as it jolts, past the signal boxes. Away, away, she thinks, away from anywhere that anyone knows her name. Even here in Shrewsbury she was recognised as the daughter of Mercy Newton, the killer, in the end.

As the world passes by, faster and faster outside, she closes her eyes. She has not slept for so long now that she is light-headed – she might be flying, for the speed of this train gathers momentum and off it takes her, away from it all, away from everything.

The one true impulsive thing Maria Newton has ever done is this train journey. For as she stood there at the station and looked at all the destinations she might choose from, she did not choose London, Manchester or Birmingham. She chose Cardiff. It will be the making of her, she tells herself. Or the undoing. She cares neither one way nor the other, as long as she is as far away from Mercy Newton as possible.

Good God, but when she gets there Cardiff is the largest maze that Maria Newton could ever have imagined. From the train station she treads timidly into the streets, but after a while finds that she has reached the docks, though they are nothing like the little port at Bridgnorth. Ships, huge great cargo ships, are unloading, and everywhere is busy. Everywhere is a melee of people, boxes and crates, and men half-dressed hauling huge great boxes onto wagons, cussing and stopping to drink from flasks, kicking at stray dogs that whisp their way between legs. She does not tarry here, but steps into nearby streets, looking for 'room to let' signs, but these places seem filled with nothing but public houses and insalubrious-looking dens. Men, and women too, sit or lounge in doorways, half-soaked, and a fight is breaking out at the top of the street. She spies on the corner of a street half-way up a building a sign signifying the name of the place, and instantly takes heart – Whitmore Lane. Whitmore is a name that is, if not dear to her, then at least well-known. The name Whitmore has been part of her life for as long as she can remember, and to find it here in such a monumental city filled with such heavy accents, with so many people and so much dirt, noise and clamour seems luck above luck, for all the rest of it fills her with terror and dismay and she is already sore that she got on the wrong train. London would not be this grim, she is sure. It is a sign, she thinks. And so she gravitates to Whitmore Lane, which makes her think of Thomas Whitmore, the man whose land her father took care of, the man who stood for her Uncle John and whose son now stands for the justice due to her poor dead grandmother. Whitmore Lane then will stand for her.

The lane is thronged with people, and she slips between them, tiny thing that she is, and finds what she thinks looks like a kindly, older lady standing in a doorway leaning on a stick and smoking a pipe, and says,

"Please, are there lodgings hereabout?"

The woman grips her pipestem between her lips. She is broad, tall, covered in so many layers that she might well be less broad beneath it all, and her teeth that grip the pipestem have gaps between them and one is gold.

"Why, today is your lucky day, girl," she says, and her accent is not one that carries a Welsh lilt, but English, perhaps Birmingham or Wolverhampton, Maria thinks, and instantly likes her. "There is a room come free here just recently. And for you, girl," she eyes Maria up and down, "I'll knock a bit off."

Maria stands for a moment in the muck of the lane. She looks up the lane where a huge, tattooed man is standing with two dogs on bits of rope watching two boys fighting in the dirt, and then she looks down the street where two whores are stroking opposing shoulders of a man whose eyes are rolling back in his head. She is afraid. The place is filled with voices, cussing, sailors calling to women, women calling to anyone who will hear them, but at least nobody here knows who she is. She wants to get off the street, to close a door and sit alone and cry. And so she nods.

"I'll take the room."

The woman sighs with satisfaction, steps stiffly down out of her doorway leaning heavily on her stick, pipe still in her teeth, then leans the stick up against the door post, one hand holding her skirts out of the muck, the other held out to shake hands. Maria looks down at it.

"Mrs Prothero," the woman says by way of an introduction. "This is my house. I'll be your landlady, so to speak. Welcome, Miss...?"

"Newton," says Maria, for here there is no value to that name so she needn't hide it. "Maria Newton. And I'm a seamstress by trade; if you know of any work going, I'd be grateful to hear of it."

Mrs Prothero drops her hand, takes out the pipe and laughs and laughs. "There are trades that'll earn you a sight more than sewing, girl," she says once her mirth has subsided. "Come on in, child, and we will get you settled."

Maria's room is small, damp and cold. The house is full, every room is full. The noise from the street is almost as loud in here as it is out there. But she is, for the time being, alone. She sits on the bare mattress, with her little bundle of things on the boards at her feet, her bonnet beside her, and sobs.

Sobs for her grandmother. Sobs for her suffering. Sobs for her soul.

And she cries for herself, because now that her mother is a murderer Maria is alone, and Mrs Prothero seems to be the only person in the world who cares about her.

Indeed, to compound this theory, there is a knock upon the door and in hobbles Mrs Prothero observing this girl crying, throws down a pile of old blankets and clothes she has gathered for this poor, belonging-less girl and seats herself with a whoomph down on the mattress, wraps her arms about the girl, pipe between her lips and mumbles, "Cry it out, girl, get it off your chest, and see if there isn't something Mrs P can do to help set things right."

Maria lays her head on Mrs Prothero's doughy shoulder, but nothing on earth would make her tell this woman the cause of her tears. Mrs Prothero passes her a bottle.

"Medicinal. Take a drop, dear, on the tongue and you'll forget all about it."

Maria reaches out, takes the bottle that is offered and lets a drip form. A warm feeling spreads from her tongue, down her throat.

Instead of crying now, she sniffs and says, "Were you limping then, when you came in?"

Mrs Prothero snorts, then sets to with a coughing fit that makes her pipe smoke come out of her nostrils. Maria sits back until the woman is finished and then says,

"Have you hurt yourself? Can I help you at all?" Although she feels light now, as though she couldn't help even if she wanted to. Mrs Prothero offers her the little bottle again. She takes another drop.

"I spend much of each day in bed, if truth be told, girl," Mrs Prothero tells her. "Bedridden largely, am I. But I like a smoke and a look out into the world, and today I was fortunate enough to meet you whilst I was having a look out, and so I say that in't a bad thing, is it? But my old legs and my old hips and my old back, they've done enough for one day, and so I'll be getting back to bed shortly. So yes, there was a limp, but no, there's nothing that can be done for me at present." She takes her pipe from her mouth, holds it in one hand and fishes about on her tongue for a stray piece of tobacco or hair perhaps. "We must exchange your rent, girl, before I go. And tomorrow once you are settled, we must talk about meeting the rent more reliably. And tonight I'll send word over to The Lame Chicken in Charlotte Street, just the next street up, to have you a beer and a bite to eat ready for seven o'clock, for that's my nephew's pub and he's a good lad, and I'll see he doesn't take a penny from you in return."

At this Maria is pleased for she is hungry, although she feels as though she knows not how her legs work now, and perhaps she might fly there instead of walking. She is warm, now, and the world seems brighter, more fluid about her.

"Thank you," she says, her words coming more languidly. "You are very kind. I have an inheritance which I believe will be due before the month is out. And then I will repay your kindness in full." She wonders vaguely how long it will take for the newspapers to print the story over here in Wales. How long does it take for news to travel? A few days? And how long once a death penalty is given does it take for a gaol to hang a murderer?

"Do you have friends?" Mrs Prothero asks. "People who are waiting to hear from you?"

Maria blinks slowly. "There are the Ellises in Shrewsbury," she says. "And I have friends in Wolverhampton too. The Biddles." She feels she can tell Mrs Prothero anything now.

Mrs Prothero nods. "And family?" she asks.

Maria shakes her head. "I have none," she says, and these next words come from her gut. "I'm the last of us. Thankfully."

Mrs Prothero smiles. She sits Maria up and wipes her eyes with a thick, grimy thumb. "Which is where your inheritance comes in, no doubt. Now then," she says kindly. "Let us settle the first week's rent in advance now, and then I'll get back to bed and rest my old bones, you'll take your supper at The Lame Chicken, and tomorrow'll be a new day for the both of us." She smooths Maria's hair. "And don't get talking too deeply with the other girls who live here just yet," she says. "They take a little while to warm to a person. Nip out and nip back in again, and get your head down."

Maria nods. "Yes, Mrs Prothero," she says, whereupon the older woman stands, reminds Maria of her terms, holds out her hand, and Maria counts out most of the coins her uncle gave her, although some of the coins seem to double, then triple in Mrs Prothero's palm. Nothing is as it should be. Mrs Prothero looks over each coin, then replaces the pipe between her lips and limps slowly from the room, clicking the door latch down behind her.

For perhaps an hour Maria Newton sits and listens to the noises of the house. Her head is swimming from the medicine Mrs Prothero gave her, but she feels infinitely better about the future. She hears Mrs Prothero climb heavily back down the stairs, for her room is on the ground floor. She hears her speak with someone and then close her door upon herself. Voices cross on the stairs outside her room, more doors open and close. Smells rise: smoke, onions, fish frying. She crosses to the window and peers out, though the windows are thick with grime. There is laughter out there and an argument. A couple are pushing and shoving each other, the woman screaming and clawing at the man who is fending her off and calling her a drunk. Someone is singing loudly off in one direction and someone else joins in from the other. The two singers grow louder and closer until they meet just below her window and sing a raucous music hall song about a fishmonger and his wife before shaking hands and slouching away in their respective directions. She catches sight of herself in the reflection of the dirty window. She is usually pretty enough to walk with her head held high, although she is slight like a bird, like her grandmother. But for a moment reflected in that window, she looks like her mother. She shudders.

When she steps out into the street a wolf whistle makes her jump, but she finds that the drink has given her courage. She turns to the whistler, winks and then strides out towards The Lame Chicken, her stomach rumbling.

The day after her arrival, Maria takes a drink with Mrs Prothero. She is then taken by the elbow into the hallway by her grandson, James Loynes, and informed that Mrs Prothero runs one of the most notorious brothels in Cardiff. He warns her that if she cannot pay the next week's rent, Maria will be expected to work for her or she'll be out on her ear with a beating to boot. She stands staring at him, her mind hazy, for the drink seems stronger than anything she has taken a sip of before. Rum but filled with the crushing strength of the ocean.

"I'll pay," she tells him, holding the banister to steady herself. "I'm a seamstress."

The man laughs heartily in her face. "We shall see," he tells her. "We shall see."

Maria must find work, but for now her head is spinning again and she stumbles out into the street trying to work out how she will find a job quickly. Even if she does, she will not be paid straight away. She churns her situation over and over in her head. She must either find a position where she lives in or she must stay here. There are no other options. She will inherit nothing any time soon.

She stands there in the middle of Charlotte Street surrounded by ale houses, gin houses and whores, and stares at the shit-spattered ground, churned up beneath the feet of lecherous sailors and drunken dockworkers, and realises that she has been given a sentence of her own, unwarranted. With a sickness rising in her gorge, she turns and steps into the nearest gin house. What had she expected, being of cursed blood? Her mother has not only sealed the fate of her poor, dead grandmother, but by living and keeping Maria out of her inheritance, she has sealed her daughter's fate as well.

The Second Trial: Summer Assizes

Recollections of Thomas Whitmore, MP

Apley Estate, Bridgnorth
26th of July 1849

With my upcoming election for membership of the Royal Agricultural Society, the case of Miss Mercy Newton weighed heavily upon my shoulders. All the summer occupations of a landowner were upon me, and this case badgered me as I went about my work; Miss Newton ought to have been executed at the gallows four months ago. Who could have predicted that the trial of this woman would take so many months of all our lives? That a crime as heinous as this might be so difficult to pin upon a woman? Nevertheless, Phillimore and I were back at it, ready for the summer assizes, exploring any avenue possible to secure the right verdict.

Huddlestone did indeed, as he had uttered to Miss Newton at the end of her spring hearing, appeal that Lord Justice Coltman's discharge of the jury back in March, with the assertion that it was not within Coltman's legal power to do so and that having once been on trial for a death penalty and no verdict being given, that it was unlawful to try her for a second time.

This indeed was a huge issue for the case. Following my own investigations into the rarity of this second trial, I had discovered that only once before in the legal history of our great nation had a murderer been given a second trial. And never had this occurred for matricide. One was either guilty or not. To hang or not to hang, that ought to have been the question. But nothing about this case had progressed simply from the start.

Needless to note, young Mr Huddlestone's appeal was ignored and Miss Newton's case was to be heard again before a new jury in July of 1849. Prior to the hearing, I sought Mr John Whatmore, for his assertion that Mary Corfield was not a credible witness must be quashed.

There were three John Whatmores living in Bridgnorth at the time of the trial. Having made enquiries, I found the one I sought down at the river port, at the Hop Pole pub early one evening. It soon became clear that not only was he a drinker, but he was also a man who disliked Mary Corfield and more so, it transpired, her brother, William. As soon as I entered the establishment, he made for me, recognising me from the trial.

"I meant what I said about Mary, she's a bad sort," he breathed at me, and I ascertained from the calamitous jumbling of his consonants that he had been hard at it since the end of his workday.

"Allow me to sit with you a while," I said, guiding the fellow to a table. "Rum?"

"Indeed!" The man was positively jubilant. He sank his rum like a true docker, and I needed barely mention his interruption of the case, for he told me all about it then and there, as I forced the nasty, cheap stuff down in sips.

"That Mary, her brother, William bloody Corfield, he's a swindler," he gabbled. "And Mary's no good either. The lot of those Corfields are up to no good."

"Are you sure you made her out on the night of the 4th of December, and are you sure of the time?" I asked him gravely. "You see, Mr Whatmore, it is of importance to the case. If Mary was indeed not abed, then both the prosecution and the defence must re-examine all that has passed. It will take many hours of work, many days, nay, weeks, to rebuild the case if what you say is true."

Whatmore tipped his glass to catch the last few drops. "I saw her," he said, and those three words were definite. "She was there, at the gate talking to a man." With that he slammed down his glass and raised his eyebrow at me, which I took to indicate a request for more rum. I obliged.

"I must put it to you," I told him, as we waited for our top-ups. "That if Mary Corfield was at the gate so late that night, then she is a liar. And if liar she be, then a woman's life hangs in the balance. Think on your conscience, Mr Whatmore. Think on your dates. The 4th of December, Mr Whatmore. Can you be certain?"

Our rum having arrived, Whatmore nodded. "I know well that Miss Newton's life might be forfeit, Mr Whitmore. But I know well my own habits too. I'm here every Saturday, Mr Whitmore," he said nodding. "Without fail. Every single one." The rum was at my lips before his words sank in.

"Saturday?" I asked. "But the 4th of December was a Monday."

Here he paused but only for an instant, for he was too addled now for much of this to make sense. "Yes, every Saturday," he repeated. "Every Saturday, eh, Mr Whitmore?"

I put down my rum. "What about Mondays, Mr Whatmore? Are you ever here on a Monday?"

Whatmore snorted. "I'm nursing my head on a Monday, sir," he slurred. "For a Sunday is often a merry one too."

I sighed and cast a glance about the place. It was full of smoke and tired-looking men straight from the dock. "I put it to you that you in fact saw Mary Corfield at the gate on a day that was not the 4th of December," I suggested. "And I also put it to you that you hold some sort of dislike for her, perhaps due to the dealings of her brother."

"William Corfield is a cheat," Whatmore assured me, his words tumbling together with the ease of the inebriated.

I eyed the fellow, satisfied that his testimony was worthless and that Mary Cofield's credibility was intact. "Thank you for your time, Mr Whatmore," I said and pushed him my rum. "I shall not take up more of your evening."

Miss Newton herself was once again dressed all in black, a veil about her bonnet, but this time it was pinned back a little to reveal more of her face – no doubt Huddlestone and Kettle had advised her that if the jury could see her cry, they might feel all the more lenient; this at least, would have been my advice were I to defend a case such as this. Haggard now, she appeared sharp at the edges and thinned from prison rations and worry. Upon observing her wasted demeanour, I leaned towards Phillimore.

"One would put an animal out of its misery if it presented such a ragged façade," I whispered. "Let this be quick and not drawn out, for the sakes of all of us."

Most charitably, Phillimore wished for a swift conclusion and hanging too, that the prisoner need not bear more distress.

It was odd now to be able to see her face. Mr Huddlestone and Mr Kettle both smiled at her, and she nodded back to them, but her down-turned mouth, set deep in its lines and wrinkles, did not turn upwards to smile in return. She was composed, but it rather came across as though she were already dead inside.

Twelve new men sat on the jury. Their names and professions were announced: a saddler from Ludlow, a butcher from Newport, two gentlemen from Shrewsbury, a farmer from Cressage, a draper from Oswestry, a cabinetmaker from Ludlow, a currier from Oswestry and the rest more farmers. Might the farming community be more inclined to find this woman innocent, I wondered? Do farming folk stick together? Miss Newton's father was a farmer, I recalled, from my investigations. A farmer who already had three children upon his marriage to Anne and was not much older than his sons when he married her. Many of the Newtons were, in fact, farmers. Might she have some sort of extending reach we were not informed of?

Mr Baron Rolfe would judge this second trial; it transpired that Lord Justice Coltman had died.

Before it all began once again, I saw Kettle lean towards the prisoner, and although there were some hushed voices about, I overheard his words.

"Just think," he said quietly. "Today you could walk free. Dyer has seen to it that you will walk from here a comfortable woman."

She nodded but her face did not alter. I shuddered to think that this conclusion might occur. Yet I had heard of Miss Newton's good fortune – Richard Dyer, her paralytic old employer, had died shortly after her arrest, purportedly from the shock of it all, and word had spread amongst the legal men in Bridgnorth that in his will he had made provision for her: twenty pounds and a little house on Church Steps. Of all the women in all the world to profit from death, this creature appeared to be the most successful I had ever known. Not only in that should she walk free from here, she would have these willed articles from Mr Dyer, but she would also gain her mother's money – five hundred pounds, the details of which were known to everyone involved in the trial. Miss Newton would gain two hundred pounds in her hand and the rest would remain in the bank for her to gain the interest. Not only that, but Anne had been about to take receipt of one hundred pounds inheritance when she died. If Miss Newton were to walk free, she would be a wealthy enough woman. The injustice of it all rankled me. She must not be allowed to profit from her crime. Phillimore and I must secure a guilty verdict or else, I knew, I would find it impossible to continue as a law man.

Huddlestone had not forgotten the assertion that Mary Corfield had lied about her whereabouts on the night of the murder. Although Whatmore was not brought forward, I feel certain that Huddlestone and Kettle would have interviewed him just as I did as soon as they possibly could. Instead, he set about questioning the girl about her morals and her feelings toward Miss Newton, whether in fact they were enemies.

"I am sure I have never thought of myself as Kitty's enemy," Mary Corfield returned. "I always felt respect for her as an older, experienced servant of the house. I felt much pity and friendship towards her mother too."

Every so often I noted Miss Newton whisper to Mr Huddlestone or Mr Kettle, but nothing new arises. By the end of the first day, Mr Phillimore and I were heartily pleased with our case and felt we had put forward the most compelling argument.

The following day the coroner's case was put forward but Mr Coley, whose evidence was helpful to the defence in the previous trial, was absent; he too had died in the intervening months. A blow for them and a sad removal of a learned man from our midst, but still his death marked out a more providential prospect for Phillimore and me. I could only continue from this point with a renewed vigour, in that one of our obstacles had been overcome by His divine will in calling one of His sheep back home.

Miss Newton was noticeably shocked at the announcement of Coley's death. "But Coley might have saved me," she said audibly to Huddlestone. "There is nothing and nobody here today that might do the same." And with those words, she let her hand stray to her throat.

Yet today, annoyingly, in Coley's absence, the defence

brought forth more medical men, whose theories backed their case. In a counter offensive and having got wind that this would be the case, Phillimore and I had unearthed our own experts, and so the medical argument continued with vigour.

"The burning on the door posts at such a height can only have been made from the deceased making her way out to the brewhouse," came one expert opinion. "She leaned upon the doorpost, thus causing the burning at such a height."

"Nay," arose our opposition to this theory. "The prisoner, dragging her mother who was ablaze through the doorway, rested for a moment, perhaps from fear or mayhap doubt, confusion or even weakness. The fresh air from outside raised the flames into a blaze."

"Ask about Coley," I heard Kettle hiss to Huddlestone. "What of his evidence? Let them read it out. Let it be heard even if he is not here."

"How might Mr Coley's evidence be read here today?" Huddlestone ventured.

Mr Baron Rolfe nodded. "I will take it upon myself to read the notes out from the report compiled of the last trial," he announced, taking up papers hurriedly placed before him. He shuffled them, squinted for a moment, read them aloud and Coley's opinion is heard about the room. After this, the medical men dived into a discussion of asphyxiation, until at length it was time for Mr Huddlestone to summarise and so he stood.

"I address the jury on behalf of Miss Mercy Newton," he said. "That she who was admittedly drunk that night along with others who later attended the scene, aroused by the cries of Mary Corfield, ran downstairs and found her mother, her own mother, on fire in the brewhouse. She threw water upon her to quench the flames. Setting aside, sirs, the prejudice initiated by her earlier language towards her mother, there is no single fact in this case contradictory with our defence. It is impossible, after even a coroner's jury refusing primarily to put the prisoner forwards to answer the charge when she was tried at Bridgnorth and after the jury at the last session having been sequestered for nearly twenty-four hours being unable to agree upon it, to say that she is guilty."

Mr Baron Rolfe addressed the jury. "You must acquit the prisoner unless you are entirely convinced that Anne Newton, the deceased, died by suffocation, for the medical witnesses whose evidence we have received prove that suffocation was the cause of death. You have been informed, gentlemen, of opinions on how this might have occurred and the various modes by which suffocation might have arisen. There is one account, sirs, that satisfies all: that she was suffocated by a mode of which we cannot ascertain. If you see no rational explanation to the case except that the prisoner was guilty of suffocation, then she is guilty. But if you see any other rational explanation for it, she is not guilty."

Was this the summary of a man on the side of justice? To end with the possibility of her innocence? Good God, the man was positively leading the jury! I turned to Phillimore and noted that his face was as flushed with rage as I believed my own to be.

It was half past seven when the jury retired, and Phillimore and I took again to our port as we had done whilst awaiting the verdict of the first trial most readily.

"This must go either way," Phillimore stated most obviously. "There cannot be another case of no verdict. For this to have been the case after the initial inquiry and after the spring assizes, today is the day we will know if our case has been victorious."

"That blasted fellow Rolfe seemed more bent towards the defence," I muttered in the bitterest of tones. "If this verdict is one of innocence, I do not know that I shall continue to work in law, Phillimore. I cannot on my conscience see this murderer walk freely and consider myself a success."

Outside it was still light, and having been sequestered in the court all day my internal clock was adrift. "What time is it?" I remember asking.

It was nine in the evening. Late for a verdict.

"Perhaps it will be read in the morning," Phillimore said, but he had seen my face, and I know that I must have projected some of what emotion had overcome me; it was as though time was playing out once more as though we were stuck in a treadwheel. No verdict yet, and as the night darkened still nothing, until Phillimore rose and announced his intention to go to bed when there came a runner from the court.

"One of the jury has been taken ill, of the cholic," I read out, crumpling the paper in my hand. "For God's sake, will this woman never swing? The jury is to meet again in the morning."

Phillimore patted my shoulder. "There will be a verdict, I have no doubt, by then," he said. We parted and once more I lay upon a hard bed and did not sleep because of that woman. The second person ever to have gained a second trial for murder. Surely it was impossible that there would be no verdict again.

In the morning the meeting for the verdict was delayed. Phillimore and I arrived at court to be apprised of the information that the jurors had sent out questions for the judge on different matters that had arisen in their negotiations.

"Questions?" I turned on Phillimore. "What can there be questions about? A weak jury then, who cannot decide. It will happen all over again!"

But soon we were ushered into the courtroom where Baron Rolfe, along with the esteemed Justice Earle, was awaiting our presence. Huddlestone went before Kettle, confident, a small smile at the corners of his mouth. Clearly the reticence of the jury had given him hope.

A Dr Clement was called to the stand and sworn in. I could see by the puzzled expression upon Kettle and Huddlestone's faces that they had as little an idea of his purpose as myself and Phillimore.

"Dr Clement, a Fellow of the College of Surgeons of Shrewsbury," announced Mr Baron Rolfe to introduce this man's presence, "was called last night to see to a member of the jury who was taken with a bout of cholic. Dr Clement, can you give us the details?"

I gritted my teeth. All this stalling before we must find out, we must, what would become of Miss Newton.

"I administered medicine to the gentleman last night," came Clement's reply. "And was called to him again this morning. He is in danger, particularly as there is at present a cholera epidemic in town. It is my medical opinion that further confinement here will risk his life and I have requested that the jury member be discharged."

Miss Newton gasped. Mr Baron Rolfe eyed Dr Clement for a moment. I leaned over to Phillimore.

"More illness, just like the coroner's inquiry," I whispered. "If I could work out how she'd done it, I'd say that somehow these jurors are being poisoned! How can such a coincidence occur?"

Lord Justice Earle spoke with Baron Rolfe for some moments in low, close voices. I could have yelled out in frustration and had to catch myself; Phillimore too was overcome with a fit of coughing for a moment.

"Then, gentlemen, you are discharged," Mr Baron Rolfe said with an air of gravity, and then with a little last hint of hope in his tone, "There is no hope of you agreeing now?"

The foreman stood and nodded apologetically. "Not even a

shadow of one," he admitted.

"When will I get my verdict?" I heard the prisoner whisper to Kettle. "When will I know?"

Kettle, however, did not hear her. He was whispering to Huddlestone, just as Phillimore turned to me to expound the exact same thing.

"There cannot be a third trial! It is unheard of!"

"We will reconvene tomorrow," declared Mr Baron Rolfe, and the place descended into uproar.

"There is no jury now," Phillimore stated as we toiled back to the courtroom the next morning. "There has never, to my knowledge, in Britain, been a murder trial that has run to three hearings, as well as the initial inquiry."

"And the defence will push that fact no doubt," I agreed. "There can be no hanging without a jury."

Mr Baron Rolfe looked that morning as thoroughly sick of the case as the rest of us.

Mr Phillimore stood and addressed him with the proposition we had agreed upon together, "The prosecution is perfectly prepared to proceed with a new trial, sir," he announced. "The serious nature of the case warrants that we take it to a satisfactory and lawful conclusion."

Mr Huddlestone would not hear of it. His indignation shone from his face and his voice heightened by an octave in outrage.

"I set forth an affidavit," he declared, "that the prisoner cannot be tried again without prejudice, for most of those who have been summoned as crown jurors have been in court during the trial, or read of it in the newspapers, and will already have made their minds up on the subject. We cannot be sure that a jury will be made up of those without bias."

Mr Baron Rolfe nodded. "I have talked the state of the thing over with Mr Justice Earle," he stated solemnly. "And both he and I are of the opinion that if the prisoner demands her trial be postponed," here he glances at Miss Newton, "then the demand should be granted." He nodded towards her, and she, in her bright white bonnet received his gaze before turning to Mr Huddlestone for guidance.

"There is no jury," Huddlestone told her audibly. "We cannot risk cobbling together a jury made up of people already here who have already heard all the evidence. Your case is too sensational and all will have made their minds up already. We need new men, unbiased. I believe we need to ask to postpone."

"Then what?" In our proximity to her, it was clear to hear that the prisoner was distressed. "Wait, for the next assizes? Wait until the world has forgotten me before I can have a fair trial? When will that be? I'll never see an end to this!"

"Huddlestone is right; let us not get inflamed," Kettle said quietly hushing her. "There is nothing to do but postpone."

"I would rather hang than stay in this prison for the next six months," I heard her hiss, but then after a moment's thought she closed her eyes. "Postpone it then," she said quietly but loudly enough that Mr Baron Rolfe could hear her words, and at this he gave a resigned smile, for he had worked all weekend for her and he had most definitely had enough.

"Please escort the prisoner back to her cell," was his response.

A most curious thing occurred as Miss Newton was led from the room. She looked over her shoulder and called back to Huddlestone and Kettle, "They have a plan to keep me here until I rot!" Next, turning to the guard, "They will never let me go, they're leaving me in here without a fair trial!" At last, she turned, with dark eyes then towards the jury. "It's unlawful!"

Her words rippled over the men of the jury. I saw a jaw set, a head raise, a blink and a hand move to a mouth.

I overheard one man in the crowd say, "Us versus them, that's what this is after all."

And his mate replied, "She'll rot in there. Working class people aren't worth shit off *their* shoe."

But the guard paid her no heed and ushered her onwards. Now everyone was up and leaving the courtroom, and it was all over once more. I turned to Phillimore with a sigh, as another man hissed at us,

"You bastards ought to make your minds up instead of profiteering off the poor."

Phillimore managed to shrug him away, and the tide of people swept the blasted fellow out into the street.

"She's clever," Phillimore noted as we made our way out of the courtroom. "Just a few words and she's pointed the public in a new direction." He paused to light a cigar.

"There is nothing to fear on that account," I reminded him although the words came heavily to my tongue. I was awash with despair at this outcome and had to bluff my way towards his departure for fear of letting it show. "Don't you recall the mob in Bridgnorth who wanted to see her swing from the gibbet? A few words from her will do nothing to sway that blood-thirsty bunch."

He nodded and I watched him turn away. I stood there in the street as the first spatter of rain hit the brim of my hat and felt that Mercy Newton had undone me. There, as the people passed by, I saw the unfurling of all my work, all my efforts, rolling away down the street trodden into muck beneath their feet. The good name I had made for myself as a man of the law had been shattered. A woman had murdered her mother and I had failed in two trials to secure a conviction.

It was time to admit defeat.

I was not the man I thought I was.

I clambered with relief into the carriage and sat back in the shadows as far back as I could to hide my despair. I would retire, I determined. Mercy Newton had the better of me.

Chapter Thirteen

Maria Newton

Cardiff

July 1849

Maria Newton lies on her back staring at the ceiling. Her customer is already dressing himself.

"Leave the money on the side," she tells him. "Make sure it's not short or I'll shout for James." She reaches out and takes up a bottle of beer that sits on the floorboards. "And don't slam the door on the way out!" she calls. She swigs the beer and pushes herself up on her elbows to watch him leave. The money won't be short. Everyone in Cardiff is afraid of James Loynes.

She rises, for it won't do to lie for long after a customer has come calling. She must purge herself, wash, dress, show her face and find something to eat. This is life now. It's not much different to trying to survive in Batch Pool Lane, she tells herself, except she has monetary value now, whereas before she had none. The gin helps and so does the rum. The beer takes a little of the edge off as long as she drinks enough of it. When Maria can get hold of a little laudanum, she finds that helps too.

When she is cleaned and dressed, she saunters downstairs. James is there proprietorially seated, watching the door as he often is at the end of a long evening.

"Newton," he nods at her.

"You got something for me?" she asks, draping herself lazily over the back of his chair.

"Two things in fact," he tells her and pulls out a little bottle. "Your tonic," and he hands it to her: laudanum. James is not exactly generous with it, but he gives her enough to blunt her detestation of the men's hands on her and she takes it sometimes, though sparingly. She reaches for the bottle but he holds up his other hand. "Before you take it, you need your other present."

"What is it?" she is irritable now, eyes on the bottle. James flaps a newspaper at her.

"Read this first," he tells her. She snatches the paper from him, shoves it under her arm and then holds her hand out for the bottle.

Up in her room, she lies back on the bed and unstoppers the bottle. Just a drop, just enough to let her sleep tonight so that she can't smell her last customer on her sheets. The newspaper lies on the bed beside her, but as she lifts the bottle to her lips she spies her mother's name.

These last four months Maria Newton has changed. She has knowledge now that she never dreamed of before. She is hardened to the world and built walls about her that must stay insurmountable for now; she feels she is invincible. The Curse cannot touch her here. And she has an understanding of humankind that she never had before. She can see into the depths of a person, and all it has taken is four short months in Whitmore Lane. Not once in these last four months has she thought about her mother. But now her mother's name lies at her side and she must decide whether to pick up that newspaper and read it or slip a drop from that bottle onto her tongue and sink into sweet oblivion.

The bottle hovers at her lips.

"Damn." She reaches for the newspaper. Has it been four months already? The time has gone by in a blur. She is so removed now from her old life that she might be a different person altogether. And yet she cannot ignore this damned newspaper.

Irritably she straightens it out.

Her eyes trace the words.

"Postponed?" She sits there holding the paper so tightly it tears. Is she relieved? Is she furious? She cannot tell – her emotions are blunt now. It doesn't pay to *feel* when you're lying beneath a stinking, old, sweaty docker.

She lobs the paper on the floorboards, sinks back with a groan and reaches for her little bottle. Just a drop is enough to send her off to sleep.

She wakes to a banging on her door. "Newton, can I come in?" The voice is husky, pained. The handle turns.

Maria lifts her head from the pillow. A light from a candle glimmers as the door opens and a figure shuffles inside.

"Eliza," Maria mumbles, and lets her head fall back to the pillow.

"Have you got any laudanum?" the figure asks, pushing the door to and slotting the candle into a stick on the shelf. "Or anything?"

Maria groans and pushes herself up onto her elbows. "Are you hurting again?"

Bristol Eliza sits on the bed slowly, clutching her clothes tightly as though she might fall apart, yet Maria can see the lesions on her wrists and hands, raw and open.

"They're killing me today," she says.

Maria feels about for her little bottle of precious stuff. She squeezes it for a moment, then passes it over.

"Here," she says. "Take it."

Bristol Eliza falls upon it and pulls out the stopper. "You know this is how they trap you," she breathes, holding it to her lips. "They get you stuck on this stuff until you can't live without it and then they keep you here." She knocks it back. "Until you end up like me."

"I'm cursed anyway," Maria breathes. "I'll end up worse than you." But she says it quietly because really she isn't sure if anything could be worse than what is happening to Bristol Eliza. She watches her tip back the little bottle and taps the end so that every last drop goes down her gullet. "Has it helped?" she whispers.

Eliza whimpers but her eyes are glazed, Maria can see from the dim light of the candle. Bristol Eliza was one of Mrs Prothero's working girls until she took such a beating from a bully back in '47 from which she never recovered. Wounds that never truly healed. Now her wounds are everywhere, sores that open and weep. Maria can see them protruding from beneath her sleeves, reaching to her hands. Syphilis, the sores of whores, they say, and the smell that rises from her is of flesh in decay.

Maria shrinks back against the wall and watches her sleep. Somewhere outside a clock chimes four. Four in the morning. She is dazed and fuzzy from the laudanum, but Bristol Eliza's words replay over and over.

'This is how they trap you; they get you stuck on this stuff until you can't live without it, and then they keep you here.'

She glances down at the newspaper on the floorboards. Back in Batch Pool Lane, that newspaper would have been used for making twists to start the fire, patching up draughty holes in the windowpane and wrapping food. But here it will go on the fire, blaze for a moment and then go out. The poverty of Whitmore

Lane is different to the poverty of Batch Pool. Here she will never starve to death. She won't work herself to the bone and shrink until she is a defenceless little old lady to be mauled to death by her own kin or frozen to death because she cannot afford coal. She will go out with a blaze like this newspaper, she thinks. Like Bristol Eliza – once the beauty of Whitmore Lane, the whore the sailors all wanted, the talk of Cardiff.

That's the story she's told herself these past four months. That's the lie perpetuated by the rum, the laudanum, James Loynes and Mrs Prothero. And it's true she can afford food now, has a roof over her head and a real bed to sleep in, although none so fine as the one she once slept in at The Watering.

Even so she knows she does not want to be trapped here. Her mother's trial is postponed but surely she will hang for what she has done. And then Maria will stand to inherit five hundred pounds.

Enough to start afresh.

She cannot afford to become an opium addict and let it slip her by. She has been wary of these little gifts so far sneaked into her hands by James Loynes and she must remain so. She will, she promises herself, save up what laudanum is given to her for Eliza so that she may escape her pain for a few hours more than she otherwise might. Just a drop here and a drop there will Maria take as she has thus far. Not enough to be a habit. Just enough to sleep well once in a while.

Maria wraps a shawl about herself and settles down to doze, but the smell of Eliza's sores is pungent in her nostrils. She will be sixteen soon, she thinks. Sixteen, and what might have become of her if she had not been a Newton? As she drifts to sleep, she thinks of Edward Biddle back in Wolverhampton, of his friendship and his patience, and wonders if it really would have been so bad to have settled with him. Then she remembers, she wanted to protect him too.

Bristol Eliza turns onto her side but cries out in her slumber from the pain of it. The little empty bottle falls from her and thumps onto the floorboards.

She won't go out in a blaze, Maria knows, watching over her. All that talk of her dying in a blaze of triumphant, infamous glory from Mrs Prothero is rubbish. It is all part of their plan to keep Maria here. To drug her, sell her and use her up until she is a shell, like Eliza. No, Eliza's end will be long and lingering. It will be hellish.

She shudders.

If the curse of the Newtons is real, then the demise of Eliza ought to be her own fate, for she can think of nothing more torturous.

As soon as her mother hangs, Maria Newton will have her freedom from this place. She prays it does not come too late.

The Summer Months

Recollections of Thomas Whitmore, MP

Apley Estate, Bridgnorth
July to September 1849

No matter that I had retired from legal representation, the matters of my constituency meant that I was thrown forthwith into circumstances that threw that woman's name up time and time again. There was no escaping her, no release from the damned name of Newton, despite the fact that she was still behind bars.

At the end of July cholera broke out. Bridgnorth was no stranger to it – there had been a previous crop of it back in 1833, but this time the hold it took upon the town was devastating. A meeting was called on September the 7th at the guildhall to devise a means to arrest the progress of the disease. This being so soon after the second trial and my decision to retire from the legal nature of my capacity forthwith, I entered the guildhall with trepidation. I had conjured up a million ways these esteemed men might go about berating me politely for my failure. As I sat down there beneath those same stained-glass windows that had looked down on Miss Newton at the coroner's inquiry, it was clear that these men were solely focused on the purpose at hand. There was no small talk. We commenced immediately with the meeting.

"Forty-nine deaths between the 9th and the 15th of August," Thursfield announced. "Thirty-seven of these from the Asiatic cholera, and it is growing stronger and more malevolent by the day. In the month of August alone more people have died in

Bridgnorth than the normal count for a whole year."

"It is not only the progress of the disease that must be addressed," Jones stipulated. "The factories are closed for fear of contagion; wages are not being paid. The people are starving."

"Is there a means of tracking the disease?" I asked. "Of monitoring the spread to ascertain its course?"

Thursfield agreed. "We would do well to keep track of it," he agreed. "There might be deaths of lone inhabitants that go undetected, and the spread of other diseases will be rife under those circumstances."

"How then might this be put into place?" Mr Richards, another of our number, pondered, but I had already devised a solution. I might have failed the town when it came to Mercy Newton but I would not fail it now.

"House-to-house visitations must be undertaken," I posited. "Daily reports and a committee set up for these to be reported back to."

This was agreed on instantly. "Might I also put forth the suggestion that cleanliness was seen to arrest the disease back in 1833," Jones added. "We need to ensure that houses are clean. Men need to be employed to go forth, whitewash and cleanse the lowliest of the dwellings about town."

We concurred fully with his suggestion.

"And those starving for want of income since so many workplaces are shut down?" Thursfield reminded us.

I could see no option but charity. "We must appeal to the wealthy and the charitable," I said. "Subscriptions must be created for the purpose of supplying essentials – medicine and food – for the poor. I myself will make a donation to begin with."

This met with general applause, and I sat back satisfied that with this gesture I would win back any faith I might have lost in my dealings with Miss Newton.

The charitable donations began immediately and men were engaged within the week to begin the task of cleansing homes.

By the 20th of September we had divided the town into districts and gathered together gentlemen willing to take part in the house-to-house visits. Myself, Jones, Richards, Mr Nicholls, Mr Parson and others all determined to track this disease, and set out on our rounds with the sound advice from Mr Thursfield, 'Do not accept food, nor drink. Do not go inside the dwelling. Do not stand closer than six feet from the doorway. Do not touch or otherwise come into contact with any item from that home, including dogs or livestock.'

Every other day I took my round, and at first the people I visited were wary, for I was their squire and their MP, but within a week or two, having grown used to my face and bored by their lack of contact with their fellow man, they soon grew to confide in me in ways most unexpected.

"Bit of a blow with that Miss Newton case, I'll warrant," one said to me, and I winced when first I heard her name, but increasingly as they let down their guard, she became much of what they wanted to talk about.

"It's not right," one told me. "Locking her up like that all these months and none of her trials coming to owt."

"Deserves to hang," another said, a man who was well known to beat his wife black and blue on occasion. "Murdering her mother like that; deserves to swing."

Through the rest of September and into October my rounds continued, and I gave more to the charitable fund for the poverty of these people was eye-watering. Without work they were indeed starving, and as the year turned cold many were freezing too.

"I heard how she said they meant to keep her there without a fair trial," one said, as I handed over bread, carbolic and wood for the fire, and noted down that all were still alive inside. "I heard tell that these medical men are all arguing amongst themselves. A pawn she is, just a pawn for the egos of the rich. It in't right."

This man I remembered from the first mob outside the prison when Miss Mercy Newton was first arrested. A most ghastly character he had been then, one of the most imposing of the lot, his eyes filled with hate and dark with murderous longings. Now here he was shrunken from hunger, frightened out of his wits at the prospect that the cholera would get him and demonstrating such an about-face in his stance towards Miss Newton that I almost dropped my notebook.

I approached the situation with caution, but I was compelled to advance nevertheless.

"Sir," I said carefully, for he still had the tattooed forearms and scarred knuckles of a man who fights illegally for money, no matter that they were half the size they had been eighteen months prior. "When Miss Newton was first arrested there were people who wanted her strung up in the streets."

"Aye, and you can count me in that number," he cheerfully confessed, passing the sack of firewood to a child inside but keeping the loaf in his hand.

"Then what has changed?" I asked him. "As one man to another, pray enlighten me; how has public opinion in one so vehemently opposed to Miss Newton altered so severely?"

Here the man scratched his head. "Look at me, sir, and look at you," he said slowly. "I'm left to starve whilst you go home to your mansion house and your servants. I'll be taken by the cholera most likely, whilst you shan't be brought to that shitty end, if you don't mind me saying it. You will rise above it and go on, whilst I am wrought asunder, and that is the way of the rich and the way of the poor. In't fair, is it? Just like how that woman has been left to rot whilst a load of poncy doctors argue over her head. I heard tell that most of them weren't even here to see the body, so how do they know what they're talking about?" He ripped off a corner of the loaf and shoved it into his mouth, chewed it awhile, then pushed it into his cheek so that it bulged, whilst he added, "When all is said and done if they can't prove she did it, they ought to let her free. Surely that's the law?"

I stared at him for a moment. My heart sank. "Yes," I admitted. "That is the law."

"I'm glad you think so, squire," he said. "For all your efforts to hang her, I thought you was against us poor folks."

I did not expect the conversation to become an undercurrent in my routine visits the way it did. Carried with the cholera, Miss Newton's plight spread through Bridgnorth until her name was on every tongue as a synonym for social injustice.

By December 1849, a requisition was presented to Mr Jones, the new mayor, signed by many requesting an investigation into the state of sewerage in Bridgnorth, for there to be amendments and improvements. Jones, Richards, Nicholls, Parsons and I, along with others, took work in hand to oversee this, for the decreasing population of Bridgnorth was on its knees.

"Perhaps these works ought to have been carried out before this new outbreak," I wondered in hindsight. "It might have saved lives."

But Mr Marsh, one of our colleagues, merely snorted.

"Nobody, as you well know, Whitmore, will pay out for something like this unless it is proven to be needed by enough deaths," he stated. "Let the expendable people ride it out, and only when we think people of quality might be at risk ought something so expensive be considered."

I watched him take his seat, an expression of derision clear across his brow. Expendable people versus those of quality, I thought. That is exactly how the public is coming to think of Mercy Newton. She, like them, was one of the expendables. I shuddered.

This year had seen the people of Bridgnorth brought closer to starvation than ever before by cholera, their number decimated by the disease, whilst we, the rich, had played at charity, safe in our houses with our well-stocked cellars. In a town of only five thousand people, there were over the course of three months over 200 deaths. Deaths had outnumbered births by far.

"Is this not all reminiscent of social circumstances in the run up to the French Revolution?" I said aloud, then bit my tongue for I was met with frowns, and those who registered my words then turned away.

But still I was left with a creeping anxiety that something might burst, and I recalled those mobs outside the gaol and the guildhall and knew that truly if the people of Bridgnorth were riled enough there could well be disruption that went way beyond our capabilities to restore order.

What if the people of Bridgnorth were to rise, I wondered, with Mercy Newton as their figurehead? What might they be capable of?

Chapter Fourteen

Maria Newton

Cardiff

4th of December 1849

Maria is sixteen years and four months old, and she marks the anniversary of her grandmother's murder with hellish zeal. She does not often partake of the little bottles James slips her regularly, but today she will make an exception.

This day she sets out with The Grenadier, so called for her impressive stature, up Whitmore Lane and over into Charlotte Street. Children play in the gutter-mulch without shoes, next to a puddle of blood from a fight earlier in the day.

"You'll celebrate with me, won't you?" Maria says, as they step into the street. "Later, when the marks leave?"

The Grenadier is always up for a celebration. "Of course," she says. "Will there be rum?"

"I've a bottle stashed away," Maria tells her.

This is good enough for The Grenadier. "What are we celebrating?"

Maria calls to Merry Meyrick, who is stepping out of The Lame Chicken. "Merry! You'll come to celebrate later, won't you?"

"What we celebratin'?" Merry calls back, hitching her skirts and stepping through the mire.

"A murder," Maria tells her.

"Oh yes, I'll toast to that!" Merry cries, and all three set off in different directions to make some money first.

The mark she picks up today is straight from the customs house next door to Mrs Prothero's. He needs no persuasion; he's the type she prefers – there is no small talk, it is quickly over and he doesn't try to look her in the eye afterwards, so he doesn't see the disgust in her eyes. As she listens to his tread on the stairs receding, James calls up to say there is another mark waiting, and she takes a moment to wash and take a good glug of rum before he is sent up.

Desperate for this part of her evening to be over, she has to douche herself and stomach the attentions of this second man, a staggering, slurring chap with a scar on his cheek who can barely function. As he struggles out of his trousers, there is a yell from across the landing and the sound of feet pounding on the stairs, but the management of rowdy clientele is James Loynes's bread and butter, and it is nothing out of the ordinary.

By the time her mark has finished his business, and she has bundled him out of the room and washed and dressed, The Grenadier is there downstairs with James and she is sporting a freshly blackened eye.

"I gave as good as I got," she tells Maria proudly, and demonstrates a perfect right hook.

"Chap had to be helped out, he was so stunned," James laughs. "Stupid bastard; who'd pick a fight with you, eh?"

Maria can see how painful her eye is, but The Grenadier seems to regard it as a mark of triumph. Together they climb back up the stairs and share some of the rum whilst they wait for Merry.

"So whose murder are we celebrating?" The Grenadier asks.

Maria goes over to her little trunk and pulls out a box. "My grandmother's," she tells her.

Out of the trunk she takes each of the newspaper clippings she has amassed. Despite her yearnings to be rid of it all, she has clipped every single article she has found about her mother's trials. She spreads them out on the floorboards near the door.

"What are all these?" The Grenadier asks, crouching down. "I'm not the best at reading."

"This is a murder case," Maria tells her. "I've never spoken about it to anyone really. But I want to know why it would be so hard for a jury to decide on a verdict."

Merry's tread on the landing outside the door announces her arrival. "I've brought some gin!" she coos as she enters. "What's all this?"

"Let me give you the particulars," Maria says.

"I think it's a party game," The Grenadier says. "From Birmingham or wherever the hell Newton is from."

Maria ignores her. Merry opens up her gin and pours them all a measure and passes it round. Maria does not drink, not yet.

"Help me," she says, and takes hold of the bed. Together, they drag it so that it sits before the tiny grate. "Imagine this is the sofa. Merry, you can be my grandmother, lie on the sofa."

"As you wish," says Merry, and hops up onto the bed, gin in hand.

"Imagine this is a range, in a big old house," Maria indicates her tiny, unlit fireplace. "Imagine this," she picks up the bottle of rum, "Is a bottle of lamp oil, and this," she takes the gin bottle from Merry's grip, "This is a full butter boat."

"And I'm your granny!" Merry squawks cheerily, squinting over her gin.

"Who am I in all this?" The Grenadier is getting into it now the liquor is firing her up.

"You are my mother," Maria tells her. Merry and The Grenadier exchange glances. Everyone knows Maria Newton has skeletons in her closet – who here doesn't? – but this is closer than anyone has ever come before at discussing it with her.

"What I want to know first," Maria says, standing back to survey the scene. "Is how that lamp oil could get sloshed all over that sofa."

"Easy," says The Grenadier, picking up the rum bottle. "I'll pick it up and chuck it over her." She pretends to set it flying but swings it round and pours herself some.

"Why?" Maria asks. "For what purpose?"

"Because she's angered me," says The Grenadier. "And I want to get my own back."

"If it was a bottle filled with water, would you still have doused her?" Maria asks. "Did you mean for it to be a flammable liquid?"

"I just wanted to chuck something," The Grenadier says. "It could have been a piss-pot and I'd have chucked it at the old bag."

"Dirty girl!" Merry cackles from her sofa.

Maria takes a sip of her gin.

"Let's imagine the lamp oil catches light," she says. "How?"

"Oh! Oh! I knock the candle over!" Merry is animated now. "And it catches light and up I go in a puff of smoke!" She turns to Maria, eyes bright but notes Maria is not smiling. "Sorry," she says bashfully. "I forgot I'm your gran."

"I light a match and lob it at the old biddy," The Grenadier is not bashful. She's getting into character. "Serves her right for being such an 'orrible old bitch."

"Or you drop your pipe," Maria says, nodding at Merry who is settling back down again.

"If her foot is close to the fire or if there is a trail of oil on the floor, could the fire not have spat out a spark?" Merry suggests. She is using her normal voice now.

The Grenadier places a heavy hand on Maria's shoulder. "Bet you wish it was a piss-pot that was chucked," she breathes.

Maria shakes her off. "I just can't get my head round what

happened," she says. "It's driving me mad."

She sits on the edge of the bed. Merry pats her on the back. The Grenadier tips more gin into her cup and offers words of wisdom.

"Sometimes it's best not to think too hard round here."

"It's been a year and I still don't know the answers," Maria says. "Nobody does."

"Nobody but your mother," muses Merry.

"Have you asked her?" The Grenadier asks.

"I haven't set eyes on her," Maria admits. "How could I?"

Merry pats her back a little more and they sit and drink the rest of the gin and the rum until James comes knocking and tells them to settle down, that Mrs Prothero is getting tired of their din and Bristol Eliza is complaining.

When they leave and Maria is left alone in that room within which she has poorly fashioned a replica of the hearth at The Watering, Maria thinks on The Grenadier's question, 'Have you asked her?'

She pulls out a scrap of paper and a pencil stub. How can she write to her mother? At the gaol? Will a letter get to her? Maria doesn't know. Her head is spinning, the rum and the gin working together to complicate everything. What if she wrote to her mother's defence, Mr Huddlestone? Or Mr Kettle? But she knows not where they are, knows no address she could send a letter to for it to reach them. Her forehead is hot. She crosses the room to lean it on the cool glass of her window. Outside the street still retains stragglers, although all the inns have closed their doors hours since. She can see in the darkness a butt of a cigarette being smoked, and the sign on the building opposite announcing to those making their way up from the docks that this is Whitmore Lane.

She knows that name so well.

Whitmore.

Instantly she is lying on the boards, scribbling a note onto her scrap of paper. She folds it carefully into another piece of paper and secures it with wax from the candle, wincing as it burns the tip of her finger. Then in the neatest writing she can muster, she writes on the exterior:

Thomas Whitmore Esq.

Apley Estate,

Bridgnorth,

Shropshire.

She sits back and eyes her handiwork. Anne Newton taught her to read and write, although she has always known that much of Anne's enthusiasm for parenting was used up on Mercy's early days, and that she, Maria, merely caught the ragged, liquor-fired tail end of it.

This will do. A letter. She will ask. It doesn't hurt to ask, she thinks.

Thomas Whitmore is a man of the law. He is an MP. He is a squire.

She trusts that he will do what she asks.

He is a man of his word.

Petition for the Release of Mercy Newton

Recollections of Thomas Whitmore, MP

Apley Estate, Bridgnorth

January 1850

Rise, the people of Bridgnorth did, but in a most bureaucratic way. Six months after Miss Newton's second trial, an anomaly that could only be attributed to the ultimately anarchistic nature of the working man occurred. Anarchy or perhaps the prolificacy of alehouses around Bridgnorth. The cholera had all but diminished, and my fears of an uprising from a month before had been quashed by the sight of the factories up and running and the river port back to its bustling trade. I had not predicted the possibility that the people would speak out for her, but they did.

I first caught wind of the petition for the release of Miss Mercy Newton when the new mayor, Mr Jones, a man who had yet to impress me in his new position, brought it to my attention. He himself had been integral to the creation of the thing, and already it had been signed by various Justices of the Peace, along with solicitors, agents and clerks. It was gaining momentum now with farmers, drapers and shopkeepers alike.

I must say I was rather put out. Needless to note my signature did not, and would not, grace its pages.

"It has been six months since her second trial, Sir Thomas," he reminded me as if I had no idea of the thing at all. "That woman is languishing in gaol and it isn't legal to keep her there!"

I wanted to opine that she was a murderer and the fact that she was languishing at Her Majesty's convenience was rather a luxury given the alternative, but instead I merely grunted. Six months of rumblings, no doubt, in pubs and on corners, had attributed to this, and I hardly considered that it would make a difference.

"Don't you think it is time for her release?" he pressed. We were at the guildhall, discussing some aspect or other of one of the patronages I had taken on about town, and the urge came to me to laugh in his face.

"Do you recall how the people of Bridgnorth swarmed here, to this very building, on the occasion of the coroner's inquiry?" I asked him. "Were you not there? I was. I saw them, like a mob, calling out, shouting at her and throwing things. Indeed, if there had not been a considerable police presence I believe they would have torn her limb from limb. How can I now take seriously a petition signed by members of the same mob calling for her release? I can only predict that they wish her to be released so they may finish her off themselves! It would be murder indeed to allow her to walk amongst them! I'd wager she would be bumped off by one of them in no time!"

Mr Jones shook his head. "No," he said coolly. "I rather believe that public opinion towards Miss Newton has altered since then."

"Then the particulars of the case have not been shared properly with the common man on the street," I told him. "Or else they would be of the same opinion I am." I paused. "Has Mr Newell signed it?" I asked, thinking obviously of the ex-mayor whose surgeon skills had been put to the test in Anne Newton's autopsy.

"He has not," Mr Jones confirmed. He sat back in his chair. "She has come to represent something that calls to a decent man's sense of justice," he said thoughtfully.

There was, I recall, a frosty silence during which we could hear hooves pass by outside.

"You must agree, hers is an unlawful imprisonment now," he pressed. "And that to suffer her a new trial or to hang her now would be to side solely with one or another of the medical men who cannot agree on the matter. The people of Bridgnorth know better than to involve the life of an innocent woman in the quarrels of four medical men. Why, Taylor's Medical Jurisprudence states that the whole thing is a farce and an eminent work such as that cannot be ignored."

I could feel a headache approaching. "You must know, sir," I countered darkly. "That I spent months of hard work, deliberation and sleepless nights working on the prosecution of that woman. And for her to walk amongst you all would be to unleash a murderess with a cold heart and a colder conscience upon the people."

"The people want her free," he reiterated. "She is a pawn, a working-class pawn unlawfully imprisoned and all because of the egos of medical men who cannot come to an agreement. Two of whom never even saw the corpse. How can their opinions count? It is unjust. You're an educated man, surely you can see that?"

I glared at him. "They've got at you, Jones," I stated coolly. "You are too far embedded in the lives of your constituents. A man of your standing ought to step back from the gossip and the triviality of their claptrap. This is a matter of right and wrong, of legal importance that far outweighs disgruntled, ignorant pub-talk."

Jones sighed. "Not one of those medical men has ever seen a body that has burnt to death in this manner," he saw fit to remind me. "They openly have admitted as much. And only Thursfield, Coley and Newell saw the corpse, and they could not agree on whether burning came first or suffocation. All other medical opinion than theirs is void, no matter how many experts they bring in, because, Mr Whitmore, *these others did not see the corpse*. No, Miss Newton must be freed. She represents now," he breathed, "the downtrodden working class at the mercy of his masters. And the people of Bridgnorth don't like it."

I continued to glare. I may, additionally, have growled somewhat. "Mercy Newton is a murderer," I managed. "She murdered her mother and burned her. Do you really want a woman like that walking around free as a bird?"

And with that, I left him and his unfinished business, stamped down the stairs to my carriage which was awaiting below and returned to Apley with the foulest of headaches.

It was becoming increasingly obvious that if she were to be meted with the fate that ought to come to her kind, the justice system might make her a martyr to the working classes, particularly now after this petition debacle. The whole thing was more than I could stand, and my resolution to retire from it all had not wavered. The damned woman had made a mockery of my position, and I could not bear to put my name to a third trial and could hardly hold my face up when her name was mentioned. Within a week of hearing about the petition, however, I heard word from Phillimore, and within a fortnight he came to see me at Apley.

"They are saying she ought to be released," he expounded immediately upon entering my office, waving his handkerchief in the air. "Surely there cannot be another trial, not now. It is unheard of. But they are correct that it is unlawful to hold her so long without a verdict. If there is another trial, I shall have to work for prosecution once more. Whatever will happen, Whitmore?"

"What indeed?" I agreed. "Who will work with you for the prosecution?"

At this he pursed his lips. "You couldn't be persuaded...?"

"Nothing on earth could incite me to waste more of my time on it all," I assured him.

"I thought as much," was his dry response. "I will then, take up a partnership for the case with a Mr Best. Have you heard of him?"

I had but barely.

"His methods can be somewhat bullish," he reflected. "However, he has experienced various successes about the county." No matter how the conversation turned during his visit, nor how ebullient he appeared with this new partnership, it was clear from the onset that he had been hoping I would change my mind. Of course, I would not. However, the prospect of a third trial was ludicrous. When he left, I paced the library for a good half an hour before the blood stopped throbbing in my temples.

The petition, damned thing that it was, was submitted over 200 signatures strong from the people of Bridgnorth to the Secretary of State for the Home Department. Nothing I could say or do would deter the mayor from sending it.

From sources I will not name, I learned that detail of the petition along with a letter from the esteemed H. Waddington of the Home Department requesting his opinion on whether a third trial was necessary for the ends of justice had been received by Mr Baron Rolfe, who wrote at the end of January to the Home Department to confirm receipt of it. I was then informed, again by persons who will remain unnamed for the purposes of protecting their careers, that Mr Baron Rolfe and others at the prison debated at length the necessity of a third trial and ultimately it was decided that this was too important, too grievous a crime to allow the prisoner her freedom without a third trial. Perhaps without the petition Miss Newton might have languished in gaol a further year or more, forgotten about. However, although the petition failed to see her freed, it did invoke the wheels of motion to set her forth for the spring assizes in 1850. A full year and four months Miss Newton had been imprisoned at this point with no verdict, and public opinion had, to my mind, incomprehensively altered towards her.

The Bridgnorth people had succeeded in making a murderer into a martyr.

The Third Trial: Spring Assizes

Recollections of Thomas Whitmore, MP

Apley Estate, Bridgnorth
20th of March 1850

I did not stand for the prosecution, but there was nothing I could do to extricate myself from the proceedings. I found myself compelled to see Miss Mercy Newton's fate through to the end, and so although I did not work with Phillimore, I secured myself a seat in the courtroom as a Bridgnorth MP and Justice of the Peace, so that I might observe the proceedings.

I had with me in my pocket an epistle, if one could call it that, which had appeared on my breakfast tray back in February. It had the look of something that had been scribbled, read, reread and thumbed until the writing was all but indistinct, then put in a pocket or bag and forgotten about, for the pencil address on the outside was faded and rubbed to make it all but illegible and the paper itself was flattened. Perhaps it had been hidden beneath a mattress or a pillow. Whatever its history, I had been struck with surprise upon opening it to discover that it was a message for Miss Newton.

Dear Sir, (The note read)

I write to you as the MP for Bridgnorth to pray that you pass this message on for me, as I know not how to gain an answer otherwise. For I know that you have dealings in the trial of Mercy Newton, and I would hear from her lips the truth.

Pray pass this note from your hand unto hers and see that she answers me full and true. For all I wish to know in this world is this:

Did you kill her?

For this I thank you, sir, and remain ill at ease until this matter be settled.

Yours truly,
Maria Newton.

The address in the top right-hand corner of the thing was so faint, so thumbed, that I could make out little, although part of the address looked like my name, making me rather confused as to whether it was the address of the sender or if she had rewritten mine once more on the inside. Without course to pass the note on, for Huddlestone and Kettle were over in Shrewsbury for much of their time in the run up to this third trial, I had held onto this pitiful message until this day. It burned a hole in my pocket now, for I knew that in all good conscience I must pass it on to the prisoner's defence that they may place it into her hands. There was no return address, no way for the prisoner to give an answer. It was as though her daughter had shouted her question into a void, just to let it out.

Straight away it was obvious that Phillimore was flustered, although my replacement, Mr Best, appeared hard-nosed and possessed of a vindictive brow line, if truth be told. His eyes were a little too close together and his brow glinted with sweat before the proceedings had even begun. A new jury sat before the bench, but of course they had all heard of her, all read about her case or had it read to them from the newspapers. Not a man amongst them could be impartial. Each would have cast their own judgements in their own homes already over a pot of tea or a tot of rum. Mercy Newton was a famous woman now, and the streets about the Shire Hall were lined with people who waited to hear the verdict, and inside the courtroom was packed. Everything felt different this time. I must admit, from the start, I could detect the stench of defeat.

Mr Justice Patteson presided, a new judge.

This time, Miss Newton kept her face on show. She was weary of this there could be no doubt. Her tears flowed before she could be seated.

Hours and hours seated upon those hard benches, repeating that night again and again and throughout, she sobbed, and the jury watched her tears. Mr Ridley stepped forth.

"There were burns upon the kitchen door in some places," he described. "Burns also on the doorpost of the brewhouse."

"At what height would you say these burns were?" Phillimore questioned. "Head height? Ankle height?"

"From the ground up to about waist height," Ridley posited. "Some small markings a little higher."

"The sort of marks that might occur were a burning body dragged through a building?" Best suggested. "In your opinion?"

"In my opinion," Ridley asserted, "those marks would be precisely the sort to arise from such an act."

Here all faces turned to Miss Newton, and I know that every man there in that jury was imagining the same scene that had sprung to my mind's eye. The scene of Miss Newton dragging the burning corpse of her mother through that doorway out into the night, to deposit her on the threshold of the brewhouse, where she smouldered until the hammering rain or her daughter using a bucket of water from the barrel therein to douse her. I observed Best rub his whiskers, a sign, I was coming to note, that he was more than satisfied with what he had heard. A mark of well-hidden glee. I, myself, felt a jolt of electricity within that this expert opinion was in favour of the prosecution. As in the previous trials, however, this simple, linear explanation would not hold for long. Mr Newell stepped forth then, to put confusion into the minds of the jury.

"It is my opinion that the woman was alive when she took flame," he stated solemnly. "From the burns on the sofa material I have ascertained that she was in a sitting-up position when she was set alight. Whether accidental or from purposeful means I know not. However, I am completely certain that the deceased was sitting upright when the burning took hold of her."

I watched Phillimore whisper fervently with Best. Miss Newton appeared to shake her head slowly, but her face remained deadpan. Yet the grotesque implication of this announcement did not fail to run its ghoulish fingers up my spine. I found myself imagining a burning woman fleeing the kitchen, her mouth a gaping black hole as the flames ripped through her oil-sodden garments, desperate to get to the water-butt in the brewhouse and douse herself. There were men in the jury, I am sure, who would have imagined the same, yet they might have still harboured enough doubt of Miss Newton's guilt to guess that the flames had come from an accident with Anne Newton's pipe. However, in my imagining I saw Mercy Newton standing there by the fire behind her, an empty oil bottle in her hand. Whatever explanation was the truth, we would never know the true story now, but my very bones knew that the woman in the dock was guilty of the demise of her own mother. It would be a travesty to let her walk free.

No matter which explanation the defence, or the prosecution for that matter, explored, nothing could sway my own opinion; a woman does not douse herself in oil before sleeping. Miss Newton had soused her mother and much of the sofa in lamp oil. I wanted to shout it from the damned rafters. The whole trial was an injustice to common sense. Whether she struck a match on her living mother, left her oil-soaked mother sleeping with a smoking pipe or smothered her with a cushion and then set fire to her corpse, in my opinion, Mercy Newton killed Anne Newton. The woman deserved to swing.

The jury appeared an attentive group of men but how were they to name a cause of death as the law stated must be done? I admit I had experienced cause to question my own reckoning a number of times throughout the trials. The arguments of the medical men often created a confusion of possibilities within my own brain regarding what might have occurred that night. This had led to my questioning myself at various times throughout the trials. As in her previous trial, I found myself wondering how a jury of men called in from their farms and cabinet-making were to account for it all?

Young Mr Huddlestone and young Mr Kettle were in high spirits indeed. Their frequent glances to their client and their constant nodding or note-taking belied an optimism I truly did not feel, however, Mr Best did his utmost to try to sway the jury.

He called forth Mr Thomas Deighton, the man who had held the mayorship of Bridgnorth in 1848 when Anne Newton died. This man had not been asked to step forward to give evidence at previous hearings, and I watched with interest to observe what new fodder might be gleaned from him.

"I called Miss Newton to speak with me around five months before the incident," he related. "This was in regards to her treatment of her mother and the cruelty she placed upon her. Anne Newton had grounds to take her daughter before a magistrate on many occasions, but no charges could be brought against her for mother would never testify against daughter. Therefore, I spoke with Miss Newton personally to tell her to desist."

"What was her response?" Best asked.

"That she had done it in the heat of passion and that it was caused by her mother's conduct," Deighton replied. "She appeared to me to be penitent and promised it should not occur again."

Here Huddlestone veritably beamed.

Best had not finished yet. For his final witness he called up Edward Edwards, having left him until last. "Please, Mr Edwards, as the brother of the deceased, the uncle of the accused, can you tell the jury the way relations stood between mother and daughter, that they might try to understand the motives behind this savage murder?"

Edward Edwards vented forth once more his tales of violence, "Why, not five months ago, I remonstrated my niece for striking her mother across the knees with a poker. She'd mistreated her for years and didn't show care or remorse. Smashed her, she did, with that poker. Her own daughter, Maria, always said her mother would be the death of her grandmother."

Again the courtroom heard the harsh words of Miss Newton's response to his complaints, and again they heard the particulars of the money that was to be inherited upon the death of the mother, but all of them would know it already; no man in Shropshire was ignorant to the case. Mr Edwards put across his dislike of his niece and her treatment of his sister most vehemently, in tones that clearly displayed his anger. Each testament to his niece's violence was spat out with hatred and vitriol colouring every syllable. By the time Mr Best had completed his questioning, Mr Edwards was purple with rage and his eyes flashed towards his niece with such blackness that I had no doubt were they to be left alone together, he might not think twice in re-enacting the occurrences of the 4th of December 1848 upon his niece.

At last Huddlestone rose and addressed the jury, and more than once I saw him glance in my direction.

"Words of animosity said to have been articulated by the prisoner in the past are not evidence of her committing a crime. Truly, would a murderer so vociferously declare their intention to commit a crime? One might surmise that the public announcement of such murderous thoughts might even be proof of innocence. Who amongst us has not thought or said such things in a passion?" Here he licked his lips, nodded towards me and continued, "Since the preceding trial, my apprehension regarding the result of this hearing has not reduced. However, since then, a great alteration has happened in the conducting of the prosecution. By this I mean the retirement of my learned friend, Mr Whitmore. I had hoped that the same moderate, reasonable and compassionate mode of conducting the case would have been assumed, but the words 'savage murder' and other expressions used by the prosecution would not have been addressed to the jury had it been so. They have called a witness who has never yet been seen, and I know not why Mr Edwards, the brother of the deceased, was called last unless for the intention of leaving a sting upon the minds of the jury." He looked about him then, from each jury man to the next. "Gentlemen, I have some years of familiarity with juries of this county, and I have faith that by exposing such poor conduct, it will foil itself."

There was a murmur amongst those seated, and indeed I myself almost let out a cry. Oh, clever Huddlestone! I thought. To marry this discontent with the conduct of the prosecution with the current feeling of the people, what devious wit. That very moment I regretted my retirement. Huddlestone had ingeniously used Best's tactics against him. I perceived Kettle make an encouraging expression towards Miss Newton.

Lord Justice Patteson completed the proceedings.

"This case is exceptionally curious," he told the jury. "Especially as two previous juries were incapable of a verdict.

In my opinion, the scrutiny by the three medical experts of the body was inadequate, having taken no concern to investigate the larynx, the trachea, the bladder or the rectum. Dr Wright's testimony was given without seeing the body, his judgement based exclusively on facts given from the aforesaid practitioners. Had he himself actually examined the body his views might have been substantially different. Such evidence, I believe, will impinge the duties of a jury, and I am greatly against the use of it. I advise, gentlemen, that you employ your own judgement without surrendering to Dr Wright's evidence in particular."

This speech worked in conjunction with Huddlestone's to damn the whole trial. Professionally, I found him to be the antithesis to Mr Best; where Best had tried to use his words to ensure a hanging, Patteson had chosen his to secure a release. This man, this judge, who ought to be swaying neither one way nor the other lacked impartiality too, in my opinion. Everything that we worked on, all that I had given to my part in it, the weeks and months of our lives that had gone into this case, all of it was there made a mockery of. Taylor's blasted Medical Jurisprudence had got to him too.

Miss Newton sat straight-backed, her lips pursed, her eyes dark, tears having made her face rather grubby despite the use of Kettle's handkerchief. Her gloved hands were clasped primly in her lap. Patteson summed up the evidence succinctly once more and then added a phrase that ought never to be spoken to a jury in a case of such evident guilt: "If there is even an element of reasonable doubt, give the prisoner the benefit."

My heart sank. It was a call for capitulation. It was a call for the wrong verdict.

It was half-past ten in the evening when the jury retired. Huddlestone was nowhere to be found, but I accosted Mr Kettle, who had stepped outside for air, and gave him the note from the prisoner's daughter.

"Why send it to you?" was his incredulous response as he pocketed the thing.

All I could do was shrug. "I am her MP; I am honour-bound to pass it on," I suggested.

"She will want to write back," Kettle said solemnly.

"There is no return address," I told him. "She will be disappointed."

I met Phillimore and Best standing, dazed, out in the corridor of the Shire Hall.

"Patteson is for her," I breathed. "That damned petition, those damned contrary folk who wanted her hanged will now see that she goes free."

"After everything, after the evidence of her treatment of her mother, after all..." Phillimore trailed off.

Best harumphed and declared he needed a cigar.

We turned to go, to wait, as we had done on the other occasions, to take port together, but no sooner had we left the building than a call came for everyone to go back inside.

A verdict was to be announced. It had taken this jury just twenty minutes to come to a conclusion that had not been reached by a coroner's inquiry and two other juries these last sixteen months.

Miss Newton stood weakly clutching the bar. Huddlestone, I remember clearly, kept fidgeting with his pen. Kettle was clenching and unclenching his fists. Best and Phillimore, being greater in years, status and experience, remained as placid as their bodies would allow, although Best was twitching his collar in a most unseemly fashion. I must confess the turmoil within me had begun another headache. As the room filled, I saw him reach into his pocket and take out the battered little letter and hand it to Miss Newton with a few words. I watched her mouth drop open with surprise and then she held the letter to her heart and glanced in my direction. Our eyes met for the first time. Where there might have been hatred before, now I only saw her eyes fill with gratitude and her lips mouth the word *thank-you*. I nodded.

"Your verdict, gentlemen?" Justice Patteson asked gravely.

The foreman stood. I watched the lip of Miss Newton's bonnet raise to the heavens, as though she was praying; her eyes were closed and her cheeks were wet. Her hands remained firmly gripping the bar, just as her murderous cousin's hands had done before her. I remembered how unwillingly he went to the gallows, his pleading words and the sentiment of my father at my side, 'There is a clear choice, the law or the collapse of society. These people need you to have a firm hand, Tom.'

There must be no space in me for pity for the creature whose tearful eyes and grateful lips had just thanked me.

'Sometimes you will feel that the law is harsh. Sometimes you might feel it is more barbaric than the crime itself. Yet still we must uphold it to save all that is civilized.'

The foreman cleared his throat. My head pulsed. Phillimore was noticeably sweating. Miss Newton prayed.

"Not guilty."

The foreman smiled. Lord Justice Patteson nodded. I found myself clutching my cane with a grip that felt like a man drowning and it the only thing keeping me afloat.

"Not guilty?" Miss Newton whispered, and Huddlestone turned, grinning like a maniac and Kettle even jumped in the air a little, whilst Phillimore, in a more professional manner, shook his head, and I sank back into my seat with disappointment.

"I'm free?" I heard her whisper again, then the place was in an uproar, and I observed her pluck at Kettle's arm to tell him something, but Lord Justice Patteson began to speak and all I could do was hold my aching head and hold onto my cane, as all about me was a furore.

I watched her go along with her entourage: Huddlestone, Kettle and various police. Then I leaned down to Mr Phillimore and murmured loud enough for him to hear over the tumult of voices, "They've seen to it that a murderer walks free amongst them, through the streets of Bridgnorth."

Phillimore cast a sour look at Best, who turned his back, then nodded his agreement. "An unrepentant killer," he agreed. "God help them all."

Chapter Fifteen

Maria Newton

Cardiff

1850

Maria Newton reads of her mother's acquittal with a hangover. She squints through the black eye she has not yet recovered from and sips her tea with James Loynes, Mrs Prothero's grandson and Little Punch, another of the prostitutes who lives here and has James's name tattooed on her arm.

She has told them all about her mother now, for it has given her some form of notoriety hereabouts.

"She's free then?" asks Little Punch, whose real name is Ann, and Maria nods, but the motion hurts her head for she took far too much gin last night. "You shan't inherit that money then?"

Maria shakes her head. Now that her mother is free she feels a creeping sensation. The curse must have been imprisoned with her, she has told herself, for she has not killed anyone, nor had thoughts of suicide herself. The odd drop of laudanum has helped of course, but this has been infrequent, for she has been as good as her word and saved any that comes her way for Bristol Eliza. But now that Mercy is free, will the curse finally come for her? She looks down at her hands. They are shaking. There is rum in her and she cannot think straight.

"I shan't go to her," she tells them both. "I still think she did it."

James yawns and pinches her cheek a little too hard. "Except the lawmen say she didn't," he says pointedly. "Now who is seeing to Eliza today?"

There is a stench about this house that can only come from Bristol Eliza's room. She needs help with everything now: changing, washing and feeding her. Little Punch is eyeing James most ravenously, though Maria knows she had two marks last night and took a slap from one of them. She sighs.

"I'll go," she says.

"There's a good girl," James calls after her. She makes sure she takes a bucket and a sponge up the stairs to the little garret where Bristol Eliza is lying, out of the way of the gentlemen callers who don't want to smell her. Maria hates seeing to Eliza now. She cannot bear what has become of her. If the curse comes for her, she is deathly afraid that it will take her in the same way.

She knocks softly on the door but does not wait to hear a call; nobody expects Eliza to respond. Softly she pushes open the door, and the place does indeed stink. She has big, open, stinking wounds on her legs and sores all over her body now that the syphilis has really set in. Her bottles of laudanum lie scattered about the floor and she groans and cries out when Maria enters, so much so that Maria scrabbles about to find one that still contains some of the drug and she applies it to Bristol Eliza's tongue. Then she sets to cleaning her as best she can. Each time one of her sores is touched by the sponge Eliza cries out, laudanum or no. She is perhaps twenty-four but could be fifty or more, for her skin is tight and haggard and her eyes are sunk deep into her skull.

Maria peels off her things, takes off the swaddling that Eliza now must wear so that she does not soil her sheets and wipes her down.

This will be her fate, she thinks, one day. One day she will develop sores and disintegrate just like this. And it will all be down to the Newton blood in her veins. The drinking, cavorting, thievery, trickery and the way she spends her days, all of it is evil, and didn't her mother always say she was ruined; that she was a Newton through and through.

"Can I bring you water?" she asks Eliza. "Beer?"

"Fetch Merry," comes a hoarse whisper. "Tell her I'm dying."

Bristol Eliza has been announcing she is dying regularly for the last two years, but this time Maria looks down at her and thinks it could well be true. The state of this girl is horrific; she might be a breathing corpse to look at her. She certainly smells as though she is putrid.

"I'll fetch Merry," she tells her and drops the bucket.

Down the stairs she goes, yelling to the bedridden Mrs Prothero, "I'm going for Merry. Bristol Eliza is dying!"

Out into Whitmore Lane she goes, past The Grenadier, who has her hand in a sailor's shirt and who hollers after her, "What's the hurry?"

She doesn't stop to explain but hares up the lane, through the muck, past the gin dens and other brothels – every other house here contains working girls – past a place where a bully has a man by the neck outside. She sees it is Lemuel Anderson as she races past, and Mary Ann Powell is there, egging him on, "Smack him, Lem, the little gobshite!"

Up to Ned Llewellyn's brothel she goes, past Swansea Sue in the doorway, who is shouting over to a sailor, "There's beds inside, and I'll take your sea legs and make you even more unsteady, sonny!"

"Merry!" she calls as she reaches the hallway. "Where's Merry? Bristol Eliza is dying!"

Ned is usually an unwelcoming, threatening presence to the wayward girls from rival brothels, loitering and taking up time when his girls might be earning on their backs, but at hearing this he comes forth from his beer glass and nods at Maria.

"I think it's true this time," she tells him breathlessly. "She's got such a stink to her; she might be dead already but for her asking for Merry."

He takes in her desperation and sees she is not lying. "I'll rouse her," he says and strides up the stairs.

Maria waits, biting her nails, in the hallway. Behind her, Swansea Sue has caught her mark and is blocking the doorway, rubbing her breasts against the half-cut young sailor who has been caught by her vulgar offerings. Ned Llewellyn is back down the stairs quickly.

"She's coming," he tells Maria. "Give Bristol Eliza our thoughts. And Mrs Prothero. It'll be a blow to her."

Maria nods, but he is already back with his beer. It *will* be a blow to Mrs Prothero, she thinks. Bristol Eliza might well have paid nothing in rent for the last few years, but Mrs Prothero has never seen her out on her ear. There is a solidarity amongst some, not all, of these thieves, and certainly Mrs Prothero looks after her girls.

Merry Meyrick is coming down the stairs, pulling her shawl about her shoulders. "Dying? Are you sure?" is all she can manage.

Maria nods. "She asked for you. She's in a bad way, Merry."

Merry is taller than Maria, slight and sharp. She is in her mid-twenties, Maria guesses, pretty enough, lucky enough too, for she worked alongside Bristol Eliza when first Eliza came to Cardiff. It might easily have been her that caught the pox. They walk in step past Lemuel Anderson who has knocked the man into the gutter, and Mary Ann Powell who is now kicking him.

"She's had her laudanum?" Merry asks.

Maria nods. "What was left of it; she will need more if she..." she pauses. "If she lives," she says slowly.

"You have been good to her, Maria," Merry says. "When

others aren't. I want to thank you for that."

"I've nursed my grandmother at times when she was beaten badly," Maria tells her. "I do what I can to help."

Merry turns to her. "You're soft, Newton. Good to be a bit soft round here, just don't let anyone else know it. You don't want to end up like Eliza, do you? Can't you go home and live differently?" Her eyes are almost pleading. This life Maria has been living, the drink, the men, the money she takes, the things she steals whilst they sleep, all of this, Maria has tricked herself into believing, all of it, is real life. The only life. But here is Merry Meyrick, telling her it isn't. Maria hardens that part of her that might betray her. She cannot be weak.

Maria stares at her. "I have nowhere to go," she tells her. "Nothing. This is my life here. This is my home."

Merry nods sadly. "Then Eliza's fate might well come to us all," she says and they step into Mrs Prothero's house. Maria leaves Merry to climb up to the garret alone, then turns back to the street and makes her way down to the water.

She eats her fill from a pie man down by the canal, standing alone and staring at the surface of the water whilst all about her there is the chaotic bustle of the boatmen. This canal is notorious, not just for the men who work upon it and their insatiable appetites for the working girls, but for suicide too. She recalls watching one of the three suicides that have occurred here since she arrived, being hauled from the water dripping, with hair like water weed. One, an old man tired of life and want, the other two girls, working girls, or as the newspapers called them, unfortunate girls. *That's what I am*, she thinks. *An unfortunate girl.* She remembers standing here, as the boatmen hauled one of the suicides from the water, next to The Grenadier, whose tall frame always gave her a feeling of safety, although Maria has learned to give as much as she gets and rarely feels unsafe here now.

"This life in't for everybody," The Grenadier had said, and they had both sighed as the body was dragged unceremoniously upwards, hair, head and arms sagging, all grey and bloated, up onto the cobbles, and the water had run and run from it. Maria had wondered how close she had come to making a decision like this, to end it all, that night she got on the wrong train and came to Cardiff. She had run out of options that day. She might easily have thrown herself in the Severn instead of coming here.

Now she stands and stares at the water whilst a boatman whistles at her and others curse and sing as they unload boxes and sacks from the barges. One particularly high-pitched whistle breaks her reverie.

"Come and see me later," she calls to the whistler, her bluster coming back in an instant. "Top of Whitmore Lane. I'll be outside The Shields and Newcastle at seven!"

Then she throws a crust of her pie to a forlorn-looking duck and turns to return to Mrs Prothero's. When she does arrive, however, the place is all a-fluster.

"The mayor's wife is coming!" Little Punch yells at her as she enters. "Put a duster about the place; Mrs Vachell'll be here within the hour!"

Maria is unquestioningly swept along with preparations. She mops the floor, whilst Little Punch dusts and her sister, Catherine Owens, follows behind her polishing with the dregs of some beeswax she's found in the cupboard. The Irish girl, Eleanor Kelly, lights the oil lamp and takes the mat outside to beat it, and Mary Lawson and Elizabeth Vine have finally pulled themselves from whatever stupor they have been in and are sweeping the stairs and wiping the front windows. Mrs Prothero has even hauled herself out of bed and is propped up in a bathchair in the parlour, overseeing the proceedings.

Shortly there is uproar once more, as a carriage halts outside.

"She's really come!" cries Catherine Owen, a tear in her eye.

"To think!" breathes Eleanor Kelly. "After all the lip we've given her kind over the years!"

"Open the door, James, open the door!" prompts Mrs Prothero, and James prises himself from the chair in the corner of the parlour from where he has been eyeing up these half-crazed women and steps to the door. With the confidence and showmanship of a true bully, he opens it and announces,

"Why, Mrs Vachell, you do us a great kindness, please, step this way!"

The wife of the mayor of Cardiff is here with a chaperone, a huge, bearded, suited man who scowls at this young, muscular upstart, even as Mrs Vachell smiles.

"Thank you," she says, and James grins. He doffs his cap, which he rarely removes from his greasy head, and leads the way past the open parlour door. Inside, Mrs Prothero calls her thanks to Mrs Vachell, and the other girls smile and utter thanks. A few drop a curtsey for which they will be mercilessly teased about later. Then up, up she goes, past all their efforts with dusters and beeswax, up to the garret to Merry Meyrick and Bristol Eliza.

"Why is she here?" Maria asks watching her go. This woman, this well-spoken, important woman soiling her shoes on their floor is unimaginable.

"To read," says Mrs Prothero primly. "She is to read the Bible to Bristol Eliza before she dies. It is her last wish, and none of us could do it."

Maria stares at her. "So you sent for the wife of the mayor?"

Mrs Prothero grins. "Why not? She's seen all these girls in and out of court many a time. And she's the only person I could think of to send for to give poor Eliza her last wish, to have the Bible read to her. She asked Merry to do it, but Merry can't read shit."

"Good God," Maria breathes, and does not let on that she might have read it for her, and instead they all strain to hear the footsteps of Mrs Vachell as she enters the garret room, and the tone of her voice as she speaks to Merry and Eliza. "Do you really think Eliza is dying?" she asks Mrs Prothero. The nod that comes is definite and sad.

"It's a miracle she's still here, girl," Mrs Prothero sighs. "In her state she ought to have gone many moons ago. Let her have her Bible session, that's what I say."

They all sit silently in the parlour with gin and wait.

Two hours later Mrs Vachell is heard coming down the stairs. By this time enough gin has passed between them all that nobody is quite right. Merry is standing behind the good lady, and the good lady herself is wiping her eyes.

"She is gone," Mrs Vachell tells the assembled mob in a voice that quavers. "I am truly sorry to see such a clearly God-fearing girl go this way. My thoughts are with you all." She pats her eyes once more.

Little Punch lets out a sob. The Grenadier rubs her eyes on her sleeve. Everyone is swaying or gripping something for support. Maria wants to tell her that Bristol Eliza didn't believe a word of the Bible before she went downhill, but Mary Lawson has suddenly gripped her and is crying into her blouse.

"I will leave you all to make what preparations you must," Mrs Vachell tells them as she makes for the door. "Please accept my condolences and the condolences of my husband, the mayor."

"You're a true lady, Mrs Vachell," Mrs Prothero calls huskily as the door closes. She glances at James. "The coroner must be called."

It falls upon Maria to take the coroner up to Eliza's garret. Merry has gone back to the Llewellyn's, and the rest of the girls are already out and setting to with drink and fervour, plying their trade as though nothing has happened. Mrs Prothero has been helped back to bed and is sighing and eating cheese on her own. James Loynes is outside the house, looming, intimidating and watching everything that goes on in the lane, smoking and calling to those he knows. Maria is preparing to go out but is lingering, for she cannot bear the thought of a man's touch leading to such deterioration and suffering. Every time she closes her eyes she can see Bristol Eliza's dead, corroded face and she can still smell her with every breath she takes; the smell of her seems to have taken over the house. So when the door knocks and it is the coroner, James calls to her,

"Maria, since you're too lazy to be out there already, you'd better see these gentlemen up to the garret."

She knows James is irritated with her lingering by his tone, and she makes haste down to the door, as he tells the coroner,

"She'll be of help to carry the body if you need it."

She shivers, prays quickly that she will not be asked and takes the coroner and his man up to the garret. She sees them inside, but finds she is unable to look up to see Eliza's form, for she cannot bear it. But she knows she must wait, for James said she would be of assistance and she knows that he will be angry if she does not do what is expected of her; her fear of James's fist is worse than her fear of most else.

"A dose of the spotted dick got this one," the coroner's man says as soon as he sees Eliza's corpse, but the coroner himself is to business.

"We must move her," he says, and now she glances up to see if they will indicate that she is to help but she catches sight of dead Eliza and cries out. She has seen the dead before, but never such a sorry, oozing, maltreated body as this. Already the two men are moving her – they do not need Maria after all – but as they do, blood gushes forth from Bristol Eliza's mouth and nostrils. Maria steps back with another cry, her foot knocking against one of the laudanum bottles on the floorboards. She scoops them up out of view of these two men so that questions are not asked, pockets them quickly, retches, and rushes down the stairs and out into the street. What help she might have been to them is gone, for she cannot stomach it.

"You'd best make some money tonight, Maria!" James shouts after her. "Or you'll be out on your arse!"

At seven o'clock, she is outside The Shields and Newcastle across the street, watching, and there is the lad who was whistling earlier, looking all about for her. She ducks behind a group standing in the street so that he does not see her. She waits a while, observes and does not show herself amidst the people just yet. Does he look as though he has the pox, she wonders. How can anyone tell who is poxed and who is not? He looks young and almost innocently eager to her, but she is not naïve enough to think that this means he is clean. She thinks of James's words: 'make some money, or you'll be out on your arse...' If she must be with a man so soon after witnessing the death of syphilitic Eliza, better it be this clean young man than a filthy old one. She needs the money, and this lad is fresh from the Custom's House and will be carrying lots of it. She steps forward.

"Good evening, sailor boy," she says coquettishly, and he smiles and does not know that she would rather eat glass than lie with him.

Later when she passes him a drink, she slips a drop or two of poor dead Bristol Eliza's laudanum into it. While he sleeps, she dresses quickly, wipes away the wet he has left between her legs and delves into his pockets. There are notes inside, and whilst many of the girls would have taken the lot, Maria feels pity for this lad and only takes a few pounds, leaving him out cold in her bed. She puts on her clothes and steps out into the night to find somewhere else to sleep, that he might wake embarrassed in the morning and flee before he finds half his money missing.

He might press charges, she knows, but by the time the case comes to court, he will be unable to attend for his ship will have moved on, or if he still lingers around Cardiff, he will be too embarrassed to stand in front of a jury and have his name printed in the newspapers for being robbed after spending the night in a brothel.

As she strides through the night, she feels the pounds in her pocket. Bank of England pounds. All the way from England. And she wonders where her mother lives now that she is free. Her mother now has the inheritance she's always wanted: five hundred pounds. Two hundred of it is to go straight into her hand and the other three hundred will remain in the bank. Additionally, according to the papers, there is a further £150 from the death of an uncle and a small bequest and a cottage from the old man whose arse she wiped. She will have a lovely, comfortable little home – the sort of place they could have shared, the life Mercy always promised her. Meanwhile, she is running away from a mark she's just robbed, wondering where her next drink will come from. She's minded herself with the drugs and come this far without being stuck on them, but she is trapped here nonetheless.

Maria Newton suddenly realises she is down by the docks, past the canal. Below her the black water swirls. She stands there on the edge, with the gin still in her, the scent of her mark in her nostrils and the sight of the blood running from Eliza's nose and mouth as she was moved for the coroner behind her closed eyelids.

"I hate her," she says out loud. "I hate my mother. All of this is because of her."

And suddenly she is crying for the first time in a year, she is crying and now the tears do not stop. They are the tears of pent-up anger, frustration and hurt, of hatred for the feeling of all those hands that have run across her body and all those pricks that have delved between her legs. They are tears for her lost life, for what might have been and for this new, hardened creature that she has become. She wrote to her mother and sent it to Mr Whitmore. He will surely have given over the letter, yet there is no reply. Her mother does not even have the decency to tell her own daughter the truth. She mourns that the world is so cut-throat and unfair. Her mother has walked away from it all with money and a home, whilst she, Maria, is still here in the gutter with all these rats. Merry was right – this isn't a real life and isn't what she ought to be doing. She has built a shell of steel around herself so that she can survive here. As long as these tears last, she is inside that shell, she is her old self again and it is almost too much to bear. She stares into the water and wonders what it is like to feel it fill the lungs, choke on it and gulp it in instead of air. Perhaps the rot that took Eliza is already within her too, she thinks. Perhaps it is too late. Newtons take either the life of another or their own life. She's heard that saying in different forms enough times. Perhaps this life she is living is just another type of suicide, she thinks. Perhaps it will destroy her, just as a gun destroyed her father. Just as her mother destroyed her grandmother.

If she dies of the pox like Bristol Eliza, thinks Maria, it will all be Mercy Newton's fault for filling her veins through and through with this cursed Newton blood.

She stands there at the water's edge and gathers her wits about her.

There is no going back. There is no inheritance. Mercy Newton lives and Maria must only survive.

She wipes her hand across her eyes. She has gone over the case time and time again. She knows it all from the newspaper reports and she knows what she thinks happened. After all, she, more than anyone, knew how things were between Anne and Mercy. She knows what both of them were capable of towards one another. If she closes her eyes she can imagine it. And now she looks down at her hands, which are covered in a strange and blotchy rash, and puts her finger to her lips upon which lies a chancrous growth and she knows that all is not well within her.

She closes her eyes now and imagines the flames and her grandmother burning, her flesh turning to charcoal. Then she steps off and drops like a stone into the water below.

Chapter Sixteen
The Freedom of Mercy Newton

Mercy Newton

Church Steps, Bridgnorth
1850

Mr Jones, the mayor of Bridgnorth himself, had insisted upon chaperoning Mercy from the gaol back to Bridgnorth, presenting her proudly with the key to the cottage Richard Dyer had left for her in his will. She'd removed her glove to receive it so she could feel the metal, cold against her skin. Huddlestone and Kettle had waved her off like two proud parents at the gate of the prison, and she had breathed deeper of the air of freedom than any breaths she had ever taken in her life.

All the way from Shrewsbury to Cross Houses, Mr Jones had prattled on, telling her things about herself she had not known and could hardly bear to hear.

"Two hundred and twenty men signed the petition," he had repeated proudly for the fourth time. "You've been a symbol to them, Miss Newton, a cause to fight for. The pride of the working class will not be imprisoned by the egos of the middle classes. Nor the upper classes for that matter, Miss Newton. Your release gives hope to everyone who ever has found cause to rally for their rights. What do you say to that?"

Wearily, she had turned an eye upon him and sighed. "Does that really have anything to do with what has happened to me?"

she whispered and turned back to watch the jolting landscape go by.

From Cross Houses to Cressage, Mr Jones had decided to keep her abreast of the local news: of boys being caught stealing turnips, a woman arrested for stealing a sheet from a washing line and Betty Milner, the drunk, coming up before the magistrate. At first, she had managed to ignore his prating, but by the time they were through Cross Houses she had turned to him again.

"Mr Jones, I have suffered more than enough knowledge of arrests. I should not be bothered if I never saw or heard of a policeman, nor a magistrate, ever again. Do not bother me with such small, depressing tales."

Here, Mr Jones had given up and maintained a dignified silence until Much Wenlock, where they had finally stopped at The Gaskell Arms for refreshments. Not until Mercy had tasted a meal and supped some beer had she begun to feel more like a real person. As her prison skin had begun to slough, she had turned to Mr Jones and remarked, "If the people thought so much of me, might there be a welcome for me back in Bridgnorth?"

She could not imagine the people of Bridgnorth ever treating her with warmth, and yet Mr Jones's eyes had lit up.

"There may be," he had affirmed, "a sort of welcome waiting."

Mercy is dropped off on Underhill Street at the bottom of Church Steps as the night draws in, and she alights on the roadside, where a sheet has been strung from windows on the warehouses that announces, 'Welcome home, Mercy Newton' in huge green, painted letters. There had undoubtedly been a crowd at some point in the day but now they have given up waiting, gone home and left nothing but a few beer bottles lying about the place.

There is a small flag, dropped by a child no doubt, on the ground, and she stoops to pick it up and slips it into her pocket.

"It was a long journey and we did spend rather longer in Much Wenlock than I'd planned," Mr Jones says apologetically. "I'm sure you will be surprised, Miss Newton, when you do see your neighbours and friends again. They are overjoyed that you have been released."

Really, she is grateful that they are gone. She thanks Mr Jones and insists she does not need his help to carry her things up to her cottage. Eventually he gets the message and has the horseman drive on. As she watches it pass, and she glances uneasily back up Underhill Street towards The Watering, she spies two figures standing there silhouetted in the street, one tall and one shorter, and she can tell instantly who they are. Mary Corfield and her brother, William, are not standing there with flags or beer. Mary has her shawl clasped to her as though afflicted by an icy chill, and her brother stands protectively, his hand on her shoulder. They are lit by the light from the Hop Pole pub and their shadows are long and jagged in the empty street. Mercy stands, stares back and watches as the two of them turn from her and disappear into the darkness.

Down from the river port a whistling and voices rise, and she realises that the street might be empty but all about her is life. She lifts her chin to the sky and feels the first drops of rain.

It is time to go home.

She takes up her things and knows well her way up to the little cottage Richard Dyer has bequeathed her. It sits about halfway up the steps, looking out towards the river. Richard Dyer had always kept a tenant in it, but they have long since been evicted and she cannot now even remember their name. On the step blocking her entry are little packages, some wrapped in brown paper and some in newspaper piled up against the door. She pauses, then reaches over them and unlocks her door.

She had always considered this little place tiny, too small for a real home, but now she has spent so long in the confines of a prison cell, it will be a little sanctuary all her own. When she inserts the key into the lock, she pauses; the clanking of all the keys in all the locks that had imprisoned her for the last year and a half passes through her mind with a ghostly clamour. Now to turn her own key in her own door, to be able to go as she pleases and to lock herself away when she has a hankering for silence, well, she muses as the door swings inwards, what luxury.

She steps inside over the packages, drops her bags and then scoops up the offerings one by one. They are indeed gifts and she unwraps them individually. A couple of candles and some matches, some soap, a tin mug, a little parcel of tea, some apples, a comb, boot polish and a card with a prayer printed upon it. She shudders at this for it is similar to the one her mother pulled from her basket back at The Watering when she came for food that night it all went wrong. There is a fruit cake wrapped in a cloth and a set of three saucers. Each package contains a marvel. She has not owned anything for fifteen months.

Mercy soon makes this little house homely enough. It backs into the sandstone rock, the bedrock of the town, and looks out over the valley, across to High Rock and, if she takes three steps from the front door, she can see downriver towards Winscote Hills, towards where once her happiness lay.

She has determined to make her life in Bridgnorth a life of charity, kindness and good intention, for the people here have shown such faith in her in creating the petition for the Home Department that now, at last, she feels one of them; they have finally embraced her as one of their own and this sense of belonging is new to her. She likes it. 'There will be,' Mr Kettle had warned her, 'out there in Bridgnorth, people who still believe you guilty of murder, and you must take care not to let them bother you.' Part of her had expected her windows to be bricked on her first night in that little cottage. For all those two hundred and twenty who signed the petition, there must surely have been those who refused and wanted to see her hang. But no bricks came through the windows and no fire came through the letterbox the first night. A night when she had no belongings but her little bag, a bit of wood for the stove and a hard bed that Mr Huddlestone had managed to acquire from a relative and that Mr Jones had seen put ready for her. Even so, she had slept quite soundly and felt perfectly safe.

Upon receipt of the nineteen pounds and nineteen shillings left to her by Richard Dyer, she creates a home from this cottage with comforts. Upon receipt of the two hundred pounds from her mother's inheritance, she quickly invests this back into the bank to sit with the other three hundred so that she might have some interest from it. Only then does she realise how little this interest actually amounts to. Seven shillings and sixpence a week is not a fat lot even without a landlord to pay rent to, and suddenly she understands at last the extent of her mother's poverty and is chastened by its recognition. She is grateful there is a further hundred-and-fifty pounds inheritance from an uncle to keep her afloat.

There is, however, one last thing to resolve, one thing that has tormented her in all her time in gaol. Where, oh, where is Maria? The letter Mr Kettle handed her at the trial is hidden away, slipped inside the Bible she keeps on her shelf, the letter from Maria, demanding to know only one thing – whether she killed Anne. There was no return address, only a smudge in the corner and the name 'Whitmore' barely legible in faint pencil. She prays that one day perhaps the girl will turn up on her doorstep, for everyone in this town knows where Mercy Newton lives and she will be easy enough to find. She prays Maria finds her, and then they can talk. If only she comes to see her and finds a place in her heart to love her still. If only.

At first in the early days of her release, people drop by to give her things, actually *give* her things, not sell them to her: candles, a duck, half a dozen eggs, bread, a rag rug even, and she accepts each item graciously. She invites each person in to take a cup of tea, for she feels that each of these well-wishers must have signed the petition, and for that she thanks them from the deepest recesses of her heart. But after a year or so the gifts fade and the well-wishers die down until there is merely a nod here, a ''Mornin' Miss Newton!' there. This is indeed enough for Mercy, for she never was one who courted company.

Yet for all her freedom and all her little luxuries, Mercy is still not yet whole. She is alone. Comfortably alone, yet achingly so. Once she had a lover. Once she had a mother and she made a daughter from love. She took the people who loved her for granted and pined for the man who forsook her instead, and now she realises that she got it all wrong. She is empty. Empty but free. And just yet it is not enough. Mercy Newton wants her daughter back.

Chapter Seventeen

Maria Newton

Cardiff

April 1851

Maria Newton stands in the dock. She tried to kill herself but it hasn't worked – she had been dragged out of the water by a couple of dock workers, coughed up a lung full of water and escorted back to Mrs Prothero's by a lad who seemed to think she might reward his attentions with a free hour of her company but was rewarded only by a door slammed in his face. The curse clearly does not wish to claim her yet.

No, Maria has not succeeded in killing herself and now she stands accused of stealing the waistcoat of John Hemming, a man she would not recognise amidst the many she has taken to her bed for money.

She waits there before a jury and thinks of her mother who never wrote back. She wonders how afraid her mother was when she stood trial and hopes she was utterly petrified. Maria knows that the chances are that John Hemming will not show up; cases like this are a common occurrence in Whitmore Lane for her to be able to confidently predict the outcome.

Parts of her are itching and she cannot scratch them, not here in front of a jury. *What if it is the start of the pox*, she thinks. *What if I end up like Bristol Eliza?* Yet the chancre on her lips is healing and the rash on her hands has faded, although it is on her feet now, but who can see in her boots? All this is whirling about her consciousness as she stands in the dock but her face remains a mask. She must face this out. Never show weakness, she has learned here in Cardiff. If you show you are defenceless, you become prey.

"Since there is nobody here to prosecute," is the declaration which comes quickly enough. "Case dismissed."

"Thought as much," Maria replies and winks at the magistrate.

But for Maria Newton, when she stands on the steps outside the court and imagines her mother's first steps of freedom, nothing is dismissed.

Bristol Eliza haunts her in Whitmore Street. With every mark she takes into her bed, she thinks of the sores on Bristol Eliza's body, and these new blotches she has upon her own body are ominous. She is shaking now because of all the hours she has not had gin in the police cell waiting for her hearing. Perhaps, she thinks, it is the demons in her blood, those Newton devils, making her dither and shake. She does not want to go back to Whitmore Lane once this is over. She has seen babies pulled up from that canal. The child of Little Punch, born from God-knows-what hook-up and thrown into the water to drown, unwanted, was the last one. Lemuel Anderson and Mary Ann Powell have been transported for seven years for robbing and beating a man almost to death at The Lame Chicken. No, Maria Newton cannot live this life any longer. It is rotten and she has had enough.

The Newtons all kill either themselves or someone else. She has no hankering to murder another human being and she has tried and failed to kill herself. And there is more – it is three months since she bled.

She observes the general populace, the way they busy themselves like ants as though they all know exactly who they are, where they belong and what they are doing. She knows none of these things. She only knows that now things must change.

She sees them all, purposeful, justifying their existence somehow, yet she has always struggled to justify her own. And suddenly she knows what she must do. She turns towards the train tracks.

Chapter Eighteen

Mercy Newton

Bridgnorth
August 1851

"Morning, Miss Newton," says the butcher, Charles Brawn, when Mercy makes her way up the High Street for sausages and chops. The day is already warm, and those steps up to the Castle Walk have tired her before she has even begun her day. "You'll have seen the newspaper this morning, no doubt?"

Mercy grips her basket and observes the produce on his cold slab. "I'll have some of that smoked ham too, if you please, Mr Brawn," she tells him. She is flustered. Out in the High Street, she has just spotted Mr Newell whistling as he walks, swinging his cane, and his figure made her scurry and run the last hundred feet to reach the shelter of Brawn's the Butcher so that she did not cross his path. She stands at the counter steadying her breath as the butcher takes the ham in his hands.

"How much?" he asks. "And what about the papers?"

"What of them?" she snaps, for she is sure it will be a resurfacing of her case to which he refers; the newspapers have a repetitive habit of rewriting her story every now and then.

"Your Maria," he tells her.

She drops her basket.

Out in the street a boy is selling The Bridgnorth Beacon; she cannot bear to stand and count out the change, instead she whips the paper from his hand and hurls a fistful of coins towards him.

"Keep the change!" she tells him, and leafs through it, scanning, scanning. Maria Newton, Maria Newton, and then there at last, she sees it, those letters so familiar it hurts.

Maria Newton has come to Shrewsbury. From wherever she ended up Maria Newton has come as far as Shrewsbury. She is coming home! Mercy reads, lets the words sink in and pauses suddenly at the word, 'suicide'. She pauses. The newspaper drops from her hands and flutters to the road. She cannot read on.

All around, the town continues in its work. A carriage pulls up outside the hotel. The paper boy has finished scrabbling to pick up all the coins she threw for him and has pocketed the lot.

The butcher has finally caught up with her.

"Suicide?" she breathes. "Every Newton ends either their own life or the life of another."

He holds out her basket to her. "She's not dead," the butcher says. "Here, let me read it for you."

Mercy Newton is in such a panic that she cannot make one word out from another. "Please," she stammers, waving him towards the pages, and he takes it up and thumbs through it. "Betty Milner is in here again, I see," he notes, pointing to a column. "Drunk and disorderly on Listley Street. Her husband, old Thrasher'll be paying the fine as always."

"Please, Mr Brawn, get to it," Mercy pleads.

He turns the page, makes a sound of recognition and reads, "William Ellis and Maria Newton were brought up and charged with disturbance at Ellis's house in Barker Street, Shrewsbury. When Inspector Jones arrived there, he found Newton trying to jump out of the window."

"Oh God!" cries Mercy, and clutches his arm but he continues,

"Upon entry to the property, Inspector Jones located a quantity of knives and a chopper on the table, and the female prisoner said she would poison herself."

"Dear Lord! No!" Mercy says, but the butcher doesn't stop.

"She had laudanum for the purpose of suicide. She had been to the canal that morning and was very wet."

"Oh, what have I done? She might have frozen!" mutters Mercy remembering throwing water over her mother and declaring that she hoped she would freeze. Never did she want this for her daughter.

"It is August, Miss Newton," the butcher interjects. "And a warm one, at that." He clears his throat and continues to read, "Ellis, on being asked what had become of his wife, maintained that she ran away with another man to Stockport, allegedly some time back."

"Ellises? I don't recall the Ellises," Mercy says. "But she is alive, thank God."

"William Ellis was fined £1 in default of a month's confinement," he reads. "And Newton was dismissed on promising to leave the town and go to her friends in Wolverhampton."

At this he closes the newspaper.

"Wolverhampton," Mercy echoes.

"She's alive and well then," says the butcher. "And up to some japes I shouldn't wonder; a proper little Newton tearaway, eh, like her pa and his brothers when they were nippers." He falters. "Will you be needing that ham now, Miss Newton?"

Mercy stares at him. "Japes?" she says through gritted teeth. "Her own poor father shot himself! Her own uncle hanged himself! Were those japes?" She stifles herself from boxing him about the ears, takes the newspaper from his hand most abruptly, folds it carefully and lays it down in her basket. This is the first news of Maria she has had in over two years. Poor, sad, lonely Maria. She is, at least, alive, but Mercy has no way of finding her and given her state of mind, the question might be, how long will she remain so?

"I don't want your rancid ham," she tells him and marches off down the High Street.

The Final Account

Recollections of Thomas Whitmore, MP

Apley Estate, Bridgnorth
1852 – 1853

In 1852, I stood down as MP for Bridgnorth.

The marriage of my youngest brother, Henry, to Miss Adelaide Darby, of the famous Coalbrookdale Darby family, pioneers in a world of iron, gave us cause for much celebration, and Henry's ambitions began to grow. He expressed the desire to become an MP himself.

The election process for further MPs was found to have been corrupted by bribery across the country, and a number of elections were disputed and found to be corrupt. Indeed to my disappointment, the Bridgnorth election was one of these and was thoroughly disputed in the committee room.

A Mr William Milner and his wife averred that they and others had been offered a sovereign in one of the public houses by an agent to cast their votes for Pigot and for my brother, Henry Whitmore, who sought to take over my previous role in the town. This William Milner had then brought the possibility of a sovereign to his brother's ears, a Mr Thomas Milner, and both had gone to see the same agent, a Mr Head, whereupon Mr Thomas Milner had also received a sovereign and the promise that after the election, they would receive something else.

Following the election, it transpired that not only these two gentlemen had profited, being given another four pounds each after the election was completed, but various voting men about the town had been bribed too.

I saw Miss Mercy Newton thrice in this time, for I undertook various meetings about the town. The first time she was entering the bank as I arrived at the guildhall for a meeting. Neatly dressed and sober of countenance, she flashed me a glance too quick to respond to, before stepping into the internal darkness of the open doorway, and I was left, half-inclined to nod toward her, yet half-inclined to pretend I had not in fact recognised her.

The way she moved was quick and determined. Everything about her spoke of a woman who knew what she was about.

The vision of her haunted me throughout the day, so that I found myself, once the day's work was done and I was travelling back to Apley, considering what approach I must prepare in case our paths crossed again.

And cross they did. For as the year of 1853 brightened, I came upon her on the High Street on market day, whilst all the bustle of the Bridgnorth folk went on around us.

"Mr Whitmore," her voice was clear, her tone clipped. "I never thanked you for passing on the letter from my daughter."

I looked down at her, a slender woman she was, her hand clutching a basket. Those hands were instruments of murder, I had no doubt, but I found that this time I did not shudder.

"It was my duty as your MP, Miss Newton," I said, for I had determined that I would not pretend that I did not know her and would not shun her. I would remain professional in her presence. "I trust it gave you comfort."

"There was no return address," she told me, although this I knew already. "I still have not found her."

I touched my cane to my hat. "I sincerely hope you do, Miss Newton," I said and embarked upon the sentence I had prepared for her in case our paths ever crossed. "You must make the best of this freedom that you have and work for the good of others now. As I try to. This is an opportunity to seek God's path, Miss Newton, to work for good."

She eyed me for a moment and one lip curled at the corner. "You think God had a hand in any of this, Mr Whitmore?" she snapped. "I want no patronising from those who would have seen me hang." She turned to go but then turned back. "The name of Newton carries a curse, and the blood of Newton carries the devil," she said grimly. "And I'll thank you to remember it."

And with that, she pushed past me and was gone between the market stalls.

Despite the townsmen who had tried to fiddle the election in favour of my brother, Henry went on to be elected MP for Bridgnorth and gladly I watched his progress in the world of politics.

The third time I saw Miss Mercy Newton was on the steps of The Cape of Good Hope public house. She had a bottle of beer in her hand, was holding the shoulder of another woman and yelling something crass at someone across the street.

Had she learned anything from her trials, I wondered?

Did she value life any more now than she did before?

These were things I could never know.

I continued to follow my father's advice to work for the prosecution of those petty crimes of Bridgnorth that arose – unpaid bills, petty theft – prosecutions that were inevitable given the crimes. To maintain social equilibrium.

As my tale of her trials comes to an end, I have only one further entry to make in my account, and it is a musing, rambling of the thoughts that keep me awake in the dark hours, that keep sleep from my door.

Miss Mercy Newton made legal history.

In my opinion she got away with murder.

Is it possible when one understands the social, economical, emotional and psychological aspects of a person to forgive the taking of another human's life? Are memories really so short, so fickle, that the people of Bridgnorth could greet her each day and not shudder to recall the particulars of her mother's death? Or was Anne Newton so inconsequential that the removal of her from this earthly plane would place so indelible a dent in the conscience of the public that they did not, after so little time, really care?

Miss Newton was out there, going about her daily life and interacting with people as though nothing had happened. How many other people are out there too, having murdered, having committed the grossest of acts, walking amongst us?

The punishment must act as a deterrent, my father had said.

Yet still passion overcomes it all.

Perhaps underneath this façade of religion, class and propriety we are no better than the beasts that roam free in the forests.

Perhaps that is all we are after all.

Chapter Nineteen

Mercy Newton

Bridgnorth

1854

Mercy never wanted to end up like her mother but she has come to enjoy a drink once more despite her resolve to drink again after what happened at The Watering. Her life is small and lonely, and she finds over time that she likes to drink in company, not on her own in her little house but out in town. She enjoys carousing and flirting, and the dramatics that arise from the liquor-soaked inn-goers, the little passions and the fall-outs. She has decided that she must find a husband if she cannot find her daughter. A husband would give her company, warmth and at least a little more income.

She finds herself one evening in September in an alleyway with a man who can barely stand, and as Mercy comes to her senses, for she has imbibed a lot of gin, she realises through the drink-mist that this slurring, sweaty meatball of a man is not the sort of husband she is looking for at all. She realises, through the haze of gin, she knows his wife. The outrage that rises for the sake of his poor, down-trodden missus suddenly fills her with such an explosion of anger and injustice that she slaps him, snatches his watch and then runs, laughing, into the darkness, leaving the idiot drunk, swearing and swaying. Past the end of the High Street, where Betty Milner stands on the corner, yelling something about a bastard at anyone stupid enough to stop and listen; Mercy pays the fuddled old drunk no heed.

She sobers a little as she reaches the end of East Castle Street when the wind hits her, and she looks down to corroborate her suspicions; she is indeed carrying a watch in her pocket and it is solid and real and not a laughing matter – she has committed thievery whilst under the influence – so she takes it home and secretes it in a chest in the corner of her living room wrapped in polishing rags. The place rotating about her, she collapses into her chair and laughs herself to sleep. But presently there is a banging on her door, and she rouses herself by the faint light of the dying fire to find the drunk standing on her doorstep with a police officer, McWilliam – everyone knows everyone else round here. This sobers her up no end. She curses herself for stupidity; the drunk she accosted is no bargeman stopping by in Bridgnorth for the night, but William Milner, a brute of a man, who beats his wife and is in and out of court for petty things more often than he takes a bath. In recent years, everyone knows he and his brother made a good amount from the bribery surrounding Henry Whitmore's election. Here he is now, panting from the steps, half on, half off her front doorstep with a bobby beside him, hammering on her door.

"She took my watch!" she hears him yell. "Search her!"

"I have no watch but my own," retorts Mercy, pulling open the door, but Milner is having none of it.

"I'll knock your bloody head off!" he roars, pushing his way past her. "And scatter your brains against the wall! Move, I'll search the place myself!"

Police Officer McWilliam appears nonsensical at this, but Martha Overton, her neighbour, who has heard the commotion from down the steps, pops her head out of her door and calls, "Do you have a warrant?"

William Milner pushes past Mercy and starts to uproot the

place. "I'll not leave until I've found my watch!" he cries, and Mercy goes to him to drag him out of her house, but he throws her off, sending her sprawling into the rocking chair. Mercy is enraged. She rushes at William Milner, grabs him by the whiskers and shakes his head so violently that he cannot hold himself upright.

"You scamp," she shrieks at him. "You scoundrel! Coming here, drunk and accusing! Get out of my house!"

She rakes her nails all down his face until it bleeds and at last the Police Constable must get involved. He intervenes between the two and oversees a thorough searching of the place. Mercy has sunk down upon the chest in the corner, covered it with her skirts so that it might be a stool and refuses to move for the duration of their toil.

"No warrant," says Martha Overton, who loves a good bit of entertainment and has stationed herself in the doorway, leaning on the doorpost. "A sickening state of affairs for this woman who has already suffered so much at the hands of *your* kind." She nods at P.C. McWilliam. "No warrant," she says again to Mercy. "You'd have the right to take them to court."

Court is the last place Mercy Newton wants to go, but she sits and reflects as the two men turn her house upside down. She decides it would be better for her to accuse William Milner of ransacking her house, drunk and without a warrant, than it would be for him to accuse her of shaking his head by the whiskers and raking her nails down his face. She determines that she will lodge her complaint first.

The incident is up before the local bench within two weeks, up there on the first floor in the town hall, the very place she stood her own police trial when she was first arrested. She remembers the stained glass, wood panels and the rows and rows of pews for spectators. She remembers standing there back in 1848, having come up the back steps a prisoner and being held in the back room where the faces of kings looked down on her from their stained-glass array. This is where William Milner sits now whilst she waits to give evidence. No back steps for her now. Not ever again.

William Milner is fined 15 shillings for distress to Mercy, and she stands there before the jury, as prosecutor and victoriously eyes the furious William Milner. Triumphant as she might be in this instance, she does not want to stand before a judge and a jury ever again. It crosses her mind as she descends from the courtroom, that she must now avoid William Milner at all costs: no mean feat in such a small town.

She cannot continue like this forever, she knows that. She cannot be part of these petty, pathetic little squabbles between drunks. This whole experience with William Milner might easily have become another Anne Newton moment, something regrettable done quickly in a passion, something regrettable. She must tame herself, she thinks, or she will lose everything all over again. She will only drink with friends, she decides. She will not be in the newspapers again.

One day in the spring of 1854, there is a knock on the door of Mercy Newton's cottage that rouses her from a nap by the fire. She is not expecting visitors, but she often has visits from Martha Overton or Emma Hammond, who live not a stone's throw away and is not utterly bereft of companionship. She chuckles to herself and eyes the gin bottle on the table.

"Did we not have enough last night?" she calls out, pulling herself up from her chair. "It'll just be tea this morning!"

But when she opens it and stands back, she cannot catch her

breath. For there on the step looking up at her stands Maria, older, as thin as ever with the sharp cheekbones of Anne, but with the grey eyes of James Newton staring straight back at her.

"I've worked it out," she says breathlessly, the wind catching a strand of hair and sending it across her face. "The curse. I've worked it out. I've come here to save you."

Mercy wishes she had put away the gin bottle from last night which sits now on the table close to hand. "Will you come in?" she asks carefully, afraid that this might be some spirit or other, and that unless she tread carefully she might frighten it away. "I will make tea?"

Maria hesitates on the step for a moment, then nods.

Mercy almost laughs for joy but quashes it and steps back to allow Maria ingress.

"This is all yours," Maria says, ducking her head to get inside the low doorway. "The whole house yours?"

"Richard Dyer left it to me," Mercy says. "It will be yours one day."

Maria shakes her head. "No," she says quietly. "I don't want anything from you. Not anymore."

Mercy does not know what to think or say at this, but she swipes away the gin bottle into her skirts as she turns and sets the kettle boiling, as she secretes the gin behind her rocking chair.

She bids Maria sit in her comfortable chair and takes her seat in the rocker as the water warms. "You are well?" Mercy asks.

Maria lifts a shoulder. "Well enough. I have come to tell you about the curse," she tells Mercy. "So you can live in peace."

Mercy tuts. "That old wives' tale, pay it no heed. We are a passionate bunch, the Newtons, that is all." But she is ready to listen all the same. Years might have passed, and she might be older and perhaps a little wiser, but when it comes to the curse, she cannot be sure of anything, in truth.

"I'm not a Newton anymore," Maria tells her bluntly. "I'm a Biddle. I married one of my friends from Wolverhampton."

Mercy is overcome. "But I was not told!" she says hurt. "I was not invited."

Maria stares at her squarely. "No," she agrees without explanation. "No, you were not."

Mercy sees that this is not a time to quarrel and pulls herself up. "Mrs Biddle! Mrs Maria Biddle! Why, doesn't that sound fine!" she says and rises to see to the cups and wipes her eye quickly so that Maria cannot see her shed a tear. "And where have you been and what have you been doing all this time?"

"Did you kill her?" Maria's words hang in the air. "Did you break her nose and suffocate and burn her?"

Mercy turns to her. She spreads her hands. "How can you ask me this?"

Maria laughs out loud, cold and low. "I wrote to you, but you did not answer. But I saw you hurt her so many times. I saw you hit her with that horsewhip until her skin was hanging all off. I saw you beat her until she was crying and begging you to stop. I heard you scream that you wished she would die. That you wished she would drown, burn or get trodden on by a horse." She too wipes a stray tear, but unlike Mercy she is not afraid to show it. "Did you do it?"

Mercy checks the kettle. The water is nowhere near warm. Her cheeks are burning. "If I wanted her to die, if I really wanted it and wanted to do it myself," she says. "Would I admit it to the world so publicly, so frequently, so loudly? Would I incriminate myself so openly?"

Maria snorts. She is not frightened of this mother of hers any longer. She is harder now than she has ever been before. Cardiff made her fearless towards the worst of humanity. There is only one thing, in fact, that Maria Biddle fears, and it certainly isn't

Mercy Newton.

"That is part of the summary of your defence," she says. "I read all the newspapers. Don't quote what your Mr Huddlestone said, at me. I want the truth."

Mercy stares at her, mouth half-open. This is not the Maria she once knew; this is someone else, a stranger with Maria's face.

"There are some things about your trials that I don't understand," Maria says pointedly. "There are some details that seem to have been lost along the way."

Mercy shakes her head. "Don't be stupid," she says but her hands are shaking. "Nothing was lost. I was found innocent."

Maria shakes her head. She wanders across the room to the fireplace where she picks up a tin and makes it rattle. "I used to be so afraid of you," she tells her mother. "Of your temper. But I've met people that make you look like a little mouse, and now I'm not scared of you anymore. And I have my own theory about what happened that night. One that I didn't read about in the papers."

Mercy is growing red about the cheeks. She doesn't know if she ought to grab the girl by her neck and throw her out onto the steps or whether, in fact, she might cry. All this ought to be behind her. Instead she takes the lid off the teapot and opens her tea caddy and starts to spoon the leaves inside.

"I had drunk so much that night," she tells Maria. "Everyone had. And that is no excuse, not for anything, but you must know I had taken more rum than I had ever had, before or since." Maria waits. Mercy turns to her and tries to break the silence. "You must know by now," she says, "that when you drink that much, so much that you cannot keep your eyes open, there are gaps, black bits in your memory."

"So your defence was a lie?" Maria surmises. "You don't actually know?"

Mercy looks at her daughter. Her face is lined more than it should be, she looks older than she should. They both do, she is sure.

"I'll tell you what I think happened if you like," says Maria, not waiting to see if Mercy does like it or not. "I read the papers; Gran taught me to read just as well as she taught you. And things that were mentioned in the coroner's inquiry at the town hall were not reported in the later newspapers as being brought up as evidence in your trials at the assizes." She indicates to Mercy to check the kettle. "In the coroner's inquiry it was reported by Gran's brother, your own uncle, Edward Edwards, that Gran had not long been left £75 by their brother upon his death but she had not yet received it. No wonder you and her had been getting along so well. No wonder you were planning on papering her new lodging room. She had funds coming to her." She watches her mother who has taken herself to the fire and is wiping about the place with a cloth, keeping herself busy, unable to show her red, twitching face. She is so close to the fire that her skin is starting to sting, but she cannot look at her daughter.

"You were always obsessed with her money. You wanted some of that new inheritance money, so you were getting close to her. But you couldn't hold your temper forever." The kettle starts to whistle, and Mercy takes it up and pours, unsteadily, most of the water into the teapot. Maria settles down to rest upon the chest in the corner. "The newspapers all said that you had drunk rum that night and that Nan had only had a drop of beer. You were completely drunk. I know that. And I also know that you attacked Nan that night."

Mercy shakes her head. "My defence was straight. It was told to a jury three times. Four times if you count the hearing here. I don't have to answer to you." Her tears are coming now, her voice quivering, shaking.

"You stabbed her that night," Maria stands, preparing herself. She's seen her mother lose her temper before and she needs to be ready in case she comes at her. "In the coroner's inquiry, they said she had been stabbed with a fork. She had suffocated, been burned and stabbed with a fork. But the fork wasn't reported in any of the papers as being mentioned at the assizes."

"A fork didn't kill her," Mercy growls. She wipes her eyes and nose on her apron. "They had to find the cause of death. And they found that it wasn't a fork, and they found it wasn't me. I put the fire out. Me! I did! She set fire to herself with her own pipe, just like she did when you were a baby, and just like she did a few years before she died. And *I* was the one who doused her."

"I've put it all together myself," Maria says. "You fell out with her over money, and you hit her so hard it squashed her nose flat and then you stabbed her with a fork. That was when Mary the maid heard her shout out. And the reason the maid didn't hear anything more is because you smothered her with a cushion. And then you threw oil and lard over her to make sure you'd finished her off or to burn the evidence, and then you dragged her out, burning, to the brewhouse."

Mercy is trembling from head to foot. She is still stupidly trying to make tea, still ineffectually clanking things together. "I didn't," she says. "I never would."

"But you would though," says Maria. "I remember. You threw a bucket of water over her once and said you hoped she'd freeze to death. But this time you made sure she'd burn."

"Lies," Mercy says, then louder, "It's lies, Maria! Why would you come here, all this way, to say this?" She turns on her daughter now and Maria can see that she is seething. Were she anyone else, Mercy Newton would have knocked her to the floor.

"Whether you set the match to her or not," says Maria, and she too is shaking now but from anger not fear, "you stabbed her with a fork and she burned because of the oil you threw over her. But then she never was a quiet woman. If she cried out when you stabbed her, imagine the fuss she would have made if she had woken to find herself burning. They'd have heard her down the river in Arley. No, I believe you did away with her before all that. I believe you suffocated her – you've tried that before – and then threw lamp oil and dripping all over her and set fire to her. Or she'd have woken the whole house up with her screams."

"She knocked that bottle over herself," Mercy tries but her voice is failing her now. "I just picked it off the floor after it all, and set down the bottle, safely, on the grate."

Maria shakes her head. "If I had been in that jury," she says darkly. "I'd have found you guilty. She died because of your actions that night. If you had been anyone else, if you hadn't been a Newton, she would be alive today."

Mercy cannot contain herself any longer. She takes up a cup of the scalding tea and hurls it in the direction of the chest, but Maria has already moved from the spot, and the tin mug hits the wall and tea splashes about.

"I believe you did kill her," Maria tells her mother. "Even though you didn't have the decency to write back to me, to tell me yourself. You're a coward and you have lied your way to freedom. And I came here today to tell you that. And to tell you that I am not afraid of you anymore." She hunches her shoulders defensively, clenches her fists and holds them the way James Loynes taught her back in Whitmore Lane. "And if you try to hurt me," she tells her mother, "the way that you hurt my gran, I will make sure that you don't get up."

Mercy stares at the tea splashes on the whitewashed wall. She takes in her daughter standing there defiantly before her, confidence oozing from her unlike any meeting they've ever had before.

"What are you going to do?" breathes Maria. "Set fire to me too?"

Mercy falls to her knees. "Maria, let's not quarrel. You're my girl, I want to know you. Let's put this behind us, now it's been said. Let's..."

Maria does not let her finish. "I don't think so," she tells her mother, and she touches the mug that lies on the brick floor with her toe. "I shan't take a cup if it's all the same," she says. "I don't drink tea with murderers."

She licks her lips. She makes for the door.

"Wait!" Mercy cries out.

Maria turns one last time.

"How can the curse of the Newtons be lifted?" Mercy asks from the floor, tears stinging her eyes. "What did you mean?"

Maria Biddle sniffs. "There is no curse, you stupid woman," she tells her mother. "It's the booze. Nan was an alcoholic, I've read of it. She couldn't live without it. And it made her evil. And you, you can't take your spirits. You get spirits into you and you do awful things. You hurt people and you can't remember half of what you do. Give up the drink before you do something else you will regret." She eyes her mother. "Temperance. Before it is too late." She brushes down her skirts. Mercy stares at her. She thinks of John Newton who killed his wife after drinking all day, and of her beloved James who shot himself after a week or more on the bottle. She thinks of her own mother, Anne, whose words grew cruel and vindictive when the gin was in her, and of that night at The Watering when the rum flowed down her own throat until she cannot piece together her actions the night Anne died. She thinks of drunk old Betty Milner who yells at all who go by on the corner of Bridgnorth High Street, and she thinks of how she robbed William Milner of his pocket watch after a night on the spirits, and how, drunk as a Lord, he came to ransack her home with a police constable in tow, who also seemed ten sheets to the wind. The drink is most assuredly a devil when it gets into the veins.

"Then you do care?" Mercy asks suddenly frantic. "Is that why you are here, Maria, because you want to keep me safe?" She grabs at her daughter and takes her by the skirts to keep her from going. "Is it true? If I give up the spirits, will I be safe? Are *you* safe?"

She stares at her daughter. She remembers that echoing gunshot out in the woods, the panic between herself and William Newton and the dogs barking and howling locked in the stable. James Newton's body laid out in the parlour. The days she'd wept over him. He'd killed part of her too that day. Hope. That's what he'd taken from her. She'd never been able to be a mother to this child of hers because of his death. How can this girl be so convinced that the curse is not real? What does she know, what has she seen of life that Mercy has not?

"What has happened, Maria?" she whispers. "Where did you go? What did you do? How did you come to this certainty?"

Maria is silent, but she leans on the table for a moment to steady herself. Mercy pulls herself to her feet and reaches out to her, but she shrinks away.

"I birthed a child," she whispers. "Before I was wed. A poor, tiny little thing she was, well before her time. Gone. And I cannot help but think, it was a mercy, for she was not well formed. Her little face, oh God! Her face was a broken doll." She stares at her mother, who reaches again for her, but there is a world of lost time between them. "And then, when I was right again, I married Edward and he knows nothing of the child for it was not his." She sniffs. "I know not why I am telling you this," she says. "Perhaps so that you know that I have seen life, know grief, I am strong and I survived. So far." She looks about her at the little house that might have been home to her if she had not gone to Cardiff and run away from it all. If she had a forgiving, trusting heart. But there her mother looms, too large in this small place, and she knows it would not have been long before they would have gone for each other.

"Was my father violent?" she asks now. "Angry? Unstable? A drinker?" and Mercy nods sadly. "Did he kill himself because he knew I was to be born?" Maria adds, for this question has been at her lips her whole life and now she has the strength to free it.

"His own brother hanged himself," Mercy tells her. "There was a melancholy in their hearts that was not of your doing, not of my doing either." She racks her memory; what were his words? "They had the morbs," she tells her. "That's what he called it. The morbs. Morbid, they were, a darkness in them. They weren't right." She remembers how he had turned against her in those final weeks. How he had shuddered to be near her. How his family had driven a wedge between them with their hatred for her mother and their distrust and disgust in her.

"But he wouldn't have done it if I weren't to be born," Maria whispers. "That's what I've thought my whole life." She is fumbling for a handkerchief. "He wouldn't have shot himself if I had not existed."

"He would," Mercy tells her earnestly. If she can assuage the girl's doubts and make her close to her through this shared loss, perhaps she can save their relationship. Perhaps Maria will learn to love her, visit her and care for her again. "He had it in him. And, Maria, you are right about the drink. He drank for days and days before he took the rifle to himself. He would have done it over some other thing eventually, even if you had not been conceived. Of that I am sure." She passes Maria her own handkerchief embroidered MN in the corner. Maria wipes her eyes and looks down at it.

"Look at those initials, they were once mine," she observes sniffing, and passes it back. "Thank God they are mine no longer."

Mercy reaches to her again now, whilst she is distracted, and takes hold of her wrist gently. Maria winces and eyes her mother's fingers which tighten upon her.

"Newtons take the life of another or they take their own," she says quietly. "That's the curse you always taught me, the curse Gran always taught me. But I don't believe in it anymore. We make our own decisions, though sometimes we are in a corner. We are what we do, and there's no good that can come of blaming something that isn't real." She straightens her clothes and pulls her shawl closer about herself, making herself ready to leave. "You killed her in your drink, and my father shot himself in his. Give up the spirits and you shall be free of all the rot."

And she yanks herself free from her mother's grasp and steps to the door.

"Will you come back?" Mercy grabs at her again, but Maria is already at the door. "Will you come again? Where are you living? Don't go, Maria, don't leave me!"

Maria has the door open already and looks back at her mother. "It is better for us both that I go and that I never come back," she tells her and steps out onto the steps, leaving her mother sobbing as she slams the door behind her.

Chapter Twenty

Mercy Milner

Bridgnorth

1856

Mercy Newton is left then, knowing precisely where she stands. She has no family. Nobody who cares for her. She is utterly alone.

Despite the passage of time, there is no getting away from William Milner either. He has a memory that will not give her peace, constantly reminding her of that drunken night of idiocy. He is everywhere she turns, bad-mouthing, snarling in her direction at the market and shaking his head at her in church. She thinks that one day, he might brick her windows or worse. He often sits with his brother, Thomas – known as 'Thrasher' both for his fighting days and for his wife-beating – drinking in one or other of the many beer houses in High Town. Mercy knows which are his favourites and she avoids them now; it is almost impossible not to feel intimidated when the two brothers are together. In addition to their joint menace, Thrasher Milner's wife, Betty, the local drunk constantly arrested for obscenity and threatening language, is regularly to be seen around the High Street, cursing at anyone who catches her eye. Whenever Mercy catches sight of her, she slips away into a shop or an alleyway, bonnet dipped, so that she might avoid her attention. Betty is a coarse-mouthed drunk, forever charged with being drunk and disorderly, often in the papers and always in the streets after midday frequently until dark. Whenever she is faced with a fine, she is quoted about town as declaring, 'Tommy will pay it!'. Some say that when it comes to matrimonial battery, she gives at least as good as she gets. Mercy cannot stomach the sight of her, for her drunken slurring voice makes her think of Anne. Mercy avoids them all, all the Milners. The trio of them together are the stuff of Mercy's nightmares, at least, now that her nightmares of hanging from the neck have begun to wane.

It is a shock then, when in the May of 1856, Betty Milner suddenly dies. Although Thrasher is sad, he is out and about in town the very next day as though a leash has been cut from around his neck, walking, walking, dazed but sober. And he comes to sit his bulk down next to Mercy that evening as she is sitting on a bench at the top of Church Steps in St Mary's churchyard, looking out across the river, watching the sun set across the valley.

"Miss Newton," he says gruffly.

"Thrasher," she replies uneasily. "I was sad to hear of your wife's passing."

He sighs. "She was pickled," he tells her. "You'd think in that condition she'd've lasted longer."

They sit and about them swallows swoop and an early bat begins to circle.

"It'll be a quiet house you'll be keeping now then," Mercy says.

"It will," agrees Thrasher. "And my pocket will be fuller with coin than it has been for many a year now it won't all be pissed away." They sit a while longer. Then, "Did I ever say how your passion towards my brother that night you shook his whiskers and called him a scoundrel amused me, Miss Newton?" And he turns to her with such admiration on his face that she cracks a smile, and then he cracks one too. Suddenly, they are laughing together there on the bench, until Thrasher wipes his eyes and says, “I needed something cheerful this evening, and the thought of you giving his big old head a waggle is just the thing.”

Mercy reaches over and pats his hand. “I’ve lived alone ever since, well…you know,” she says.

He nods. “Since you were banged up,” comes his unrefined reply.

“Yes,” she says primly, and readjusts her bonnet. “And although it can be lonely, I have also found that it can be quite peaceful. To never have to answer to another, is quite a wondrous amount of freedom, I have found.”

She sits there next to him, feels the warmth of him beside her and remembers that cart ride with James Newton, that first day she went to live with him in Apley. She’s always liked a big strong man.

“Miss Newton, you might be right,” he says thoughtfully. Then he turns to her. “If you’d a hankering for a walk one of these days, or perhaps a pie and a pint…” he says, and she smiles.

“Yes, Thrasher, I’m sure I might. If you’d kindly tell your brother to keep away from me and stop scowling at me every time our paths cross, I might certainly see my way to it,” she jokes, but realises he is serious and straightens her face. “’Though I’ve heard that you weren’t averse to raising your hand to old Betty. If you ever were to raise a hand to me, I’d chop it off.”

Thomas Milner chews his lip for a moment. Then, “I wouldn’t expect anything less, Miss Newton,” he says.

Mercy eyes him for a moment, then nods. “Shall we start with a walk then, perhaps? Did you ever see that madman, Mad Jack Mytton, ride his horse around Castle Walk?” And she rises, and so does he. He offers her his arm and she takes it, and away they stroll.

Mercy Newton marries Thomas 'Thrasher' Milner three weeks later at St Mary's Church on the 5th of June 1856, aged 46, and breaks free then and there from the curse of the Newton name. There is no congregation there to see them standing before the altar, both dressed in black, only the witnesses present to hear their vows. The church is the fanciest place they might have chosen in Bridgnorth, seated there at the end of East Castle Street, with large, expensive townhouses flanking the street. As they step out into the sunshine, there are no family members to congratulate them, but ranged about the graveyard hang the local youths, so the newspaper reports tell. A 'strong body of the local juvenile population' have waited outside to see this spectacle, as Bridgnorth's murderess ties herself to Thrasher, newly created a widower by the death of his wife, the famous local drunk, Betty Milner. When they leave the church and turn their backs on the tall, domed tower, they are promenaded back up East Castle Street, back to their marital home on Listley Street by a large gang of lads, all singing and cajoling, whooping and laughing. Mercy Milner grips the arm of her husband hard to stop him from thrashing the lot of them, and he places his hand upon hers to clamp it to his arm to prevent her from breaking free from him and boxing them all about the ears.

Together they go, holding on tight to each other, and beneath her black bonnet, beneath her black veil, Mercy Milner smiles.

Epilogue

Mercy Milner

Bridgnorth

1865

Mercy Milner sells, or rents out, her little cottage on Church Steps and she and Thomas Milner live in his three-storey house on Listley Street in High Town. They live quietly enough, in comparison to the lives they'd lived separately, drinking a little, quarrelling at times, but keeping each other mostly steady. The Curse of the Newtons has passed through her and she has lived to tell the tale.

On Tuesday the 21st of March 1865, in the morning, the bells of St Leonard's and St Mary's churches in Bridgnorth toll, and all about the town the shops remain closed. Mercy steps out into the street, lets the bells ring in her ears and takes a deep breath. All about, shutters are pulled to and curtains are drawn. Bridgnorth is in mourning, but Mercy Milner is alive and knows it. She has outlived the man who sought to make her swing. A little thrill of triumph rushes through her veins: Thomas Whitmore, MP, is dead.

Mercy lives on her independent means and her husband's wage too, and they also take in lodgers; a comfortable existence. The curse of the Newtons seems a thing of the past, although at times

Mercy still takes a rum or two.

Then in February 1871, Mercy receives word from Edward Biddle that his wife, her daughter, Maria, has entered the Burntwood Asylum, suffering from delusions, insomnia and confusion. It is only a message brought to her by word of mouth, a second-hand confusion of words that she fails to understand when first she hears it.

"But Maria said there was no curse," she says to her husband. "She went away, she didn't drink. She was a good girl. I don't understand."

"Perhaps she ran too far," is his response.

In January 1872, Mercy hears from Edward one last time – Maria died on the 30th of December 1871, aged 38, from General Paresis and exhaustion, and has been buried in the asylum burial ground.

She consults the doctor, for she knows not what this means. When he speaks, she wishes she had not asked him there in the High Street, as everyone around them goes about their daily routines.

"General Paresis, Mrs Milner, is a mania," he tells her, eyeing her severely. "Historically considered to be the result of a promiscuous lifestyle, but recent medical assertions link the disease to syphilis."

Mercy is so shocked that she cannot speak. Then her daughter did succeed finally in killing herself. No matter how far the girl ran, she could not escape the curse after all.

Thomas 'Thrasher' Milner died in 1878 having spent 21 years with Mercy as man and wife. Within the next ten years, Mercy Milner moved from their home in Listley Street and onto the

Cartway, just up from the River Severn, a steep cobbled street surrounded by beer houses and brothels frequented by the sailors from the river. Again she took in lodgers to supplement the money she had in the bank. In 1890, Mr Huddlestone, one of her defence team, died, and Mercy might have read again of her trials in the newspaper articles that recounted his many legal triumphs; even 42 years later, the name and deeds of Mercy Newton had not been forgotten.

Then finally in the autumn of 1892, Mercy Milner, famous as a Newton, but forgotten as a Milner, died, aged eighty-three, a good enough age for the time. Sarah Milner, her sister-in-law and wife of William Milner, reported her death, which was recorded as a case of 'senile decay'. Her funeral was held at St Leonard's church in Bridgnorth, a red, sandstone church just off Bridgnorth High Street, and her body was interred at the cemetery across the river. Her grave lies about ten metres from her husband's in the same cemetery as George Edwards, the tinsmith who visited John Newton on that fateful day back in 1823, and whose visit incited the murder of the heavily pregnant Sarah Newton at Severn Hall.

After her death, Mercy's nephews, two Edwards brothers, went to court to quarrel over the money that she left in the bank – there were almost three hundred pounds remaining; the last of Anne Newton's legacy.

NEWTON FAMILY TREE

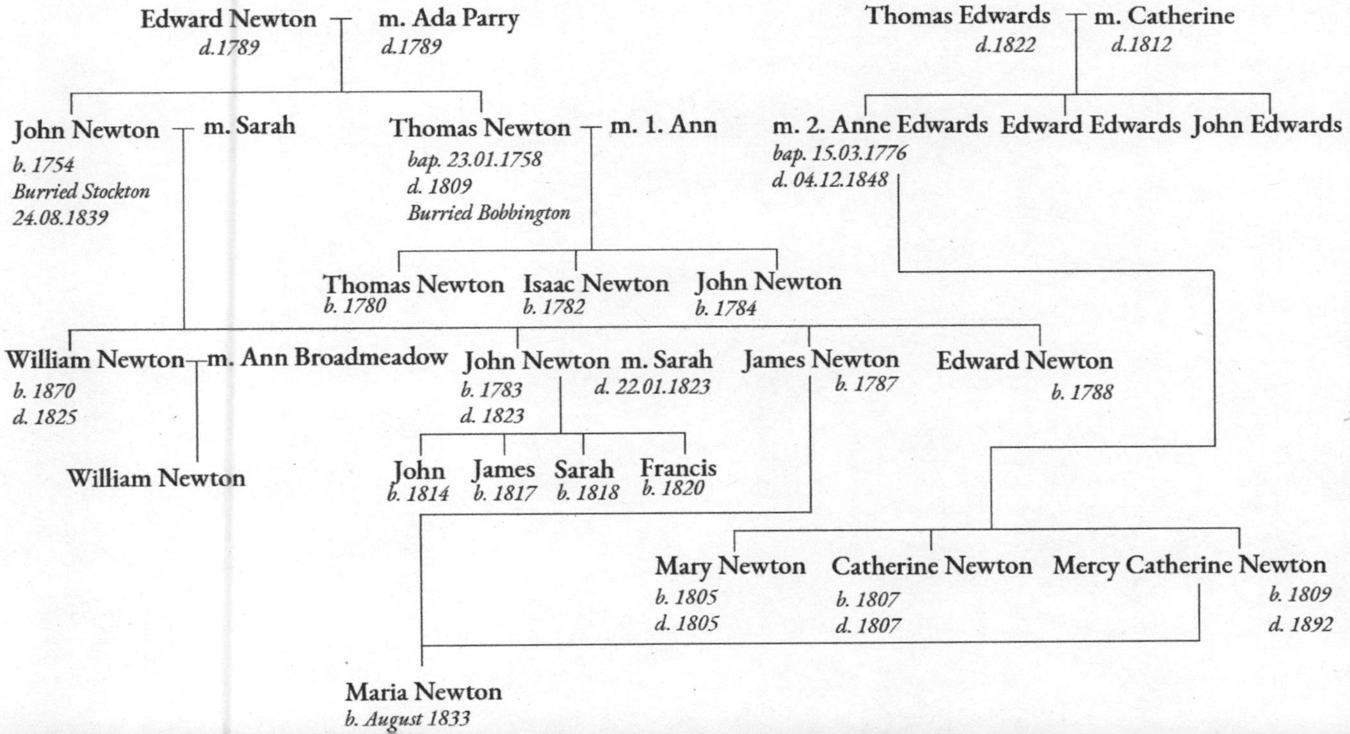

A Note from the Author

Bridgnorth is a quaint little town built on sandstone cliffs on either side of the River Severn in Shropshire. A branch of my family hails from Astley Abbots, just outside Bridgnorth. I wanted to write a story about this place, to capture the streets and the people as they were. I began with a bit of research, using old newspapers to find out some of the juicy pieces of history that had happened there.

That's when I found Mercy Newton.

The more I looked, the more I found. I discovered that I could, with old newspapers, census information, birth, marriage and death certificates, prison records, wills, old maps, location visits and even a copy of the actual petition and notes from the prison, piece together not only her life, but parts of her mother's and her daughter's too, as well as the lives of her cousin, the murderer John Newton, and his brothers. Mercy Newton was just waiting to be rediscovered. A coroner's inquiry and three trials found her finally innocent, but there were many who did not agree. Despite this, there are over two hundred signatures collected on the petition, one of which to my mirth I found to be the signature of William Milner, who she later shook by the whiskers and prosecuted in court for upsetting her peace. I believe that Mercy came to embody the struggle of the working man against the elite classes, and I believe that this is why 220 people signed the petition, and why those who lined the streets calling for her to hang in December 1848 wanted her free by March 1850. The newspapers even went so far as to describe her as a good-looking woman at her final trial, an assertion that having seen two artistic representations of her at her previous trials that portrayed her in an antonymous fashion, appears to have been written favourably to ride the wave of the whims of the readers.

Mercy Newton was at that time allegedly only the second person to have been tried more than once for murder under the British legal system. I have not yet discovered if she was the first to ever have endured three trials for murder.

In all, seven medical men were called upon for evidence during her trials: only three of these had seen the corpse of Anne Newton, and none of them had ever seen a body which had burned to death (although one had seen a death from a colliery explosion, which would have created burns of a different nature). Dr Strange and Dr Martin, who are not mentioned in the story, took part in the coroner's inquiry and their evidence was certainly used in the third trial, as reported by the newspapers. There are names and opinions enough within this account to boggle the mind without adding their input, but the reader might be interested to know that they appeared to favour the defence.

Maria's fate was the hardest to find. Once she was married, she was known as Mary and I lost sight of her for a while. She disappeared after the 1861 census until I discovered that a Mary Biddle had entered the Burntwood Asylum in February 1871, just before the 1871 census would have been taken. She died in December 1871. Her husband, it seemed, had gone to live with his father and brother. I delved deeper and, after ordering her death certificate, discovering that the age of the woman was right and the cause of death was, as I had suspected, linked to syphilis, it all fell into place.

Some small elements of poetic licence have gone into writing this book:

I do not know if Anne Newton saw John Newton of Severn Hall hang, nor indeed whether Thomas Whitmore went to the hanging with his father. However, the execution took place on a Monday, the day after Easter Day, so he may have been at home for the Easter service. It was a very public spectacle and was widely reported in the newspapers of the time, so accounts of it in the book are as accurate as the media reports.

I do not know if Mercy had a loving relationship with James Newton or if he forced himself upon her. However, the fact that Maria was baptised at the same church where he was buried indicates that Mercy wanted him there somehow, in spirit, so I took this to imply that they were lovers.

I have no idea if the bet involving Mad Jack Mytton was a pre-planned event or a spur-of-the-moment whim. For the purposes of the book, I have presented it as an event that would have interested the masses. Bridgnorth was often visited by travelling circuses and had its own racecourse, and I wonder if Mercy and James perhaps saw any of these spectacles together too.

I do not know if Thomas Whitmore went to observe the third trial. He refused to put his signature on the petition, sticking to the stance that he believed Mercy guilty of murdering her mother. To have him there to witness the final trial in the book tied it up nicely, so I allowed it for the book.

The house within which Anne Newton was murdered goes by a different name. I have called it The Watering as it was named in the 1841 census to avoid confusion, as its other (one might say more accurate) name is too similar to other locations in the book.

I do not know if Maria really did miscarry, however, given the situation she was in, the prostitution, her syphilis and the 20 years of marriage without issue, I think it is safe to assume that she was rendered unable to have children by the infection and this might have caused miscarriages or premature births.

I do not know anything about the relationship between Mercy and Maria after Mercy was found innocent. I do not know if Edward Biddle told Mercy about her daughter's illness or death. I would like to think that Mercy knew where Maria was, that they were in touch and Mercy went to her burial. However, there is no evidence to support this.

There may be other small liberties, but I have worked hard to keep integrity with the real history that I discovered, and so all life events are to my understanding as factual as historical fiction can possibly be.

What I do know is this: at least three of the four orphans of John Newton of Severn Hall survived to adulthood, married and were left money in the will of their grandfather, another John Newton, in 1849. Little Sarah grew up and married a wood ranger called Richard Perks, from Enville. James became a shoemaker in Dudley and little Frances married a labourer in Stockton called Thomas Milward. Only little John Newton, who saw his father murder his mother, is unaccounted for.

The story of this family explores morality and humanity. It explores issues that still abound today – the intricacies of familial relationships, broken homes, poverty, epidemics, alcoholism and mental and sexual health. Love. Loyalty. Morality.

These were hard, harsh times.

This book does not have a heroine.

There were none.

The prevailing force was a will to survive.

One last thing. I found the grave of Mercy Newton. And I took her flowers.

Themes

Alcoholism and Abuse

Bridgnorth had, and still has, a high ratio of public houses to population. The term 'alcoholism' was first put forth in 1849 by a Swedish physician called Magnus Huss in his book entitled *Alcoholismus Chronicus*. However, the idea of the misuse of alcohol and chronic, habitual drunkenness as a disease is an ancient concept.

The theme of alcohol in the life of Mercy Newton is ongoing. Each pivotal moment in her life, each tragedy, hangs on an alcoholic encounter. Domestic abuse, of men against their wives, was often reported in Bridgnorth during these times. Anne, Mercy and Maria were part of that cycle, although they seemingly lived for much of their lives without men. Anne was cruel and, by all accounts, an alcoholic. She abused her daughter if not physically, then certainly verbally. I am aware that she was a small woman, and if Mercy outgrew her, then any abuse she might have meted out when Mercy was a child, she would have been unable to continue with once Mercy was bigger and stronger than her. One thing is clear, Mercy disliked her mother enough to hurt her, perhaps to turn the tables. Mercy experienced periods of drinking, but in her profession as housekeeper, it might have been more difficult for her to sink into alcoholism. Maria was the victim of their dependency, both on drink and on each other.

General Paresis, Syphilis and Maria

General Paresis was also known as General Paralysis of the Insane, or Paralytic Dementia. Modern medicine recognises it as a symptom of late-stage syphilis, the onset of which can take 10-30 years to become apparent and affects approximately 7% of syphilis sufferers. The connection with syphilis was first posited in or around 1857, however, it was not until the 1880s that the possible connection was more thoroughly admitted. Symptoms included delusions, a loss of inhibition, depression, memory loss, dizziness, fatigue and insomnia. Seizures and muscular deterioration ensue, resulting in paralysis. Treatment for syphilis (penicillin) was not available until the 1940s.

Syphilis itself has different stages: primary, secondary, latent and tertiary. In the primary and secondary stages, there are symptoms which I show in the book with Maria's rash and chancre. These stages last approximately 1-2 years. In the latent stage, there is a long period of an asymptomatic nature, during which the disease is less transmissible. This was an important part of my research, as there was no real evidence that Maria's husband suffered from syphilis. The tertiary stage is where her General Paresis would have taken effect, and this may have developed very quickly so that she became suddenly delusional. I believe that her husband looked after her until he could no longer cope, at which time she entered the Burntwood Asylum, and he went to live with his father and brother.

Babies born to syphilitic sufferers can be stillborn or miscarried. Those who survive the womb suffer congenital syphilis, and before treatment was available might develop deformities within the skeleton, suffer seizures, intellectual disability and nerve palsy. There is no evidence that Maria had children in the 20 years she was married. In the book, I have suggested that she miscarried before she married, and that the child was deformed due to syphilis. She may, of course, have been infertile either naturally or due to the infection. However, Edward went on to remarry and had three daughters with his new wife within 12 years, the oldest of whom he called Mary, the name Maria was known by after their marriage. Edward Biddle lived well into the 1890s, which indicates that Maria had entered the latent stage of syphilis by the time they were married and was less contagious.

Suicide

When Maria was arrested for trying to commit suicide in Shrewsbury in 1851, it was illegal to try to end one's own life. In fact, suicide was not decriminalised until 1961. Attempted suicide could be prosecuted and could result in imprisonment. Families of those who committed suicide could also potentially be prosecuted. Maria escaped imprisonment with her promise to leave Shrewsbury and go to friends in Wolverhampton, thus removing the possibility that further suicidal attempts would occur in the town.

'The morbs' was a Victorian phrase used to describe someone suffering from melancholy or depression. Generally, this was not used to describe suicidal depression; the morbs was more a term for a temporary state of depression. James uses it in the book to try to hide the depths of the melancholia that actually permeates his family.

Of the four Newton brothers, John, William, James and Edward, only Edward survived. In March 1821, James Newton (who later fathered Maria) tried to drown himself in the River Severn. His employer, Thomas Whitmore (the old squire) sent him to Stafford Asylum. John, who murdered his wife in 1823 after drinking all day, attempted to plead insanity at his trial. Once he was executed, his brother, William, hanged himself, and then ten years later in 1833, James shot himself. Theirs was a deep-seated depression and certainly not a fit of the morbs.

Sources used for this book were:

britishnewspaperarchive.co.uk

ancestry.com

findmypast.co.uk

National Archives website

upset.victorians.blogspot.com

Mad Jack Matthews – Cardiff's Most Notorious Criminal by John F. Wake

Apley Hall: The Golden Years of a Sporting Estate by Norman Sharpe.

A vast array of old photographs of Bridgnorth provided to me by local historian, Clive Gwilt.

The British Newspaper Archives were invaluable in researching this case, and it is with the utmost thanks that I would like to acknowledge the importance of this as a national resource. It enabled me to explore and reframe the trials with such a wealth of information, and to engage in the way that witnesses spoke and interacted with the professional men conducting the trials.

Acknowledgements

Thank you to my mum, Marion Woodhouse, who reads all my work and has proved a fantastic asset in considering the time period and the inclusion of historically accurate details. To my daughter, Ellie, who has partaken of an Anne Newton forensic murder evening with me, as well as visiting Mercy's grave with me, with her droll greeting, 'Hello Mercy. Welcome to the family'.

Thank you to Steve Morris, who has had to put up with my obsession with various dead women over the last five years and will be continuing to do so for many years to come.

Thank you to Beckie Somerfield, who has been enthusiastic and interested no matter how many times I have inundated our conversations with Mercy Newton's life story. To Angela Bancroft for beta-reading and being interested in my writing for as long as I can remember.

With thanks to local historian and author Clive Gwilt for his local locational input and a never-ending stream of gratitude to Hattie Grünewald who taught me so much and gave me the confidence to carry on.

And of course, thank you to Jenna and Victoria Richards, and the rest of the team at Cranthorpe Millner, without whom nobody would have had the opportunity to read this book.

Praise for Mercy

"Mercy is a relentlessly gritty true crime tale of inequality, hardship, co-dependency, deprivation and substance abuse in industrially rural 19th century England. While it is often difficult to like, or even condone, some of the actions of the heroines, the reader is compelled to turn the page, and to hope that there is some universal justice, balance, respite... or even mercy to be found." - **DJG Palmer, author of the *Babanango* trilogy**

"The description of Mercy Newton's trials are cleverly written to demonstrate the bias of vexatious prosecution and questionable jurisprudence, keeping the suspense going throughout the book." - **Jay D. Waveney, author of *Somersham Boy***

"I was hooked from the very first line. Told with tenderness and tension in equal measure, Mercy blends fact and fiction to uncover the truth behind a story lost for over a century. It's the kind of book that lingers with you long after you turn the last page." - **Netgalley reviewer**

"The characters and world of the story are wonderfully and evocatively written. I loved every minute of the read because the characters were so real. The knitting together of the relationships between the characters was so skilful and so credible...it had me glued to the page." - **Netgalley reviewer**

"I loved the wide range of characters and the well-crafted 19th century settings. Mercy, in particular, lives on the page: agreeable, disagreeable, misunderstood, kind and loving, heartless and cruel. A satisfying read for gothic mystery readers." - **Netgalley reviewer**

